Organizational Structures

Organizational Structures

Kenneth D. Mackenzie

The University of Kansas
and
Organizational Systems, Inc.

AHM Publishing Corporation
Arlington Heights, Illinois 60004

Contents

Foreword

The growing awareness of the importance of organizations in our lives has created interest in understanding them. We are interested in individual and interpersonal behavior in organizations. We are aware that organizations influence us and that through our participation we can change organizations. We realize that organizations have subgroups, structures, and task and administrative processes. We understand that organizations are affected by technology, other organizations, and by general social and economic conditions. We also perceive that organizations can be used by their members in order to achieve personal goals.

Given the wide range of problems and issues, there are many theoretical approaches, schools of thought, and very different methods for studying organizational phenomena. This diversity has resulted in a growing, vigorous, and exciting field of study. It has also given rise to a wide variety of academic courses and research interests.

The books in this series are more than a collection of separate surveys. They have been integrated to provide a clear picture of the scope of organizational behavior, to insure consistency in approach, and to portray coherently the relationships existing across subproblem areas. Each book cross references the others, and together they provide an up-to-date working library for any person seeking to understand the field of organizational behavior.

To achieve these goals of intergration and completeness, six outstanding scholars and teachers with experience teaching in business schools were assembled to write the first six books in this project. Two are social psychologists, three are specialists in organizational behavior, and one is a sociologist. The wide range of topics was first drawn up and then divided into six groups. Each of the authors then worked with the series editor to draw up a detailed outline for his or her portion of the whole work. Care was taken to insure that each author understood how he or she related to the whole series, that each author had a theme for each chapter, and that these themes were consistent within individual books and across the series as a whole. When the independent writing of each book was completed, the author and the series editor went over each manuscript painstakingly to create a solid part that was consistent with the whole series. One of the features of this series is that each book examines its topics in terms of behavioral processes. Behavior is seen in terms of complex interrelated sequences of contingent events.

Each book is written so that it can stand alone and so that it connects across the others in the series. Thus, any single book or any combination of books can be used in the classroom. In addition to the coherence of an

integrated series, the integration itself
helped to reduce the length of each book and
hence reduce the direct costs to the student.
The author of each book had the primary responsibility of writing on his or her assigned
topics. But when a topic from another book was
needed, the author could count on its being
adequately covered. Thus, each author could
stick to specific topics and refer to the
other books for more detailed explanations for
other topics. Together these books provide
adequate coverage of the main topics, a com-
pendium of ideas about organizational behavior,
and a source of new ideas and critical references.

The books in the series were written primarily for beginning M.B.A. students at a re-
spectable college or university. Some of these
schools require two semesters or three quarters
of classes in organizational behavior. For
these, we recommend that all six books be used.
Some require a semester of classes. For these
we recommend any three of the books. Those
requiring one or two quarters should use two
or four of these books.

Kenneth D. Mackenzie
Lawrence, 1977

Preface

The topic of this book is organizational structures, and the treatment of this topic is new. My approach asks the reader to reconsider and to think about the meaning of structure, which is defined as a need-satisfying pattern of interactions among the group members. An organization has more than one structure, and these structures can and will change. The processes used by groups to change their structures are the core of the theory of organizational structures presented in this book.

The concept of structure used throughout this book is introduced in chapter 1. Given this concept of structure, one can link together the organization's structures and its task processes; these ideas lead to some new methods for measuring structure. An important problem here is connecting measures of organizational structure and measures of efficiency and effectiveness. Some new ideas and results

on organization structure change processes are
presented in chapter 2. Why structures change
and some processes by which they change are
discussed. Ideas and concepts from the first
two chapters are applied to the analysis of
administrative issues in structural change in
chapter 3. An interesting problem tackled in
this chapter is the analysis of how administrators cope with inconsistencies between the
authority structure and the actual task-process structures.

Based on the new theory, new approaches to
the ancient problem of span of control appear
in chapter 4; many other modern management
methods also serve to enlarge one's maximum
possible span of control. In chapter 5, these
ideas are applied to the theory of bureaucracy.
The approach is that most large scale organizations today are partially related to the concept of bureaucracy; such organizations are
called *buroids*.

Chapter 6 treats the managerial problem of
centralization and decentralization. The key
problem is balancing the need to maintain control and the need to avoid being overloaded.
Chapter 7 summarizes the theory and analyzes
some common organizational structures. Finally,
in chapter 8, we return to the problems of
gaining acceptance of organizational structural
changes. This last chapter also presents the
idea of organizational war and a theory of organizational growth.

This book blends theoretical topics and
practical applications. It brings together
many separate literatures on organizational
structures and seeks to assemble a coherent
and logical framework for the analysis of
problems of organizational structures. Much
of this work has been strongly influenced by
my research and professional experiences. This,
in turn, has been influenced by contact with
many students and colleagues.

The chance to teach and to work with serious
and motivated students is very precious. Their
interests, confusions, questions, and contribu-

tions have always forced me to think and re-think. The theory of organizational structures would be much more primitive than it is today were it not for their presence. I wish to ac-knowledge their contribution and to thank them by dedicating this book to all my students— past, present, and future.

1

Structures

CONCEPTS OF STRUCTURE AND THEIR IMPORTANCE

If one wanders through any organization and
gets to know its members, one cannot help being
confronted with issues and problems that concern its structures. Persons are concerned with
promotions to a higher level, transfers within
a level, and even demotions to a lower level.
The organization's structures reflect the distribution of authority and power. Systems of
governance within the organization are related
to organizational structures. Those with whom
one interacts and what one talks about are influenced by these structures. The tasks of the
organization shape these structures. Knowledge
of these structures and beliefs about them can
be used to describe and predict group behavior.
The importance of structure is clear.
  However, despite the importance of structures

to the members and the behaviors of the organization, there are surprisingly few hard facts about structures. And because there are, for practical purposes, few limits on the number and types of alternative structures, we need to know more about structures to guide our choices for working within them. During the past thirty years, there have been many developments in the study of group structures. This knowledge, however, is diffuse, spread over a number of academic areas and pockets of knowledge hard won from experience. This book gathers some of this knowledge and attempts to synthesize it in a form that is both theoretically and practically interesting.

The first four chapters are primarily theoretical. They are included to provide a language, a set of concepts, and sets of relationships out of which we can erect a theoretical framework that can be used to build up our understanding of a number of organizational problems. The next four chapters apply these ideas to problems of span of control, common techniques of management, formation of hierarchies, bureaucracies, decentralization, centralization, information overload, evolution of organizational structures, the adoption and diffusion of change, organizational growth, and organizational warfare. Reading and understanding the first chapters will make it much easier to comprehend the material in the later chapters.

Because each of us participates in a number of different organizations, and because organizations influence almost every aspect of our lives, we all have acquired some insight about organizational structures. But much of this information is unsystematic, some is profound, and some is simply incorrect. Many facts, fables, and hunches about organizational structures can be found in virtually every magazine, newspaper, television program, novel, course, and gossip session. Only in the last few decades, however, have we begun to winnow the

wheat from the chaff, to separate the important
from the trivial, to gather and synthesize our
facts about structures into a branch of human
knowledge.

A significant amount of this work has been
done within laboratory settings; it consequently bears some of the telltale marks of its ori-
gins. This knowledge tends to be concerned
more with small groups and their simple processes than with larger organizations with a
wide variety of processes. It is, however, more
systematic knowledge, and more clear. The
reader should keep in mind that the experimenter also participates in "the real world" and
his experiences there influence what he thinks
about and what he sees when he conducts experiments. And, what he sees in the laboratory
affects his experiences in "the real world."
Thus, instead of thinking of him as isolated
in a laboratory, it is more accurate to think
of the experimenter as an intellectual commuter
between his world of the laboratory and that in
which he works and plays. The reader of this
book should also attempt commuting intellectu-
ally between these pages, the classroom, and
those organizations in which he participates.

Weick (1974) has argued that one could best
improve knowledge of organizations by not
studying large organizations directly. They are
simply too complex to understand. He suggests
that we study everyday events, everyday questions, micro-organizations, and absurd organizations. We can learn from these and we can
organize this knowledge and then test its implications. Eventually, however, we should ven-
ture out to understand and to improve the
functioning of larger organizations. Thus, the
content of the first four chapters comes from
the laboratory, while the content of the next
four chapters is an attempt to put together our
systematic knowledge and apply it to organizational problems.

Consequently, there is a strong emphasis on
describing a conceptual framework for analyzing

issues of organizational structures. The framework contained in these chapters is relatively new, having been developed during the last twelve years. Numerous attempts have been made to assess the state of the art of group structures (see Shaw, 1964; and Collins and Raven, 1969; for two excellent surveys). But there is not very much agreement on the basic definitions and concepts of group structures. There is even less on the processes of structural change and problems of methodology for studying structures. This conceptual confusion makes it difficult to compare different studies and to organize the many facts and results into a coherent set of knowledge. Different scholars and practitioners emphasize different aspects of structure, ranging from a mathematical model of social choice to the ethical aspects of participation in organizations. In between are numerous studies, such as those relating technology and structure, and those attempting to establish links between measures of efficiency and group structure. Human relations have also received wide attention. However, the selectivity of each study, when coupled with confusion about concepts and measurement, makes it hard for a student to organize this mass of material into a coherent set of knowledge.

The author, having studied structural problems for over a decade, has developed a framework in which he finds it comfortable to work. This theory is presented in the first chapters. It is hoped that both the student and the scholar will find something of value in this book. But as Milton Friedman, the economist, points out, "There is no free lunch." It will take each reader some effort to learn the framework. It will be easier to understand the basic ideas if we concentrate on little organizations first. Once these ideas have been explained, they can be applied to analyze problems involving larger organizations.

STRUCTURE AS A PATTERN OF INTERACTION

The basic idea of structure is that it is an interaction pattern among a group of participants. To describe a structure we need to make a list of the participants and a table of who interacts with whom about what. We could use the names of the participants but it is analytically easier if we devise some notational system. The simplest system is to let x_1 represent person one, x_2, person two, etc. So if we are studying the structures of a group of, say, n persons, we let X_n be the list of the n members, x_1, x_2, $\ldots$, x_i, $\ldots$, x_n.

We also need some way of recording who is interacting with whom. To do this we need to describe who initiates and who receives an interaction, what the interaction was about, and some recording of the amount of interaction. A simple idea for describing the direction of interaction is that of a *channel of communication*. Suppose we start with person one interacting with person two. There are two possible directions: Person one sends to person two and person two sends to person one. The channel between x_1 and x_2 consists of the two *half-channels*, described by the half-channel from x_1 to x_2 and the half-channel from x_2 to x_1. Ordinarily, we use an arrow to represent these half-channels schematically as shown in Figure 1.1.

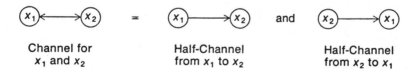

Channel for x_1 and x_2	Half-Channel from x_1 to x_2	Half-Channel from x_2 to x_1

FIGURE 1.1 Schematic representation of a channel.

The type of diagram in Figure 1.1 is very useful as a description of a structure. We build up the larger structure by combining the half-channels of every pair. For example, suppose there is a third member, x_3. There are now possible half-channels between x_1 and x_3 and between x_2 and x_3. We can combine the channels between the three pairs into a simple structure, as seen in Figure 1.2. Please note that there is no *a priori* meaning attached to the length, position and the angle of the arrow representing a half-channel.

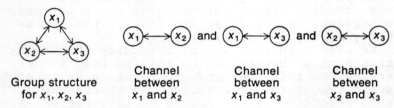

Group structure for x_1, x_2, x_3 Channel between x_1 and x_2 Channel between x_1 and x_3 Channel between x_2 and x_3

FIGURE 1.2 Combining channels into a structure.

It should be clear that this system can be extended to any configuration of half-channels and any size of group. Ordinarily, when we come to larger groups, it becomes cumbersome to draw diagrams. At some point, usually about five, it is easier to represent these diagrams in more conventional notation.

It is easy to make a table (or square matrix) whose rows represent the senders and whose columns represent the receivers. The cells in the table represent each half-channel. For the group structure of Figure 1.2, this table of half-channels would be:

$$
\begin{array}{c}
\begin{array}{ccc} x_1 & x_2 & x_3 \end{array} \\
\begin{array}{c} x_1 \\ x_2 \\ x_3 \end{array}
\left[
\begin{array}{ccc}
0 & x_1 \rightarrow x_2 & x_1 \rightarrow x_3 \\
x_2 \rightarrow x_1 & 0 & x_2 \rightarrow x_3 \\
x_3 \rightarrow x_1 & x_3 \rightarrow x_2 & 0
\end{array}
\right]
\end{array}
$$

The zeros along the diagonal represent the restriction that we do not ordinarily record interactions with oneself in describing a group structure. However, if the participants are subgroups or departments, we may wish to open up the table by adding more rows and columns to record the subunit structures. The entry $x_1 \rightarrow x_2$ in the first row and second column means that this cell in the table is the half-channel from x_1 to x_2.

The existence of a possible half-channel does not mean that it was actually used during the period we observed the group. A common procedure for recording the volume or intensity of interaction on any half-channel is to write the measures of the interactions on each half-channel in the corresponding cell. For example, suppose x_1 sends three messages to x_2, and one to x_3; x_2 sends two messages to x_1 and none to x_3; and x_3 sends two to x_1 and five to x_2. The table of interactions would now look like:

$$
\begin{array}{c}
\begin{array}{ccc} x_1 & x_2 & x_3 \end{array} \\
\begin{array}{c} x_1 \\ x_2 \\ x_3 \end{array}
\left[
\begin{array}{ccc}
0 & 3 & 1 \\
2 & 0 & 0 \\
2 & 5 & 0
\end{array}
\right]
\end{array}
$$

This table shows that there were 13 recorded interactions and exactly how they are distributed according to sender and receiver. A table of this type is easy to construct and it is easier to use than a diagram. The corresponding diagram would be:

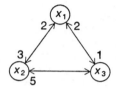

where the number of messages sent is recorded on the head of the arrow. If the reader would construct both a table and a diagram for a five-person group, he will note the greater simplicity of constructing a table. For larger-sized groups, diagrams cannot, in general, even be constructed without overlapping arrows. The table is also easier to manipulate computationally.

Let R be a symbol representing the *table of interactions*. We can now use the list of participants, X_n, and R to describe symbolically a structure. We write:

$$S = (X_n; R)$$

So if one knows X_n and R, S is a complete description of this structure.

The table of interactions, R, is defined with respect to some method of counting. One simple way is the number of interactions. For another purpose, R could represent authority with entries of 1 in the ith row and jth column if person x_i has authority over x_j and 0 if x_i does not have authority over x_j. One could use a volume measure such as dollars to describe a structure of sales among a set of firms and customers. There is no limit to how one can construct R. This means that one of the key problems in studying group structures is to decide upon X_n and what it is that one wishes to record in order to construct R. These decisions will depend upon the purposes of the study and the theory one employs in the study. There is no set answer for how to study an organizational structure. This is why there is such stress on describing a framework for conducting a study. The framework can be used anywhere, but the facts in any given instance are not transferable across organizations.

The careful reader will have noticed that structure is spoken of in a plural sense. There are many structures in an organization. For example, even in a five-person laboratory group up to nine structures have been observed. The

members may share information in a different
structure than one they use to make a decision.
There are different structures for different
task-oriented activities and still others for
friendships and socializing. There can be temporary structures for solving what appear to be
temporary problems. In any organization, one
sees subgroups and substructures. There is
often a sizeable discrepancy between what the
structure actually is and what it is designed
to be. Some authors speak of formal versus informal structures to capture this distinction,
which is painfully evident in most organizations. This author finds it very helpful to
compare actual structures with the "official"
structure. The discrepancies provide major
clues about many organizational problems.

Notational systems for multiple structures
have been devised (Mackenzie, 1976a, b), and
methods for aggregating and disaggregating
multiple structures and for performing many
types of analyses have been developed. Although
these are beyond the scope of this book, some
of the main ideas linking task processes and
structures are discussed in the next section.
But before going on to consider these problems,
it will help to provide a few figures for multiple structures corresponding to Figure 1.1
and the table of interactions R. We shall return to these ideas in later chapters.

To draw a figure of a typical channel between
two persons when there is more than one type of
structure, one replaces the arrow of Figure 1.1
by a set of arrows as in a quiver used in arch-
ery. For a pair interacting on three different
dimensions, one would have:

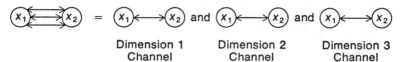

| Dimension 1 | Dimension 2 | Dimension 3 |
| Channel | Channel | Channel |

FIGURE 1.3 Schematic representation of a channel for a
multiple structure.

Let R_1, R_2, and R_3 represent the tables of interactions on dimensions 1, 2, and 3 respectively. Then we can view the composite table, R, as a three-dimensional array much like the three pages of a notebook in which each page represents one of the tables of interaction.

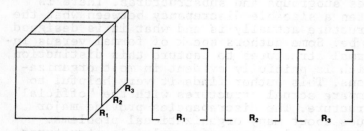

FIGURE 1.4 Schematic representation of a table of interaction for a multiple structure.

A STRUCTURE IS A NEED-SATISFYING PATTERN OF INTERACTION

The description of a structure as a pattern of interactions shows how one could depict the sender, receiver, and intensity by a list of participants and a table of interactions. The entries in each depend upon the content, and different types of content can be placed in different structures. It is argued that, in most cases, there are a number of different structures for a group. There is, however, no mention of why persons interact the way they do to create a structure. It will be argued here that a structure represents a need-satisfying pattern and that as the members' needs change, or if they can think of better ways of interacting to satisfy their needs, the structures may change.

Without delving into all of the mysteries of human needs, we can still consider the proposition that a structure represents a need-

satisfying interaction pattern. Let us first
distinguish between the ability to perform an
act and the advantages one might associate with
the performance of an act. There are many acts,
such as driving on the wrong side of a road,
that we can do even though we may choose not
to. The person who can perform an activity is
called a *controller* of that activity. The person
may or may not exercise his right to control
for many reasons, such as a determination of
his expected net benefits or need satisfaction.

Next, let us argue that a person will exercise his control whenever he believes that this
will benefit him more than not exercising his
control. Now if we recall the definition of
half-channels, it is clear that a member controls those half-channels originating from himself. For example, if we have a four-person
group, there are three half-channels originating from each member. For person x_1, these are

$$(x_1) \rightarrow (x_2) \quad (x_1) \rightarrow (x_3) \quad (x_1) \rightarrow (x_4) \quad . \text{ So, if } x_1$$

controls his half-channels, then x_2 controls
his, etc. A structure reflects the decisions
of its controllers. In other words, a structure
represents the interaction decisions of a number of controllers. These interlocking decisions are made to achieve some net satisfac-
tions. Thus, a structure represents a need-
satisfying pattern of interaction.

Further, if an interaction decision by one
of the controllers is judged to be unsatisfying
or less satisfying than some alternative decision (after allowing for the "cost" of making
changes), one would expect the structure to
change. In some cases the structures of a group
appear to be *stable*—the distribution of half-
channel usage does not change. This stability
is especially interesting because each of the
members, by controlling his half-channel usage,
can at any time change the structure. Thus, a
stable group structure represents a form of
unanimity or agreement among the members about
how to interact.

This stability may be very fragile, because any member can cause a change by his own actions. Having tracked group structures since 1962, I have found structural stability to be more rare than structural change. Structures change for many reasons. Any change in membership causes an immediate change in structure, and then the adjustments by the group to this change can cause major structural changes. Structures change and evolve as groups gain experience and learn who can do what. Any number of effects originating outside the group can set in motion structural change processes. Errors, emergencies, and other special problems creep into the system and cause structural changes. Incompetence and changing bases of influence can also cause structural changes.

It is a major conceptual mistake to view an organizational structure as a static, one-dimensional entity. It is far more useful and correct to view organizations as having a number of structures that change. The key question involves the reasons why and the processes by which groups change their structures. Unless the structures are reasonably stable, the usual question of how structures influence behavior does not make much sense. Structures represent need-satisfying interaction patterns; they are more the result than the cause of behavior. Structures represent behavior patterns. Sanctions may be applied to members who seek to change structures. A stable structure can represent established norms for how to interact. Clearly structures do not change anything by themselves. It is the persons involved in maintaining these structures who can affect behavior.

RELATIONSHIPS BETWEEN STRUCTURES AND TASK PROCESSES

PROBLEMS AND TASK PROCESSES

Let us begin with the belief that most behavior is purposive. This does not mean that a person

can always articulate the reasons for an act,
but it does mean that there is more regularity
in behavior than what one would believe with
assumptions of randomness. We assume, further,
that a person seeks to join an organization
because he expects some net benefits and that
the organization lets him join because it expects to have a net benefit from his participation. We assume, with March and Simon (1958),
that this participation is maintained so long
as the inducements to belong are in excess of
his costs or contributions necessary to participate. This calculation includes analysis of
alternatives. For example, if a young executive
is making $20,000 a year in his current job
and could make $35,000 in another job, he may
change jobs even though he would be willing to
participate in his old job were it not for the
new offer. He may still turn down the offer because of other considerations such as possibilities for advancement, the type of work, job
security, etc.

Organizations carry out a number of different
activities and they can vary markedly in how
persons behave to accomplish these activities.
There is no simple, unique interaction pattern
to solve most problems. It is, therefore, useful to differentiate the *problem* to be worked on
and the processes that ensue to solve it. Our
main interest in this section is how the type
of problem affects the type of *task processes*
employed by an organization to solve it. The
task processes affect the dimensions over which
the organization's structures are defined.
Thus, knowledge of the problems leads to an understanding of possible task processes and
these, in turn, influence the dimensions of the
different structures for the organization.

Most organizational problem-solving involves
much more than merely calculating a set of numbers or choosing from among a set of alternatives. Most involve more than a single person
and involve processes (see Tuggle, 1978, Chapter 1). Many organizational problem-solving

processes and operations can be conceived as
having a number of stages that describe progress towards some acceptable end. Persons interact at the various stages and they may have
different structures at different stages. The
problems worked on may range from completing
the manufacture of a routinely produced product
to those of administration, control, and reorganization.

Most organizational problems take time to
find and solve, involve the interactions of a
number of persons, and are describable in terms
of a sequence of stages called *milestones*. These
milestones are designated by a list, M. The
first milestone is M_1, the second is M_2, and so
on until the final milestone, designated as M_F.
Furthermore, there is some order in the sequences by which any given milestone is reached
from any other milestone. One can draw many
conclusions concerning the group's efficiency
and effectiveness by studying the number and
sequence of milestones and how these milestones
are reached as a group goes from the beginning
milestone to the final milestone. These conclusions and the way they are derived are the core of
the theory of organizational structures presented in this book.

Consider the construction of a house. There
are a number of milestones to be reached before
construction begins. These might include ar-
ranging financing, obtaining building permits,
lining up suppliers, filing site plans, purchasing land, and obtaining architectural plans.
Each of these stages involves other persons
such as bankers, city planners, real estate
brokers, building subcontractors, lawyers, and
architects. Different sets of people are involved in different stages. Assuming that these
milestones have been reached, our builder can
begin construction. Many houses require that
land be cleared, foundations dug, house
footings set, foundations poured, framing constructed, plumbing installed, electrical and
heating work completed, roof finished, brick-

work laid for a fireplace, outer shell made,
and construction of windows and doors, stair-
cases, and interior walls completed. Cabinets
are installed, as are plumbing and electrical
fixtures. The walls are finished; rugs, tile,
and other flooring are installed. Doors are
hung; sidewalks and driveways are poured.
Painting and other interior and exterior fin-
ishing is completed. In some cases there is
some landscaping. The home has to be inspected
to insure compliance with local ordinances.
Financing is a continuing problem and a buyer
must be found.

An experienced builder can describe these
milestones and specify the order in which different milestones are to be reached. Some of
the possible orderings are considered necessary, such as completing the installation of
plumbing and heating after the framing has been
completed and before the walls are completed.
Other sequences, such as putting in a fireplace
after completing the walls, are wasteful. Departures from the original design and interrup-
tion of the building sequence are usually
wasteful and expensive. Deviation from a normal
plan may be necessary, however, because of the
unavailability of materials and labor, the
occurrence of weather, or because the buyer
changes his mind.

The use of concepts such as milestones for
complex projects has long been a fixture in
management literatures and operations research.
There are Critical Path Methods (CPM), program
evaluation and review techniques (PERT), and
other scheduling methods. The use of milestones
is also applied here to organizational problem-
solving. However, we seek to identify the structures by which the milestones are *reached*, and
we have to worry about criteria for reaching a
milestone. We can link the structures for
reaching the milestones and the order in which
they are reached to evaluate the overall structures and efficiency of the group.

Let us now, to be specific, examine these

ideas in the context of a little laboratory
organization that is solving a series of
simple problems. The experimenter describes a
problem to five subjects who are then going to
solve it. The group must organize itself while
solving a sequence of similar problems. Probably one of the simplest problems is the *minimum list of symbols problem* used by Faucheux and
Mackenzie (1966). In the minimum list of symbols problems, each member of the group is
given pieces of information, such as a list of
numbers. The problem to be solved by the group
is to combine each person's information, construct a list containing each person's information, and agree upon an order (the solution)
in which to present it to the experimenter. In
this problem, if any piece of information is
omitted in a solution, if any piece of information is used more than once, or if any of
the five members turns in a solution with a
different order than any other, the solution
is judged to be incorrect. The group must then
keep on working on it until the solution is
correct before being allowed to begin work on
the next problem. Typically, the groups are encouraged to work as fast as possible. The milestones are easy to specify: M_1 (begin) which is
signaled by the receipt of the original information from the experimenter, M_2 when one person has all of the information from the others,
M_3 when all members have all of the information, M_4 when a minimum list is compiled, M_5
when they agree on it, M_6 when they agree to
submit it, and $M_7 = M_F$ when the correct solutions have been turned in to the experimenter.

There are many ways of solving this sort of
problem. For example, the group members can
send data to only one person, who then compiles
the list, and who then sends it to each member.
The members can then submit it to the experimenter. This solution procedure can be de-
scribed by the sequence: $M_1 \rightarrow M_2 \rightarrow M_4 \rightarrow M_7$. In
another solution method, every person sends his
information to every other person, each member

constructs a minimum list, they negotiate over
the minimum list, and after arriving at one
they agree to submit it and do so. This solu-
tion procedure is described as $M_1 \rightarrow M_2 \rightarrow M_3 \rightarrow M_4 \rightarrow M_5 \rightarrow M_6 \rightarrow M_7$.

This problem seems easy enough, but if mistakes are made or if someone sends in a solution prematurely, the group can spend hours on
one simple problem. The record is three hours
for one of these problems. Some groups have
solved them in under three minutes. This wide
variation in performance makes the problem of
determining which milestones are reached and
how they are reached very important, both to
the group members and to the experimenter who
is observing the problem-solving processes.
Learning which processes and structures are
more efficient is of great interest to those
running an organization. It is, therefore, not
surprising to find the members of a group
worrying about how to organize themselves to
complete these problems. One can observe the
effects of experience and of disputes on the
organization and efficiency of such groups.
One can observe power struggles, sophisticated
treachery, and earnest cooperation in these
little organizations. The members may not yet
be experienced businessmen, but the study of
such group processes yields many insights for
real-world organizations.

Consider how the groups can exchange the information received from the experimenter. One
way is to choose a person who receives all
such information and then sends a list to all
members. Another way is for everyone to send it
to everyone else. The structures are:

	x_1	x_2	x_3	x_4	x_5
x_1	0	1	1	1	1
x_2	1	0	0	0	0
x_3	1	0	0	0	0
x_4	1	0	0	0	0
x_5	1	0	0	0	0

Structure #1
Group chooses x_1 as "hub."

	x_1	x_2	x_3	x_4	x_5
x_1	0	1	1	1	1
x_2	1	0	1	1	1
x_3	1	1	0	1	1
x_4	1	1	1	0	1
x_5	1	1	1	1	0

Structure #2
Everyone sends information to everyone.

Both structures allow the group to reach milestone M_3, which occurs when each member has all of the information. Structure #1 requires 8 messages and structure #2 requires 20 messages. But, if member x_3 does not send in his information, the group cannot proceed. If member x_3 makes a mistake or if x_1 makes an error, the group may not reach M_3. Some members send the information more than once. Such messages are *redundant*. Some member may persist in sending information after M_3 has been reached. Such messages are called *untimely*. And, if the group does not reach M_3, but proceeds further to M_5, they may be forced to return to M_3 at a later time. Incorrect solutions may require the group to return to M_1 and try again. Redundant and untimely behaviors seriously affect group performance.

For a given type of problem, one can describe the list of milestones M_1, M_2, ..., M_F. These are subscripted in logical order from the beginning to the end of a problem. Groups can skip some milestones, and groups can interact to reach milestones so as to give different milestone structures. We can describe each milestone structure by keeping track of the messages for each milestone. We can look at the set of messages to determine which ones were timely and necessary, which redundant, and which untimely. If a group's behaviors are *timely*, the arrows connecting the milestones fall into a path such as

$$\boxed{M_1} \to \boxed{M_2} \to \boxed{M_3} \to \boxed{M_6} \to \boxed{M_F}$$

But if the group is reaching the milestones out of logical order, the arrows connecting the milestones will begin to exhibit loops such as

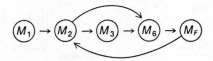

Every untimely milestone involves one or more loops.

TASK PROCESSES AND ROLES

The organizational problem determines the list of possible milestones for the task processes. The groups interact to reach the milestones. There is a *milestone structure* for each milestone. These milestone structures can be aggregated to describe the *role* of each member as well as the role of the entire group. Thus, there is a logically close relationship between the behaviors of the members and the task processes. To describe the roles of each member, we use a table where the members are designated by the rows and the activities engaged in by the columns. There is a one-to-one relationship between the structures and the table of roles, if we designate the activities according to the usage of half-channels for the various milestones. A role matrix for a little laboratory group following $M_1 \rightarrow M_2 \rightarrow M_3 \rightarrow M_7$ and using structure #1 is given by:

	Activities for M_2				Activities for M_3				Activities for M_7				
	$x_2{\rightarrow}x_1$	$x_3{\rightarrow}x_1$	$x_4{\rightarrow}x_1$	$x_5{\rightarrow}x_1$	$x_1{\rightarrow}x_2$	$x_1{\rightarrow}x_3$	$x_1{\rightarrow}x_4$	$x_1{\rightarrow}x_5$	$x_1{\rightarrow}E$	$x_2{\rightarrow}E$	$x_3{\rightarrow}E$	$x_4{\rightarrow}E$	$x_5{\rightarrow}E$
x_1	1	1	1	1	1	1	1	1	1	0	0	0	0
x_2	1	0	0	0	1	0	0	0	0	1	0	0	0
x_3	0	1	0	0	0	1	0	0	0	0	1	0	0
x_4	0	0	1	0	0	0	1	0	0	0	0	1	0
x_5	0	0	0	1	0	0	0	1	0	0	0	0	1

Here an entry is 1 for both the sender and the receiver for M_2 and M_3 and 0 otherwise, and an entry is 1 for M_7 if the member sends his data to the experimenter. We call the *role matrix*, R.[1] The role matrix for structure #2 will have more columns, and if the task processes involve more milestones, there will be more sets of columns, a set corresponding to each milestone. The entries into the role matrix, R, can be classified according to whether they are timely, redundant, or untimely. We can thereby subdivide R into three component role matrices: the *timely role matrix*, R_T, the *redundant role matrix*, R_R, and the *untimely role matrix*, R_U. That way R is the sum of its three component role matrices. The entries in R_T are either 0 or 1. Any excess timely messages are included in the redundant role matrix, R_R. All untimely messages are placed in the untimely role matrix, R_U.

Mackenzie (1976a) discusses many refinements and procedures for tabulation of the entries in role matrices from the interaction data. It is beyond the scope of this short book to delve into these extensions, but one should keep in mind that the problem determines the milestones, each milestone has a possible structure, one can combine the many structures into a role matrix, and one can subdivide the role matrix into its timely, redundant, and untimely portions. These ideas demonstrate the linkages between task processes, structures, and roles.

ROLES AND ORGANIZATIONAL LEVELS

The timely portion of the role matrix, R_T, is used to determine the *organizational level* of each group member. The level of each person is judged by his behavior and not by his position title or job description because, in real life, the formal title or position is often a misleading description of the actual task processes in which he engages. When the formal positions coincide with the task processes, the procedure for determining levels will faithfully reproduce the formal system. But when the formal system is inconsistent with the task processes, this procedure will highlight the discrepancies. And, by locating and analyzing the discrepancies, one uncovers many clues to the causes of inefficiency and high costs, and locates previously unsuspected problems for management. For example, if person

x_1 is formally designated as the supervisor of
a project and x_6 is not assigned to the project,
then the appearance of x_6 in the role matrix at
level one and the absence of x_1 in the role
matrix raises questions. Why is x_6 doing this
and why isn't x_1 involved? It could turn out,
for example, that x_1 is incompetent and x_6 is
the one to whom members turn for help and
guidance. Or, it may turn out that x_6 is interfering in the duties of x_1.

The basic idea for determining organizational
level is that the activities of an immediate
subordinate are a subset of those of his immediate superior. If one is the vice president
for production, the plant managers reporting
to the vice president work on a more restricted
set of activities than the vice president,
whose responsibilities cover the activities of
each plant manager in addition to his responsibilities to the higher level, executive vice
president. Thus, the entries in the role set of
the superior contain those of his subordinates.
The executive vice president is also the superior of the plant managers, but he is not
their immediate superior in this example. The
phrases *immediate superior* and *immediate subordinate*
are used in order to separate the interacting
superior-subordinate pairs from those who are
hierarchically separated by more than one
level.

By examining the timely role matrix entries
for every pair in the group, one can determine
whether or not member x_1 is an immediate superior or immediate subordinate to x_j. In many
cases x_i and x_j are not in an immediate-
superior—immediate-subordinate relationship.
They can be colleagues on the same level or
just members on different levels.

Procedures for determining the actual level
of each person have been developed, allowing
one to move directly from the role matrix to
the determination of organizational level. For
example, one can start by considering each

person to be a possible candidate for level one. One then examines all pairs to discover whether or not one or more of these are subordinate to others. The subordinate ones become candidates for level two. These are then examined to find subordinates of these subordinates on level two. If there are some, they are assigned as candidates for level three. This comparison process is repeated until every member has been assigned to a level.

For example, suppose the timely role matrix is given by:

		a_1	a_2	a_3	a_4	a_5	a_6	a_7	a_8	a_9	Level
	x_1	1	1	1	1	1	1	1	1	1	1
	x_2	1	1	1	0	0	0	0	0	0	2
Members	x_3	0	0	0	1	1	1	0	0	0	2
	x_4	0	0	0	0	0	0	1	1	1	2
	x_5	1	1	0	0	0	0	0	0	0	3

The header row above the matrix reads "Activities" spanning a_1 through a_9.

Then, for this timely role matrix, x_1 is on level one, x_2, x_3, and x_4 are his immediate subordinates on level two, and x_5 is the immediate subordinate of x_2 and is therefore on level three. An organizational chart of this group is given in Figure 1.5. Note that Figure 1.5 includes both the level and the activities relating each pair in the group.

TYPES OF STRUCTURAL RELATIONSHIPS

The organization chart in Figure 1.5 is extremely simple because all positions are hierarchical and exhibit only immediate superior-subordinate relationships. However, there are other interesting and practically important relationships that can be derived from the timely role matrix and the procedure for determining

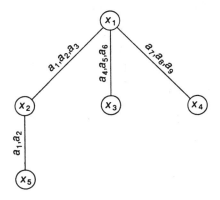

FIGURE 1.5 An organization chart based on the timely role matrix indicating the activities between members.

levels. Two important ones are *cousin* and *uncle-nephew* relationships.

If we use the analogy of a patrilineal family tree, an immediate superior corresponds to the father and the immediate subordinate corresponds to the son. Thus, in Figure 1.5, x_1 is in the position of father to x_2, x_3, and x_4 and grandfather to x_5. Members on the same level are analogous to siblings or cousins. there are functional activities describing relationships among members of a level, we call these cousin relationships. There are also relationships between a cousin at this level and immediate subordinates of another cousin on the next lower level.

Consider the timely role matrix on the following page, where there are four entries (circled) not in the previous role matrix for Figure 1.5. The organization chart for this matrix is given in Figure 1.6.

The four extra entries set up two cousin relationships between x_2 and x_3 and one each between x_2 and x_4, and x_3 and x_4. The cousin relationships based on activities a_1 and a_4

Activities

	a_1	a_2	a_3	a_4	a_5	a_6	a_7	a_8	a_9
x_1	1	1	1	1	1	1	1	1	1
x_2	1	1	1	(1)	0	0	0	0	0
x_3	(1)	0	0	1	1	1	0	0	0
x_4	0	0	0	(1)	0	0	1	1	1
x_5	1	1	0	(1)	0	0	0	0	0

Members

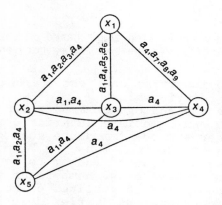

FIGURE 1.6 An organization chart indicating immediate-superior, cousin, and uncle-nephew relationships.

also set up two uncle-nephew relationships be-tween x_3 and x_5 and one between x_4 and x_5. Thus, the four extra entries in the timely role matrix created four cousin and three uncle-nephew relationships.

Cousin and uncle-nephew relationships reduce efficiency. It may be initially necessary to have such relationships, because a group may not know how to solve a problem and may wish to determine itself which person should do what activities. However, when one observes a group

seeking efficiency over a succession of problems, cousin and uncle-nephew relationships
tend to be eliminated because they can cause
conflicts, delays, and redundant and untimely
behaviors. Many organizations maintain standing
committees or appoint committees and task
forces that create temporary cousin and uncle-
nephew relationships so that new problems can
be solved without disturbing the regular task
process.

It should be recalled here that structures
represent need-satisfying interaction patterns
and that as needs change, or as persons perceive that needs could be better satisfied with
another structure, then the structure of a
group changes. If any group discovers better
ways of solving problems, either by altering
the milestone sequence or the structure for a
milestone, the structures may change. Along
with these structural changes will come changes
in the role matrices and in the problem-solving
processes. The structures of a group are dynamic. The reasons for change and the processes of
structural change are at least as important as
the structures themselves. For example, environmental and technological changes can set
off many structural changes.

MEASUREMENT OF STRUCTURE

The definitions of structure, task process,
role matrices, and levels given previously
also describe what information is *required to determine* the structure of a group. Ideally, such
complete information is available and, if it is
possible to obtain it, one can measure the
structures. However, any structure represents
a pattern of interaction involving many pairs
of relationships. Most questions about the
performance of an organization are scalar. For
example, one might wish to know the output,
profit rate, market share, effectiveness, and
other measures for an organization. It is quite

natural that one should wish to compare such scalar measures with measures of structure. In order to facilitate such comparisons, it is necessary to characterize an organization's structures as a scalar. Thus, an important problem associated with the measurement of a structure is capturing salient features of such patterns in terms of descriptive scalar measures. One may wish to examine the structures to determine the degree of structural centralization, the degree of participation, and the degree of hierarchy for the purposes of explaining other scales such as rate of output, efficiency, and measures of effectiveness.

There are a number of measures for degree of structural centrality (Mackenzie, 1966a, 1969, 1975a; Leavitt, 1951; Sabidussi, 1966; Lewin and Tapiero, 1973). But these are measures for the degree of centrality of the overall structures and do not specify how to aggregate and calculate the structural centrality for a set of component substructures. They also do not include the capability of incorporating task-process information such as the role matrix. They are useful for certain laboratory studies, but they are less useful for more complex structures or for analyzing changes in task processes. Similarly, there is a measure for the degree of participation (Mackenzie, 1966b) that suffers from the same defects. What is needed is a measure of structure that incorporates both the direct interaction patterns and the task processes. So rather than presenting a necessarily lengthy discussion of the cited measures for centrality and participation, let us concentrate on a measure for the degree of hierarchy that has proven very helpful in numerous laboratory studies and that promises much for more directly practical work. The concept of structural centrality is discussed more fully in chapter 6.

An Index of the Degree of Hierarchy

We must recognize that the hierarchy of an organization is a matter of degree, with some organizations more hierarchical than others. Accordingly, the measure presented here measures the degree to which an organization deviates from a pure hierarchy. An organization has a number of structures and task processes. We want our measure to reflect the direction, frequency of interaction, content, *and* task processes. As we learned in the previous section, content is related to the task processes but one also needs sequence (timely, untimely, and redundant) information to describe task processes. A measure of the degree of hierarchy should reflect both the structures and the problem-solving processes. A problem-solving process containing untimely and redundant behaviors detracts from the degree to which an organization is hierarchical. If one did not consider the task processes, a pure hierarchy would consist of a concatenation of immediate superior-subordinate pairs as in Figure 1.7.

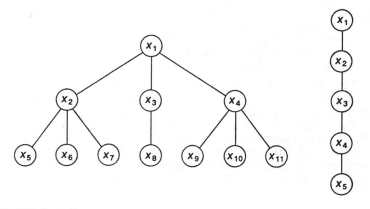

FIGURE 1.7 Two examples of a structurally pure hierarchy.

The chain of positions on the right is a simple form of hierarchy. In the left hand figure each path connecting x_1 on level one to a position in level three is a chain. Such a chain is often referred to as a "chain of command." A structurally pure hierarchy consists of many such chains.

There is an analogy to the chain in the graph of the task process. If the succession of reached milestones is timely as in $M_1 \rightarrow M_2 \rightarrow M_3 \rightarrow M_4 \rightarrow M_5 \rightarrow M_7$, the task process is a chain, too. And, if the task process contains untimely and redundant behaviors, the loops destroy the chain. The task process graph of the succession of reached milestones is a time-ordered chain. The chain graph of a structurally pure hierarchy is an interaction-determined chain. Our main assumption is that when we are examining the degree of hierarchy, it is necessary for both the structure and the process graph to be made of chains in a pure hierarchy.

A *pure hierarchy* has four main structural properties and one main task process property. The structural properties are:

1. There is only one member on level one.
2. Each member is assigned to a level.
3. All nonzero relationships between members are immediate superior-subordinate.
4. The role matrix entries for all members on a level are disjoint.

The main task process property is that all behaviors are timely. There are no redundant or untimely behaviors.

Now, if we denote the number of behaviors that are redundant or untimely as U_T, the total number of non-untimely behaviors as T, the number of cousin behaviors as C, the number of uncle-nephew behaviors as U, and let H denote the *degree of hierarchy*, then

$$H = 1 - \frac{U + C + U_T}{T + U_T} \qquad (1.1)$$

If there are no cousin behaviors, there will be no uncle-nephew behaviors. If there are no cousin behaviors and no untimely behaviors, $C = U = U_T = 0$ and $H = 1$. Thus, this simple formula satisfies our main properties by being 1.0 when we have a pure hierarchy. If there are some cousin and untimely behaviors, H can be interpreted as the fraction of behaviors that are consistent with a pure hierarchy. Thus, we call H a measure for the degree of hierarchy.

An Index for the Degree of Task Process Efficiency

The goal of efficiency is often cited as a prime organizational goal. Members are exhorted to become more efficient, but neither those exhorting nor those being exhorted understand exactly what it means to become more efficient. This is because the management literature has not been very clear about what it has meant by the word. Because the index for the degree of hierarchy is linked to a measure for the degree of task process efficiency, it is important to define what is meant by this phrase.

The concept of efficiency in the physical sciences is reasonably clear, in principle. It is the ratio of useful output to total input measured in energy terms. Thus an inefficient engine uses more energy than it produces in work. One conjures up an old steam engine. The more holes it has and the more steam that can escape before the piston is moved, the less efficient the steam engine. Different fields and devices have different operational definitions of efficiency, but all are related logically to the underlying concept. If one seeks to use such a concept, one has to ask and answer a series of questions: (1) What is the process for which we seek to measure efficiency? (2) What is the total amount of input? (3) What is meant by useful output?

If one answers these questions in succession for a problem-solving group, one concludes: (1) we seek to measure the degree of efficiency of the task oriented behaviors in a group's task process for solving a problem; (2) the total amount of input could be the total number of task oriented interactions used in the task processes to solve a problem; and (3) the useful output is related to the number of problems actually solved. More specifically, if a group produces one solution in 50 interactions and, by examining the milestone sequence, we determine that only 25 were actually required, the efficiency would be 0.50 (25/50). If the group's 50 interactions had been reallocated, it could have solved two 25 interaction task-processes. In fact, of the 50 interactions, 25 are "wasted" and 25 are useful. Therefore, the efficiency is 25/50 = 0.50.

But, even if we accept this as an approach to defining the efficiency of task-process behavior, we still have to find a way of knowing the minimum number of messages required to complete a given task process, especially when we know that the task process can change and will vary from group to group even for the same set of problems. One procedure is to examine the task processes actually followed by a group, using the distinctions between timely, untimely, and redundant milestones. The list of reached timely milestones actually employed by a group is taken from the data. For each of these reached timely milestones, one can calculate the minimum number of interactions required to reach each milestone. This minimum varies with the nature of the milestone and the size of the group. Let m_T denote the minimum number of interactions necessary to reach the set of timely reached milestones in the task process. Let n_T denote the actual number of interactions taken to reach the end of the task process. Then the *degree of task process efficiency*, E_T, is given by

$$E_T = \frac{m_T}{n_T}$$ (1.2)

The values of E_T will vary as the group learns how to solve its problems and as it organizes itself to solve them. The numerator, n_T, will depend upon the actual timely task process and will vary with how each group goes about completing its task processes. The values of E_T can be computed for each problem. The value is E_1 for problem one, E_2 for problem two, and so on. Now, if a group is given a succession of similar problems to solve, one can monitor the group and obtain a sequence of values for E_T.

Measures of *effectiveness* such as time per problem, number of errors, the number of messages, have been used as measures of efficiency. This is logically incorrect. For example, time per problem is a measure of velocity. Just because a group solves a problem quickly does not mean that it is necessarily efficient. It could have been fast and wasted enormous amounts of energy. Similarly, a group could be very inefficient and not make any errors. A measure such as the number of messages is not adequate because the number depends partly on the task process used as well as on how each milestone was reached.

There are other measures of effectiveness, such as level of profit, total time wasted, meeting of schedules, number of finished products per hour, and so on. Effectiveness measures are essentially the degree to which some standard has been met. There are any number of such standards, just as there are any number of goals. Consequently, calling an effectiveness measure an efficiency measure is, in general, an unsound procedure. However, in many cases certain effectiveness measures do correlate well with a measure of efficiency.

Mackenzie (1976b) has calculated the degree of hierarchy (equation 1.1) and the degree of task-process efficiency (equation 1.2) and found close agreement. The correlation coefficient between H and E_T ranged from 0.89 to 0.99 on nine separate experiments involving close to 700 problems in total. Figure 1.8 is a graph of H and E_T in value but the value of H is always less than or equal to the value of E_T.

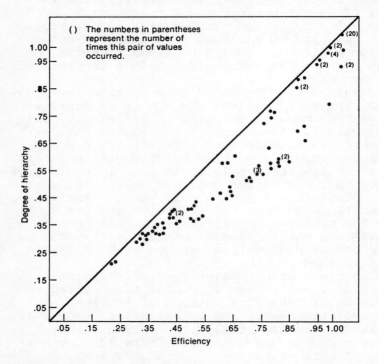

FIGURE 1.8 The plot of the degree of hierarchy and efficiency for the Faucheux-Mackenzie A problems.

Calculating H depends upon the values of U, C, U_T, and T and the detailed formulae and procedures for doing this can be found in the cited study. The values of E_T depend upon the values of m_T and n_T. H depends upon the structures and the task process. E_T does not specifically include any details of the structures. The two measures are usually different because they involve different variables and include different aspects of a task process, even though both are defined on a task process and role matrix, R. Both measures are always less than or equal to 1.0. However, it is possible for the value of E_T to be 1.0 while the value of H is small. This can happen in a task process with different milestones where each milestone structure is a wheel but different persons are the hub for different milestones.

The degree of hierarchy, H, is also significantly correlated with three measures of effectiveness: time per problem, number of errors per problem, and number of messages per problem. As groups become more hierarchical the time per problem, the number of errors per problem, and the number of messages per problem drop to lower values. These correlations, for the same data as the correlations between H and E_T , hover between 0.5 and 0.7. They are significant but far less so than the relationships between H and E_T.

One of the implications for the relationships between H and E_T, $H \leq E_T$, is that as groups become more hierarchical in structure and process, their efficiency will increase. However, as we shall see in chapter 5, a hierarchy of structure and process may differ markedly from a pyramid of officers, which is often confused with a pure hierarchy. If the task processes for the pyramid of officers are inefficient, the degree of hierarchy will decline as the task processes become inefficient, no matter how carefully the authority is defined and task processes are described in some organization manual. H depends upon both the actual interaction patterns *and* the task processes. Pyramids depend only upon the idea of formal authority hierarchy. The phrase *authority hier-archy* is used in later chapters to describe pyramids. Authority hierarchies are a special case of hierarchies.

The finding that the degree of hierarchy is less than or equal to the degree of task-process efficiency ($H \leq E_T$) provides a practical clue about how to increase efficiency. Suppose that you are in a structural "hierarchy" and you notice that there is a low degree of task-process efficiency. Because $H \leq E_T$, one should be able to increase E_T by increasing H. But H can get increased by decreasing the numbers of cousin and uncle relationships, and the number of untimely and redundant behaviors. One knows that uncle-nephew relationships between two levels can only occur when there are cousin relationships on the higher level. So, the simple procedure is to start "cleaning house" at the top. Eliminating cousin relationships on level one will eliminate uncle-nephew relationships between levels one and two. It will also elimi-nate some of the cousin relationships on level two, which reduces, in turn, the number of uncle-nephew relationships between levels two and three and the number of cousin relation-ships on level three. This will in turn cause similar decreases on still lower levels. It can be shown that by starting from the top and working down toward the lower levels of a structural hierarchy, one can rapidly increase H. Eliminating cousins and uncle-nephew rela-tionships can also reduce the number of un-timely messages. Some practical limitations to this "ruthless" method of organizational change for increased efficiency are discussed in the next section.

DATA LIMITATIONS MAY PREVENT REALIZATION OF MORE IDEAL MEASURES OF STRUCTURE

A thorough analysis of task processes, struc-tures, and roles can be made using the ideas

presented so far. It is expensive to conduct
such a study and one would have to know one's
purposes for making a study before collecting
data. *Ceteris paribus,* the larger the unit being
studied, the greater the cost. An analyst or
the manager hiring the analyst has to balance
possible gains from making such a study against
the costs. A rule of thumb is to start near the
top (and below the one paying for the study)
and work downward until the increase in costs
exceeds the increase in benefits. Persons on
higher levels usually draw higher incomes, require more resources to operate, and affect
more issues and people than those on a lower
level. The cousin relationships at a higher
level create uncle-nephew relationships with
the next level and these, in turn, more cousin
relationships at the next lower level, and so
on.

Some problems may be insoluble because of
financial and legal considerations or because
of job security. A system with many procedural
checks may deliberately create cousin and
uncle-nephew relationships and even untimely
controls. It may be impractical to make changes
in personnel or job assignments because of the
requirements of the law and because of an
organization's need for some people. For example, a small hospital may have to tolerate
disputes between its only pathologist and the
administrator of the hospital because both are
needed and no replacements are seen to be possible. In some universities, there may be a
tenured faculty member, judged to be ineffect-
ive, who is kept on because the "costs" of re-
moving the professor may exceed any forseeable
benefits. These costs may include time, legal
fees, and a breaking of trust that could lead
to more serious issues lying beyond the original. For example, the faculty could form a union
as a protest.

Practical political considerations should not
be ignored. On the other hand, serious

problems caused by untimely and redundant behaviors, or by manifold cousin and uncle-nephew
relationships, should not be ignored, especially when the organization is subject to market
forces. It is useful to know the nature of the
problems in order to reach a judgment about
how to handle them. Experienced administrators
learn to pick the issues for a fight carefully.
Knowledge of the task processes and structures,
and measures such as the degree of hierarchy,
can be useful in making a reorganization decision. Just remember that in many cases the
"cure" may be worse than the "disease."

One practical consideration, the size of the
organization, may not be decisive in performing
a structural analysis of task processes. At
first glance, it would seem obvious that because the number of possible half-channels
grows faster than the number of persons, increasing size would make such analysis too
costly. Add to this the knowledge that larger
organizations have many more task processes
than smaller ones. However, larger organizations tend to have hierarchical structures and
limitations on the activities for descending
levels. As a result, it is realistic to think
of the 10,000-person organization as a network
of many smaller organizations working on special
problems. Practically, most of the possible
half-channels are never used and usage within
the subunit is often much greater than usage
between units. Furthermore, because of the
"linking pin" function of the leader of a subgroup who is a "follower" in a higher group,
the usage of possible half-channels between
units is limited in the number of persons and
task processes involved.

Another feature of large organizations is
that the detail or specificity of the behaviors
becomes greater as one moves down from the
highest levels. This means that the specification of the task process milestones and activities change with the organizational level. The

activity element in a role matrix at a high level may open up into a much larger number of activities at each succeeding level. The number of columns in the role matrix, R, increases as one goes lower in the same manner that increased magnification shows more detail. At the higher level one can deal with more aggregated activities such as sales or production than at a lower level where one is concerned with sales and production of a specific product or assembly line.

Consider a university. There are many levels between the president and the chairman of a department of management. The task element of the president to provide teaching for the students is usually not specific about who gets assigned to a particular course. This task element becomes much larger and more detailed for the academic vice-president who has to worry about teaching for his various professional schools and colleges. The specificity increases for a dean of a school of business who must consider his departments. The level of specificity becomes even larger as the department chairman decides which professor is to teach which courses.

A structural analysis of a task process can be made at each level for each organizational unit. The number of persons and the number of task processes involved usually remain relatively small. There are practical constraints on these quantities because of the difficulties of assembling, disseminating, and processing information. Thus, the analytical nightmare of a role matrix with 10,000 rows and thousands of columns is not a realistic problem. Instead there are many small role matrices for the various suborganizations. And these are linked by the increasing task specialization and specificity of activity as one examines the task processes of successive units. Furthermore, because of the specific purpose of making a study, often only a relevant suborganization is analyzed.

However, even though making a structural analysis of a task process may be much less difficult in practice than it would seem in theory,
there are severe limitations in performing such
analyses. First of all, this type of information is usually not collected systematically.
It costs money and time to collect data. The
ideas presented here about structures, task
processes, and the measure for the degree of
hierarchy are new and could not be expected to
be used yet. Some of the data may exist in information systems, personnel files, accounting
records, memoranda, and in memory. But such information has not been collected systematically
enough to perform thorough structural analyses
of task processes. Second, some of the information may be considered confidential and thus
made unavailable. Third, some recorded information is incorrect, either by accident or intent.
Fourth, some recorded information may be out
of date or revised to be consistent with what
the organization ought to be rather than what
it is. Fifth, some managers are so busy that
they do not take the time to consider problems
of task-process structures. For these, the
argument that they are so busy because of unresolved or poorly solved problems of task-
process structures simply falls on deaf ears.
Sixth, the authority system may be so far out
of synchronization with the system of task-
process structures that a manager may feel it
is hopeless even to try. This is especially
true for middle managers who have reason to believe that even if they solved these problems
at this level and below, the confusion at
higher levels would undo carefully thought out
plans overnight. The problems arising out of
inconsistencies between the structural hierarchy and the actual task-process system are
discussed in chapter 2.

SURROGATE MEASURES OF HIERARCHY

It is hardly surprising, then, to learn that
very few studies of problems of task-process

structure have ever used more than simple summary labels to describe organizational structures and simple measures for properties of
organizational structures. Evan (1963) has
pointed out a number of surrogate indices of
hierarchy of authority: span of control, number of levels of authority, ratio of administrators to production workers, time span of
discretion (maximum length of time an employee
is authorized to make decisions on his own initiative which commit a given amount of resources to the organization), the degree of
centralization in decision-making, and the degree of limitation on the rights of management
to make decisions. Some of these quantities are
very easy to calculate and are in widespread
use. They have a drawback in that they lose the
interconnections of an organization's structures and the relationships between the task
processes and these structures.

Surrogate Measures of Process

There are many analyses of production and information flows made by those who do "systems"
work and who manage or set up management information systems. Operations research analysts
and others involved with problems of scheduling
work flows have studied task processes extensively, although there has not been very much
work on the relationships between the logic of
task processes and the structures of the organization (Gerwin and Christoffel, 1974). However, there are many instances of the use of
process analyses of physical flows such as the
flow of materials and parts in the assembly of
an automobile or the system for routing paperwork flows in administration. The analysis of
decision-making processes is technically lagg-
ing behind the analysis of physical flow
processes.
    These are attempts to give global descrip-
tions to types of task processes. For example,
we have job shops and flow shops describing the
essential characteristics of production

according to whether or not each unit of production is made at a small or a large number of
work stations. The degree of role variety
(Tyler, 1973), task-contingency models of work-
unit structure (Van de Ven and Delbecq, 1974),
role differentiation (Morley, 1974), and type
of technology (Perrow, 1967; Lynch, 1974; and
Hrebinink, 1974) represent other attempts to
describe task processes.

SOME CHARACTERISTICS OF TYPES OF ORGANIZATIONAL STRUCTURES

A simple calculation is that if every "boss"
has n subordinates (span of control is n), then
there are $n^0 = 1$ persons on level one, $n^1 = n$
persons on level two, n^2 persons on level
three, n^3 on level four, and so on. Another
simple calculation will show that if the size
of the organization (measured as the number of
people) is fixed, then the number of levels
becomes greater as n becomes smaller. An organization whose average supervisor has a small
span of control has more levels than another
organization with the same number of people
but a larger span of control. Thus, the number
of levels is a clue about the average span of
control, and knowledge about the average span
of control is a clue about the number of levels.
Organizations with a larger number of levels
(or small spans of control) are called "tall"
and those with a smaller number of levels (or
high spans of control) are called "flat."
  Numerous studies have compared the performance of centralized vs. decentralized structures (Leavitt, 1951; Guetzkow and Simon, 1955;
Faucheux and Mackenzie, 1966); in these
studies, a structure is centralized if all messages flow only on channels connecting each
person to one position called the "hub." A
group is said to be decentralized in this literature if everyone interacts with every other
person. A variant of this is the study of

Carzo (1963), where he called the organization
"tight" vs. "loose." The tight organization was
a three-level hierarchy and the loose was decentralized. There is some evidence to support
a conclusion that, although some studies have
shown a superior performance of one type of
structure over another, other factors besides
the availability of channels are more decisive
(see chapter 2). These factors involve more
detailed analyses of task processes and group
structures.

Sometimes organizations are described in
terms of the type of participation in governance. There are autocratic organizations wherein the rule follows the line set by its head.
Autocratic organizations are often described as
authoritarian. One variety of an autocratic
organization could be "despotic" if the main
characteristic is a reduced emphasis on productivity and a heightened emphasis on loyalty
and obedience. Some organizations, especially
some volunteer clubs, are called "laissez-
faire" because each member essentially "does
his own thing." Somewhere in between the autocratic and the laissez-faire organization is
what is called a "democratic" organization.
The label "democratic" can mean that officials
are elected for fixed terms to govern. It has
also been used to describe "participatory"
democracy, in which the members vote on both
the leaders and the policies involving the
functioning of the organization. More will be
said about such organizations in chapter 7.

SOME BASES FOR DIFFERENT STRUCTURAL ARRANGEMENTS

Most organizations, even if they are structural
hierarchies, have to decide upon the basis for
defining the roles of its members. The main
idea is to determine the important (to the
organization) task processes. Then, with respect to these task processes, those who are to

be interacting frequently should be able to do so easily and as directly as possible. Those who need to interact infrequently should be assigned to different suborganizations. The basis for segmenting the members by function will depend, too, on economic considerations such as transportation costs, economies of scale of production, administration, and distribution.

Some organizations with local markets and high transportation costs may organize around geographical centers. Some organizations having a variety of products that involve different task processes to produce the products may be organized about product lines. Some organizations such as General Motors have a number of divisions, by make of car, for instance, in order to foster competition and to reach different market segments (Cadillac vs. Chevrolet). Some organizations have different technical and administrative processes. The same basic process (e.g., oil refining) can produce a variety of products (fuel oil, asphalt, aviation gasoline, and stock for plastics).

Another variety of differentiations is according to the basic business functions such as productions, marketing, finance, systems, research and development, and personnel. In such an organization the knowledge specialties of an organization can be coordinated and brought to bear on a number of organizational problems.

ORGANIZATIONAL STRUCTURES AND MANAGEMENT

An organization has a number of members who interact in different ways in order to accomplish some ends. One can describe the patterns of interactions in structures. One can select the structures to be studied by examining the task processes. From these one determines the role matrices and measures of the structure such as the degree of hierarchy. Basically, structures are dependent upon the needs and purposes for participating in an organization. Organizational structures are dynamic and changing. One also notices that the extant interaction patterns can affect future interaction patterns. There is some degree of regularity and control on behavior even though there can be many forces to change the structures.

Structures can be changed, and by changing the task processes and the structures, managers can rearrange the pattern of interactions and the sequences of these interactions to accomplish specified ends. Many studies have demonstrated the way organizational structures can affect productivity and the direction, frequency, and content of interaction. It is not always possible to force changes in interaction patterns, but it is usually possible to alter the basis for need satisfaction of the members so that they will reorganize themselves in desired ways. Studies by Mackenzie (1976b) have demonstrated how, by indirect control over incentives, the groups will alter their structures and problem-solving processes. It has also been shown experimentally that it is much easier to gain acceptance of a given structure if the desired structure is reasonable and need-satisfying to the members. It takes much more pressure to get compliance to an unreasonable structure and problem-solving process. Members have needs and they interact in pursuit of these needs. If the requirements of the job conflict with these needs, it will take more incentives to gain compliance and cooperation. It is impractical to insist on organizational structures that are seen as less acceptable than another set if this other set can do the same job. The selection of an organization's structures is a joint act among its leaders and followers. It is extremely important because these interlocking decisions determine how the members are to interact to accomplish the purposes of the members and its leaders.

In some cases, in fact in too many cases, the organization's structures are considered the sole prerogative of a set of leaders. These persons usually have rank and some legal basis for the authority from which the rank is derived. The ranks recognize persons and often serve to differentiate competence and function. Often the levels and the differentiation of the roles in the role matrix follow the rank system. Such systems can function efficiently, but there is always the danger that new problems requiring newer structures cannot be solved effectively because the rank structure impedes the need to reorganize. Problems can become converted to how to enforce the existing rank system rather than how to solve the problem. Such systems can become unresponsive and overly rigid.

The organization members will set up "informal" structures to "get around" the formal rank structure. In many universities, for example, the rank system (president, vice-president, dean, chairman, etc.) for administration of facilities, admissions, payroll, parking, teaching assignments, research grants, security, etc., is out of touch with the research and teaching activities. There is often a sizeable gap between the authority system and the system of task process structures. Lippitt and Mackenzie (1974) call this an authority-task gap and see it as a major source of committee formation. Faculty and students cross department lines to teach and do research. The "managers" of a university really do not manage much except the administrative functions. Some accept this gracefully and others try to get control over the research and teaching task processes.

The attempt to control an organization by exerting more control is often dysfunctional, especially when it is the control system itself

that is a prime source of the lack of control.
In too many cases, the failure of a control
system stimulates solutions which extend the
controls. And because the original basis was
not appropriate, the new controls will fail,
which will stimulate even more controls. This
process is known as Finagle's law. Unfortunately, there are too many examples of this law.
The antidote for Finagle's law is less control
and a change is the basis for control.

NOTES

[1]Note that the role matrix R contains the same information as the composite structure R across the three
milestones. The information is just rearranged from a
table with persons on the rows and columns to persons
on the rows and communication activities on the columns.
This is why the same symbol R is used for both structure
and role matrix.

REFERENCES

Carzo, R., Jr. "Some Effects of Organization Structure
on Group Effectiveness." *Administrative Science
Quarterly* 7 (1963): 393-424.

Collins, B. E., and Raven, B. H. "Group Structure: At-
tractions, Coalitions, Communication, and Power." In
The Handbook of Social Psychology, edited by Lindzey
and Aronson, vol. 4, 102-204. Reading, Mass.: Addison-
Wesley, 1969.

Evan, W. "Indices of the Hierarchical Structure of Industrial Organizations." *Management Science* 9 (1963):
468-477.

Faucheux, C., and Mackenzie, K. D. "Task Dependency of
Organizational Centrality: Its Behavioral Consequences." *Journal of Experimental Social Psychology* 2
(1966): 361-75.

Gerwin, D. and Christoffel, W. "Organizational Structure

and Technology: A Computer Model Approach." *Management Science* 20 (1974): 1531-42.

Guetzkow, H., and Simon, H. A. "The Impact of Certain Communication Nets upon Organization and Performance in Task-Oriented Groups." *Management Science* 1 (1955): 233-50.

Hrebiniak, L. G. "Job Technology, Supervision, and Work-Group Structure." *Administrative Science Quarterly* 9 (1974): 395-410.

Leavitt, H. "Some Effects of Certain Communication Patterns on Group Performance." *Journal of Abnormal and Social Psychology* 46 (1951): 38-50.

Lewin, A. Y., and Tapiero, C. S. "The Concept and Measurement of Centrality—An Information Approach." *Decision Sciences* 4 (1973): 314-28.

Lippitt, M., and Mackenzie, K. D. "A Theory of Committee Formation." Working Paper No. 86, School of Business, University of Kansas, 1974.

Lynch, B. P. "An Empirical Assessment of Perrow's Technology Constructs." *Administrative Science Quarterly* 19 (1974): 338-56.

Mackenzie, K. D. "Structural Centrality in Communications Networks." *Psychometrika* 31 (1966a): 17-25.

_____. "The Information Theoretic Entropy Function as a Total Expected Participation Index for Communication Network Experiments." *Psychometrika* 31 (1966b): 249-54.

_____. "The Structure of a Market." In *Management Science in Planning and Control,* edited by J. Blood, pp. 167-216. New York: Technical Association of the Pulp and Paper Industry, 1969.

_____. *A Theory of Group Structures, Volume I: Basic Theory.* New York: Gordon and Breach Science Pubs., 1976a.

_____. *A Theory of Group Structures, Volume II: Empirical Tests.* New York: Gordon and Breach Science Pubs., 1976b.

March, J. G., and Simon, H. A. *Organizations*. New York: Wiley, 1958.

Morley, E. "Human Support Services in Complex Manufacturing Organizations: A Special Case of Differentiation." *Administrative Science Quarterly* 19 (1974): 295-318.

Perrow, C. "A Framework for the Comparative Analysis of Organizations." *American Sociological Review* 32 (1967): 194-208.

Sabidussi, G. "The Centrality Index of a Graph." *Psychometrika* 31 (1966): 581-603.

Shaw, M. E. "Communication Networks." In *Advances in Experimental Social Psychology*, edited by L. Berkowitz, vol. 1, 111-49. New York: Academic Press, 1964.

Tuggle, F. D. *Organizational Processes*. Arlington Heights, Ill.: AHM Publishing Corporation, 1978.

Tyler, W. B. "Measuring Organizational Specialization: The Concept of Role Variety." *Administrative Science Quarterly* 18 (1973): 383-92.

Van de Ven, A. H., and Delbecq, A. L. "A Task Contingent Model of Work-Unit Structure." *Administrative Science Quarterly* 19 (1974): 183-97.

Weick, K. E. "Amendments to Organizational Theorizing." *Academy of Management Journal*, 17 September 1974, pp. 487-502.

2

Structural
Change
Processes

WHY STRUCTURES CHANGE

A group structure is a need-satisfying pattern
of interaction. The interaction pattern, or
structure, is defined by a list of its participants, X_n, and a table of interactions between
all pairs of its members, R. In symbolic form,
the group structure S is described by
$S = (X_n; R)$.

A group can have more than one structure, and
these structures can change at different rates.
Structures change whenever there is a change in
the list of participants and/or whenever there
is a change in the table or matrix of interactions. So the question of why structures change
asks why is there a change in X_n or in R. An
answer to the question of why structures change
should include why changes occur and why, in
some cases, changes do not occur.

48

Recalling that each member of a structure is a controller of his own half-channels and that a structure represents a need-satisfying pattern of interaction, structures will change when, for whatever reason, any member (or set of members) decides that his needs might be better served in another group or, if he stays in a group, with a different usage of his available half-channels. If his needs are not being satisfied, or if he believes that his needs might be better met by a change, then he can change, and will do so provided that the net gains, after allowing for the "costs" of changing, are believed to favor the change.

This general proposition that changes occur when a person believes that change is favorable is straightforward and simple. It is hard to disprove, and it seems quite reasonable. The implications of this proposition start off being simple, but as we delve into subsidiary questions in order to ask about the detailed processes of how these changes occur, how fast they occur, and when they occur, we quickly get into a set of interesting issues.

The purpose of this chapter is to establish the main proposition and implications of our definition of structure as a need-satisfying pattern of interaction. After defining structural change, our first task is to review several studies concerning the preferences for channels and structures. This is followed by a discussion of a number of processes used when groups change their structures. Chapter 3 will analyze a number of administrative problems in coping with changes that may involve structures and processes.

DEFINING STRUCTURAL CHANGE

Most groups have a number of structures. Any change in any substructure is a structural change. For a given substructure, say $S = (X_n; R)$, there is a structural change when-

ever the list of members, X_n, changes and/or
whenever the matrix of interactions, R, changes.
The matrix of interactions changes whenever the
entries in R change. Any change in the list of
members causes changes in the matrix of interactions. Many changes in R occur without changing the list of members. Thus, the main concern
in structural change centers on explaining
changes or no changes in R.

This reasoning can be extended to a set of
structures by considering the changes or no
changes in each of the matrices of interactions
R_1, R_2, and so on, for each substructure S_1,
S_2, and so on. Changes in one substructure can
affect the type and amount of change in another
substructure. It is possible to consider
changes in each half-channel for each structure.
However, it is more convenient to examine
changes in the timely portion of the corresponding role matrix, R. The role matrix exhibits in summary form the activities of each
member. The timely role matrix exhibits the
basic problem-solving pattern more clearly than
the role matrix, which also includes the redundant and untimely behaviors. Further, by
studying changes in the timely role matrix, we
can also see the effects of each change on the
degree of hierarchy and task process efficiency.

The entries in the timely role matrix, R_T,
are 1 if a person performs or takes the responsibility for the performance of an activity.
Otherwise, the entry is 0. There are two cases
of change and two cases of no change in each
entry in R_T. These are described in Figure 2.1.
If person x_i performs or takes responsibility
for performing activity a, then the entry in
R_T, designated by r_{ia}, is 1. If person x_i
neither performs nor takes responsibility for
performing activity a, r_{ia} is 0. The two possible changes are: (1) $r_{ia} = 1$ becomes $r_{ia} = 0$
and (2) $r_{ia} = 0$ becomes $r_{ia} = 1$. In case (1)
the activity a has been *dropped* by x_i, and in
case (2) the activity a has been *added* by x_i.

The two possible no changes are: (1) $r_{ia} = 1$ remains $r_{ia} = 1$, and (2) $r_{ia} = 0$ remains $r_{ia} = 0$.

After

	Activity performed	Activity not performed
Activity performed	No change	Activity dropped
Activity not performed	Activity added	No change

Before

FIGURE 2.1 Description of the two possible changes and two possible no changes in an entry in R_T for a group member for an activity.

There can be many attempts to influence these changes and no changes. Often as much effort is expended to prevent change as to cause it. The two conditions of no change are not behaviorally trivial, because even though the result of a change process is no change, the behaviors and processes to accomplish this are significant.

We are concerned about both the two possible changes and the two possible no changes in studying structural change. The behavioral processes resulting in a change can also result in a no change. The processes leading to no change at one time can lead to other changes and no changes at a later time. Similarly, the processes which result in change can affect later changes and no changes. The processes of change are the centerpiece of this theory. The results of such processes can set up more change processes in continuing behavioral sequences. The static condition of no change is seen to be a temporary phenomenon. Any change in personnel or task processes can set off structural change processes. The "constant" and persistent phenomena of organizations are the continuing structural shifts.

Some structural changes are easier than
others and some can occur more quickly. Usually
the length of time in the processes leading to
a change in the authority structure is longer
than changes in organizational structure, represented by R_T. The authority system lags behind the changes in organizational structures
but it, too, is subject to change. This gap between the authority system and the task-process
system is analyzed in chapter 3. Minor adjustments in half-channel usage are simpler than
changes in overall structure. For example, a
structural change from an all-channel structure
to a wheel structure in a 5-person group means
that 12 of the 20 half-channels have been
closed (12 drops in Figure 2.1) and 8 half-
channels have remained open (8 no changes in
Figure 2.1). This is a more extreme change than
a dropping of a channel. This extreme change
requires the consensus of all five and the
dropping of a channel requires only the decisions of a pair on a portion of their half-
channels.

Net Benefits

Because each member is a controller of his own
half-channels, he can decide whether or not to
open or close his half-channel to any other.
His decision can be described in terms of net
benefit. There are some possible advantages and
some possible disadvantages associated with
each decision to open or close a half-channel.
There are also advantages and disadvantages associated with the process of change that could
occur in implementing the decision. Let us assume that after considering these advantages
and disadvantages, the member acts as if he
computes his net benefit for the change or no
change. Let us further assume that his decision to change or not to change will be made on

the basis of which action yields the greatest
expected net benefits.

It follows then that if someone, say an experimenter, were to take actions to alter the
expected net benefits for using certain channels, he could start up processes that might
cause the group to alter its structures. And if
he could cause these change processes to operate, he could study them in detail. Furthermore, if some of his actions resulted in changes
that were consistent across groups, in that
stable structures began to emerge out of these
change processes, he could gain an understanding of how each of the controllers managed to
arrive at the strong consensus required to fix
the entry in every entry of the timely role
matrix, R_T. Knowledge of the speed and timing
of the change processes resulting in consensus,
represented in a stable structure, would also
allow a fuller appreciation of the processes
that would yield information for predicting
structural changes.

The approach is simple. First, we posit a
simple notion of a net benefit function incorporating as variables some of the possible
events and rewards controllable by an experimenter. This can be used to guess at the direction of change in channel usage in terms of
more or fewer channels being used. Then, by
systematically varying the magnitudes of these
variables, one can predict the tendency to
change the usage or non-usage of those half-
channels affected. The predictions are then
checked by conducting a laboratory study to see
whether or not the actual behavior of groups is
or is not consistent with the predictions.

It should be noted that this approach is made
without specific knowledge of each individual's
net benefit function for usage of his half-
channels. Lacking this information, one can
only hope to explain the direction of change in

terms of more or less channel usage and show
that the direction of change taken is consistent with the reasoning. This type of explanation is weak, but the results demonstrate that
by systematically altering what are presumed to
be the net benefits to using channels, one can
cause changes in group structures. At a minimum, these data are consistent with the thesis
that structures represent need-satisfying patterns of interaction. These data, however, do
not "prove" it. A few of these studies are
briefly described in the next section. The
reader can judge for himself whether or not it
is reasonable to assume that structures represent a need-satisfying pattern of interaction.

Let us conjure up the following actions by an
experimenter: (1) he can impose a money price
for using channels; (2) he can impose a "time"
price for using channels; (3) he can offer a
bonus for certain actions; and (4) he can impose a social cost by using an obnoxious person
as a confederate. Let us also assume that he
can vary the magnitudes for some of these actions such as varying the price. If we assume
only that: (1) on the average, the group evaluates the net benefit of an action in proportion
to the magnitude of the action, and (2) the net
benefits of combined actions can be added and
subtracted, it is then possible to posit the
form of a net benefit function for a subject's
deciding to open or close a half-channel. One
does not know the precise rules for comparing
the net benefits for different types of actions
but one should be able to conclude whether or
not the net benefits have increased or decreased as a result of the experimenter's actions.

To be more specific, let us assume that an
experimenter can vary the size of a benefit and
that the "benefits" can be positively and negatively valued. For example, he can charge money
for the use of a half-channel. He does not know
the precise relationships between the channel

price and each member's net benefit function.
However, it would seem reasonable that most
subjects in the experiment would prefer spending less money than more money. Then, as he
raises the price of a channel, he should expect
a reduction in the number of channels used.

CHANNEL-RENTING EXPERIMENTS

A series of experiments designed to test immediate implications of a structure being a
need-satisfying interaction pattern were run by
Mackenzie (1976b). The same type of problem was
presented to each group. This problem, called
the *network decomposition problem*, requires more
complex inference, and takes longer than the
minimum list of symbols problem described in chapter
1.

The network decomposition problem begins with
each subject receiving a portion of a network.
The subjects are to share this information and
to construct a network out of the pieces given
to them. They are then asked to interpret the
network by decomposing it into two parts under
strict rules for decomposition. There can be up
to three correct solutions. The group must find
all of the correct solutions and submit them
for approval to the experimenters. If any one
of the subjects submits an incorrect or incom-
plete solution, the group is informed that the
solution is incorrect. The group must keep trying until they have a correct answer. In the
channel-renting experiments, each group had to
solve the same four problems in the same order
before they were done.

Subjects were compensated for their time. The
network decomposition problems were explained
to the assembled subjects before the experiment
began, and the subjects were encouraged to work
as fast as possible. During the experiment they
could communicate only by written messages,
which the experimenter picked up and delivered.

Faucheux and Mackenzie (1966) used both the network decomposition and the minimum list of symbols problems. There was a strong tendency to form all-channel structures for the network decomposition problem and wheel structures for the minimum list of symbols problem. In a later experiment, it was learned that if groups were forced to solve the network decomposition problems in a wheel structure, the performance was at least as good as that when they were in an all-channel structure. Thus, we learned that a wheel structure could be used to solve the network decomposition problem even though, when there were no restrictions imposed on channel usage, the subjects worked in an all-channel. Where there was a high cost (defying the experimenter and physically disrupting the group), they could function in a wheel, and when there was zero cost, they would function as an all-channel. This suggested that if there were variations in these costs, one could obtain different channel usages.

The first channel-renting experiment allowed each group to have channels forming a wheel structure for free, and imposed charges for additional channels of $0.00, $0.01, $0.05, $0.10, and $0.25. Each group had the same cost per channel on all four problems. Because there are 10 channels in a 5-person all-channel structure, and because there are 4 channels in a 5-person wheel structure, there were 6 channels that could be rented. The groups were allowed to remake the decisions for what channels to rent at the beginning of each problem. The experimental choice of channels is illustrated in Figure 2.2. Each subject was paid $6.00 for completing the four problems. If any channels were rented, the charge for the channels was deducted from the $6.00. Note that at $0.25 per channel, if the group rented all six on each of the four trials, the total charge would be $6.00 and the subjects would receive no pay for their work.

Channels available for free   Channels available for rent

FIGURE 2.2 Descriptions of first channel-renting experiment.

The channel-renting procedure was simple. Each subject received a "channel-renting form" on which he marked his choice for channels to be rented. They could rent none, one, two, ..., six. The individual choices were made independently and turned in to the experimenter, who then computed the choices. The decision by one subject was binding on the others. If one wanted a channel, each had to pay for it. But if all five wanted the same channel, they only had to pay for one.

The results are shown in Figure 2.3. This curve establishes that as the price charged per channel went up, the groups selected fewer channels. This is consistent with the argument that, holding all other factors constant, the net benefit for using a channel declines as its price goes up. The downward sloping curve in Figure 2.3 is consistent with the proposition that follows from structure representing a need-satisfying interaction pattern. The renting of all of the channels at $0.00 channel charge confirms the earlier work by Faucheux and Mackenzie (1966).

What is very interesting about Figure 2.3 is how close the curve is to the axes. There seemed to be little preference for other than a wheel or an all-channel. Even at a low charge of $0.05, the average group rented less than one channel. There is scant evidence for choices of structures whose structural central-

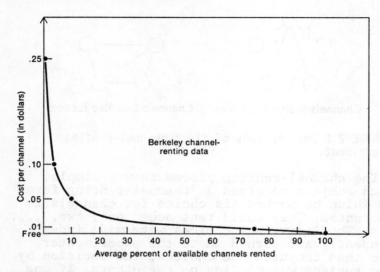

FIGURE 2.3 Channel-renting curve for first experiment.

ity (see chapter 6) is intermediate between the wheel and the all-channel.

Three later experiments were performed using the same approach. In the next experiment, the method of payment and channel charges was changed. An introductory psychology course had a requirement that every student participate in experiments for five hours during the semester, and each subject was given three hours of credit for the experiment. Psychology credit time (in minutes) was used for channel prices. The curve had the same shape as in Figure 2.3. An incentive was introduced to rent more channels by announcing that the first subject to turn in a correct answer to a problem would receive a bonus of one-half hour's credit. Because there were four problems, a subject could conceivably earn a total of five hours of credit. Reasoning that it would take time for a hub to compile and send out all the individual member data and that the hub might "play games" to insure that he would earn the half-hour bonus, it was predicted that the benefit of the half-hour bonus would result in a greater number of channels being rented. It did. A third variation was to see whether or not persons would spend to avoid an obnoxious confederate. To accomplish this, an assistant acted as the hub and was obnoxious. The subjects rented more channels in this variation. The main results are shown in Figure 2.4.

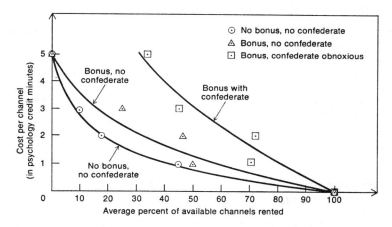

FIGURE 2.4 Channel-renting curves from the channel-renting experiments.

The subjects changed their problem-solving processes as a result of the bonus. Where there was no bonus, the typical group went through the milestone sequence for the problem. With the bonus, the incentive to get it caused the subjects to bypass intermediate milestones to submit an answer before going through each stage with the others. And, after a subject had "staked a claim" on the bonus by turning in an answer, he would then try to solve the problem in a more normal way. The bonus groups had many more untimely behaviors. They took longer and made more errors.

These four channel-renting experiments produce results that are consistent with the idea
that a structure represents a need-satisfying
interaction pattern. By varying his actions to
influence the evaluation of the net benefits of
a channel, an experimenter can cause changes in
group structure. The main implications of an
underlying net benefit function were also sup-
ported. The results also indicate that these
needs are not limited solely to money. The
bonus experiment and the one with the obnoxious
confederate suggest, too, that the underlying
task processes are not independent of the kinds
of incentives and actions taken by the experimenter. The reluctance of groups to select
structures intermediate between the wheel and
the all-channel suggests that not only is there
a possible net benefit function for channels,
but there also seems to be one for overall
structures. In the next section, several experiments on preference for structures are presented.

EXPERIMENTS ON PREFERENCES FOR TYPE OF STRUCTURE

Many writers have remarked on the acceptability
of different group structures. The wheel is
often described as authoritarian, directive,
and efficient for simple problems. The all-
channel is described as democratic, not so efficient for simple problems but preferred for
complex problems. Persons are described as
being happier in an all-channel than in a
wheel. There are data to support such claims
and there are data that refute them. We learned
from the first channel-renting experiment that,
at zero costs, groups would form all-channels
for the network decomposition problem. But at
channel costs as low as $0.05, wheel groups
tended to be the chosen structure. Thus, there
does not appear to be much difference in preference between the wheel and the all-channel
for solving these complex problems.

There are many other structures, such as a circle or a chain. The experiments on preferences for type of structure attempted to determine the preference order for wheel structures, chain structures, circle structures, and all-channels. These structures are illustrated in Figure 2.5. The absence of chains and circles in the previous experiments suggested that both the wheel and the all-channel are preferred to these two structures.

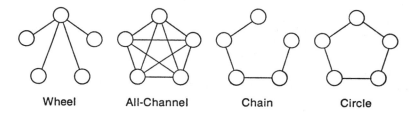

Wheel   All-Channel   Chain   Circle

FIGURE 2.5 Four prototype structures.

The procedure on the first two experiments was almost identical to the procedures on the channel-renting experiments, where there is a money charge for channel-renting. The exceptions were: (1) that each subject was only given an amount of money equal to the maximum total cost if the group rented every channel each trial, and (2) the groups were given the channels forming a chain or a circle for free instead of those forming a wheel.

The observed lack of choice for either the chain or the circle may reflect a belief that it is more difficult to coordinate the message-handling with the problem-solving stages because of the need to relay messages and co-ordinate all of these information flows. If this is the case, then the subjects' beliefs are consistent with the more precise evaluation of these problems made by Simmons (1974). Our purpose is to establish an order of preference and not to study the details of the information-processing problems. However, we can

examine some of these problems in order to have
a basis for explaining the observed preferences.

Imagine a problem requiring extensive mes-
sage-passing for eight possible milestones. All
kinds of mishaps could occur. Someone might
forget to relay his information, and errors
could be propagated without correction. It
would take four messages for a message to move
from one end of a chain to the other. Most
milestones require two-way flows. The chance
that a message would not be received or an error remain uncorrected is large. Questions
about data or any step of the task process
might not get relayed. In short, the possibility for clerical and message-handling errors is
very large. The preference for a wheel seems
reasonable because it involves a minimum number
of messages and there is always direct access
to a coordinator (the hub).

In the chain structure, there is some clue
provided about who should serve as coordinator.
For example, it would take, on the average,
more messages using one of the end men than one
of those in the middle. The configuration of
the structure gave some clues about whom to
pick as coordinator. The circle graph is a
little more confusing than the chain because
all members are equally likely to be coordinator and there are more possibilities for confusing two-directional flows of messages.

The wheel structure should be preferred to
the chain structure and the chain structure
should be preferred to the circle structure. If
the wheel structure is preferred to the chain
structure, a typical group should be more willing to incur the costs of renting channels to
break out of a chain structure than a wheel
structure. Hence, we would expect that the
channel-renting curve for the chain structure
should lie above and to the right of the one
for a wheel structure (as in Figure 2.3). Similarly the channel-renting curve for the circle
structure should lie above and to the right of

of the chain structure. Both channel-renting
curves for the chain and the circle should be
downward sloping to the right.

The results of these first two experiments
are shown in Figure 2.6.

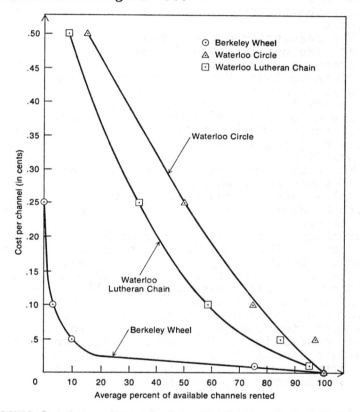

FIGURE 2.6 Comparison of channel-renting curves from
Berkeley Wheel, Waterloo Circle, and Waterloo Lutheran
Chain experiments.

Interestingly enough, the channels rented for
$0.50 cost were those that would establish the
possibilities for forming a wheel. These data

show a decided preference for the wheel structure over either the chain or the circle structure. Any of these four structures could be
used to solve the problems. Some groups just
gave more thought and took more care in organizing the structures to reach the various milestones.

The results from these two sets of experiments are consistent with the assumption that
structures represent need-satisfying patterns
of interactions. Not only can one cause the
groups to alter structures as a result of
changing levels and types of benefits, but
there also is a preference for some structures
over others. More detailed analyses of problem-
solving processes are consistent with these
conclusions.

The next steps required are to compare the
preference for a wheel structure relative to
an all-channel structure. This work was done
with H. Wedderburn. Before describing the experiments, it will be helpful to examine the
advantages and disadvantages of both forms of
structure. These two deserve extra care to
compare because they are: (1) extremes on a
scale of structural centrality, (2) the most
common structures observed in small groups,
(3) the most discussed because some studies indicate a choice problem of trading off member
satisfaction and group efficiency, and (4) the
most confused in being understood. A more up-
to-date discussion of these two structures also
illustrates numerous theoretical points about
group structures introduced in chapter 1.

RELATIVE PREFERENCES FOR WHEEL AND ALL-CHANNEL STRUCTURES

CHARACTERISTICS OF AN ALL-CHANNEL STRUCTURE An
all-channel structure has the advantage that
direct contacts are possible between any pair
of members at any time. It is excellent for

sharing information. An all-channel contains
every intermediate structure as a subgraph.
An all-channel also has the advantage of being
relatively easy to modify. Selectively using
those channels that are already open and that
involve only implicit voting to close is easier
than explicitly recalling to open previously
closed channels and to close previously open
channels. It places minimum barriers on its own
reorganization. An all-channel structure allows
a group to avoid direct decisions about leadership, division of labor, and process. Initial
estimates of abilities to solve group problems
may be incorrect. The all-channel has the advantage that one person can be considered for
possible leadership positions without having to
depose another. By avoiding a commitment to
another, more restricted, structure until after
the group has gained experience with the problem and with each other, the group is in a
better position to pick its structures. In effect, an all-channel is suitable whenever a
group does not know what it is doing.

An all-channel structure also has many disadvantages. First, too many messages are sent,
reducing efficiency. Second, processes are
likely to take longer because of the large
number of cousin relationships. All-channels
have low degrees of hierarchy. Third, for some
problems, the coordination of individual efforts will be more difficult in an all-channel.
For example, the minimum list of symbols problem requires every member to have the same list
of symbols in exactly the same order. Gaining
agreement on the order could be very difficult
in an all-channel. Fourth, if some members are
more willing to contribute than others, and if
some are also judged as more effective with the
group problems than others, the all-channel
does not take advantage of these differences.
When it does, it usually ceases to be an all-
channel. Thus, for problems that can become
well-defined and for which there is an incentive

to make the definition and implement it, the
all-channel is unstable. The instability of the
structure and of the processes of all-channel
groups is a major disadvantage. Whenever some
members believe that another organization is
more suited for solving group problems, they
will begin to form appropriate structures. Efforts to enforce an all-channel will involve
heavy costs. Often this sort of issue is resolved by allowing a structure like a hierarchy
to form for solving the problem and maintaining
an all-channel-appearing structure for non-
task-oriented processes. This way members can
"feel" they are in an all-channel without, in
fact, being in one.

CHARACTERISTICS OF A WHEEL STRUCTURE A wheel
group structure can be very flexible in its
task processes. The hub member can take on many
roles, ranging from an autocrat to a mere
switchboard operator who routes messages. The
hub can be consultative. He can be a judge or
referee of the efforts of others, or he can be
the problem-solver. The hub can behave differently for different milestones. For example, he
can be very "bureaucratic" about disseminating
data and consultative about forming solutions.
The hub member can be used as one of the spokes.
A wheel can also be inefficient and have a low
degree of hierarchy. It may involve extra processes of checking and double-checking because
the hub member does not wish to take responsibility for an answer or because some of the
spoke members do not trust him. Wheel groups
eliminate uncle and cousin relationships but
not redundant and untimely messages. On the
other hand, if redundancy and untimeliness are
eliminated, the wheel is capable of maximum
hierarchy, efficiency, and if this satisfies
the members' needs, stability.
One should differentiate between a wheel
structure that is chosen by a group and one
that is imposed on a group by an outsider

(e.g., an experimenter or a legal statute). A
wheel that has been adopted by the group reflects both the identity of the occupants of the
positions in the group and the task process.
In short, a group whose structures *evolve* into
that of a wheel has decided upon its structures
and task processes in such a way that the resulting group structures are need-satisfying.
On the other hand, the group whose hub is imposed by an outsider has solved only the problem of who occupies which position. The selection of task process remains unresolved. If the
imposed hub can establish task processes that
satisfy group members, the effects of imposi-
tion may be minor. However, if the imposed hub
is technically or socially inept (unable to select a task process or interpersonal relationships that satisfy the group members), recalls
may occur. These recalls may lead to unanticipated consequences such as hostility, altered
processes, and changed structures. One changed
structure is the replacement of the imposed
hubs. Just about anything can occur if the hub
is imposed. Imposing a hub for a wheel may or
may not lead to difficulties. The main problem
is that picking a hub is not the same as selecting the task process. This still must be
done. The behavior and competence of the hub,
the tolerance and competence of the spokes,
the social norms of the groups, the incentives,
and the group problem can affect the manner in
which the task process is resolved.
   Even a simple analysis of the all-channel and
the wheel suggests that: (1) there is no one-
to-one correspondence between group problem and
group structure, (2) the correlation between
the type of structure and efficiency is not
unity, (3) the correlation between centrality
and satisfaction is not minus one, (4) the effects of imposing a hub on a group are uncertain, and (5) an all-channel may represent a
lack of agreement about structure. The analysis
suggests that if the goal is efficiency, groups

will prefer those structures which are the more
efficient for the solution of the group problems. Structures represent need-satisfying interaction patterns, and if one structure does
not facilitate these needs, another may form.
The structural form *per se* is not as important as
the group's task processes. Groups will alter
their task processes and structures in order to
satisfy members' needs, if they can.

AN EXPERIMENT TO COMPARE WHEEL AND ALL-CHANNEL
STRUCTURES *Ceteris paribus,* the greater the cost
of a channel, the less likely it is to be used.
There is a cost associated with choosing a
structure and task process. The more complex a
problem, the greater the costs associated with
electing structures and task processes. But,
ceteris paribus, wheel structures require more
decisions to organize than letting structures
remain all-channel. So, *ceteris paribus,* the more
complex a problem (more milestone structures to
pick), the more the all-channel is preferred to
a wheel. But, if we could reduce the costs of
organizing, the preference for the all-channel
relative to the wheel would be reduced. One
way of doing this is to have a group agree unan-
imously on a structure before it begins. *Ceteris paribus*, requiring this unanimity tends to
reduce the preference for the all-channel relative to the wheel structure.

An experiment to check this was run using
procedures similar to the channel-renting experiments except for the procedure for selecting structure. In this experiment, the subjects
discussed (using written messages) the structure they wanted *before* beginning. When they
reached consensus, we let them work the problem. They were allowed to choose a new structure before each problem. The four free channels
were any four that the group wanted.

The results yielded a channel-renting curve
that is below and to the left of all curves
shown in Figure 2.6 except for the one point

representing a $0.05 channel charge. Only 4 of
the 13 problems solved at no cost (as opposed
to 100% in earlier experiments) were solved
using all-channel structures. Eight of the 13
were solved in wheel structures. Only 5 out of
the 15[1]problems solved at $0.01 channel charge
were solved in an all-channel; the other 10
used a wheel structure. At $0.05 channel
charge, 8 were solved in the all-channel and 8
were solved in a wheel. All problems with $0.10
and $0.25 charge used the wheel. Thus, these
data are consistent with the hypothesis that
the requirement of unanimity reduces the preference of the all-channel relative to the
wheel.

The next set of arguments refers to the manner in which these groups decided to change
their group structure on successive trials.
Whenever channels that were opened or closed on
previous problems became closed and open respectively on the next problem, there was a
switch. If six channels were switched, it was an
extreme switch. Observed extreme switches were
from a wheel with one hub to a wheel with another hub, from a wheel into all-channel, or
from an all-channel into a wheel.

Recalling that, *ceteris paribus,* reducing the
costs of organizing reduces the preference for
an all-channel, we might expect that experience
in solving a problem would reduce the relative
costs of organizing. *Ceteris paribus,* the greater the experience, the greater the relative
preference for the wheel relative to the all-
channel structure. So, if there are switches,
most of them will be extreme switches. And,
with experience, more extreme switches favor
the wheel relative to the all-channel structure.

There were 22 switches and 19 no-switches in
this experiment. Of the 22 switches, 21 were
extreme. Of these 21, 1 was from a wheel to an
all-channel, 2 were from an all-channel to a
wheel, and 18 were from a wheel with one hub to
a wheel with another hub. Most of these extreme

switches followed poor performances on the earlier problem. It is significant that most switches were extreme and most were to a wheel structure.

In the earlier experiment, where the group started with four free channels making a chain and where there was no discussion about structure, there were 0 extreme switches, 17 switches, and 21 cases of no switches at all. The absence of extreme switches where there is no discussion is to be contrasted with the 53.7% for the discussion groups. This indicates that the requirement of group consensus had a strong effect on the choice of structure.

The main conclusion to draw is that the preference for the all-channel relative to the wheel structure in these experiments may reflect the fact that an all-channel structure can postpone the need to organize. Thus, it is unclear that there was a preference for the all-channel relative to the wheel. Rather, the groups did not want to go into the difficulties of attempts to organize when they were unsure of how to complete the first processes and of the abilities of the group members. When they had to make a choice in the discussion-to-consensus conditions, the choice of all-channels relative to the wheel structure was greatly reduced, comparing the choices to all of the earlier experiments. Furthermore, after gaining experience, the switches were almost all to that of a wheel. Thus, it is difficult to conclude that subjects really prefer working in an all-channel rather than in a wheel structure.

The important conclusion is that rich implications can be drawn out of the simple idea that structures represent need-satisfying interaction patterns. The preceding experiments provide numerous examples of this simple proposition. They also establish that structures can and will change and that money and other factors act as stimuli to set off structural change processes. The next section introduces several new ideas about processes for structural change. Knowing that changes occur and seem to occur for sensible reaons, one is emboldened to seek answers to the problems of how such changes come about. What do people say and do that results in structural change?

How Structures Change

The main arguments for emphasizing structural changes rather than static concepts of structure center on elementary ideas about need satisfaction. It was argued, for example, that since a structure represents a need-satisfying interaction pattern and since there are many structures, one source of behaviors leading to structural changes is the perception on the part of individual members that alternative usage of various half-channels could lead to changed levels of need satisfaction. Experiments generally support this reasoning. The needs include the usual ones of financial incentive, avoidance of unpleasant persons (our obnoxious confederate), the difficulty in organizing, and those of efficiency and effectiveness.

We shall consider in chapter 3 a number of administrative methods for creating structural changes, reacting to changes that may require structural changes, and resisting structural changes. In the remaining portion of this chapter, the intent is to introduce the ideas of behavioral constitutions and mapping functions in order to describe a number of natural processes for altering group structures. These two ideas have been used to explain how, and how fast, the structural changes reported in a number of experiments actually occurred. They also yield some insight into managerial behavior. Behavioral constitutions can be used to provide an algebra for understanding how group members process information. Mapping functions

illustrate one idea for ways to put together the
many pieces of a behavioral process in order to
make predictions about structured change.

BEHAVIOR AS EXCHANGE OF INFLUENCE

We shall probably never know precisely why we
act the way we do or why another acts as he
does. Nevertheless, there is probably a purpose
behind each act. We can often make shrewd
guesses and seek confirming evidence. In many
cases we have themes about ourselves or others
and we use this theme to organize and understand behavior. We can see a person as having
a peculiar personality or being morally committed to a general course of action. We make
use of dominant processes to understand others.
For example, a person may be seen as ambitious,
power-hungry, "uptight," gregarious, and so
forth. Social psychologists are concerned with
understanding this form of social judgment. How
one attributes intent and forms these judgments
is discussed in Jabes (1978), chapter 4). There
are no simple answers yet to understanding why
persons do what they do. This type of question
is, however, of great interest to each of us.
A common thread underlying each analysis of
intent is the assumption that behavior is purposive.

Understanding our own and another's behavior
is difficult because, given our current knowledge, behavior is seen to be exceedingly complex. Even in our little laboratory organizations, one can easily detect many social processes at work. At a most obvious level, persons are interacting in order to complete task
processes. Group members also interact to
organize themselves to carry out these task
processes. They learn from experience and this
knowledge of the task processes and the capabilities and concerns of the group members
serves to guide structural changes. The processes to complete the task and the processes

to change the task processes can set in motion
other processes such as the formation of interpersonal attraction and hostility. Our interest
here centers on the processes for changing task
processes, which, as we have seen, set up
structural changes.

In order to study structural change processes,
let us assume that every interaction can be
seen as an effort to influence the task-
process structures of the organization. It is
not assumed that each person is aware of or
deliberate about his attempts to influence. It
is assumed, however, that every interaction is
an influence on the processes of structural
changes. Some influence efforts may lead to
changes and others may stop changes. A special
case of the analysis of structural change is no
change. Let us assume that *every* interaction has
some potential effect or influence on structural
change processes. What we need is a procedure
to describe how, in the face of all these influence attempts, a group changes its structures.

BEHAVIORAL CONSTITUTIONS

One possible mechanism describing how the members of a group handle these influence attempts
is a *behavioral constitution*. Behavioral constitutions are essentially influence- and information-processing *rules* that have been invented to
describe the manner in which interacting groups
analyze and synthesize the influence attempts
by its members. Mackenzie (1976a, chapter 7)
has described a behavioral constitution for
structural changes that has proven valuable in
his studies of structural changes. This behavioral constitution was inferred through extensive and laborious analyses of message exchanges.

The main idea was to take the timely role
matrix as the anchor and to examine each message in terms of its impact on changing the

role matrix. The entries in the role matrix under discussion define the *issues*. Each influence attempt is a "vote," and votes can alter the state of an issue. There are voting rules to describe how the state of an issue has or has not changed after each vote on the issue. The reader will recall that an entry in the timely role matrix is unity if the member performs or takes responsibility for the performance of an activity. Otherwise the entry is zero. Each entry in the timely role matrix can be classified according to whether its state (0 or 1) is known or in doubt. If the state of an issue is known, it is considered *elected*. If the state of an issue is in doubt, it is considered to be in *recall*. An elected state is "open" if the entry is unity. An elected state is "closed" if the entry is zero. Similarly, a previously elected open state that is in recall is in *recall to close* and a previously elected closed state that is in recall is in *recall to open*.

The analysis starts by assuming every entry in the timely role matrix is elected. A recall creates the issue and the first vote creating the recall sets off an election. Voting rules are used to examine each vote as it occurs in order to ascertain the state of an issue.

There are eligibility rules. Only members whose behaviors can be affected by the changes are eligible to vote. There are three types of votes: explicit, implicit, and preemptions. *Explicit votes* are influence attempts that are explicitly stated. Examples: "George, please give me your data" or "Let George do it." *Implicit votes* are less direct and are often made by performing or not performing an activity. For example, after "George, please give me your data," George may respond by sending his data. His action would be an implicit vote to open this half-channel for data-sharing. *Preemptions* are influence attempts that, by themselves, determine the outcome of an election.

For example, George's not sending his data is considered a preemption. Preemptions are particularly interesting because in organizations formal authority is the right to make a preemption. However, the right to make a preemption may be insufficient to resolve the issue. Power is related to the capacity to make or block a preemption and have it hold. Authority-based preemptions can often be overturned, especially where there are significant authority task-gaps, and the decision is unacceptable to those who could block it. A preemption can set in motion many elections with far-reaching effects.

A number of years ago this author had a department chairman who insisted that all of the faculty should wear ties to work. The author had been wearing a tie but some of his colleagues had chosen not to wear them. They could see no reason why it was necessary to wear a tie to do research, to teach, or to attend faculty meetings.[2] A number of the faculty believed that it was not legitimate for a department chairman to dictate one's "costume." At first, his insistence was met with humor: a faculty member would wear a T-shirt with a tie; another a sweat-shirt with a tie; another a cravat with a sportshirt. His response to these abberations was to become more insistent about his request. The more he insisted, the greater the variety of dress. The greater the variety of dress, the angrier he became. The angrier he became, the greater the resistance. Soon the simple issue of wearing a tie spread to other issues. One thing led to another and within six months, he was replaced as department chairman. Of course, there were more serious problems that led to this structural change, but the tie issue, when coupled with other behaviors by the chairman, was one of the precipitating events that resulted in an ever-widening set of issues.

Another example was described by an economics professor. It seems that in the early 1950s he

was a corporal in the U.S. Army on garrison
duty in the Panama Canal Zone. The duty was
boring, and each enlisted man would make
elaborate plans for spending weekend liberty.
It was the custom for the company sergeant to
hold a formation in a clearing bordering the
jungle on Friday, followed by liberty call.
One Friday, without any advanced notice,
the sergeant announced that there would be no
liberty. The 150 men would be confined to bar-
racks for the weekend. It seemed unfair to the
men. A few members in the back ranks walked
away from formation towards the jungle. Within
a minute, all 150 men had left the sergeant
impotently demanding that the men return. Now
the sergeant had the authority to give such an
order and he had the authority to bring charges
against all 150 men. But if he pressed the issue, he would have mountains of paperwork and
would be the laughingstock of the Army. He
would probably be replaced as well. The implicit votes by the men and the explicit vote
by the sergeant resulted in a temporary structural change. As this story is remembered, all
of the men reported back to duty on Sunday
within the usual deadline. The sergeant did not
press charges.

These two examples are more exotic and dra-
matic than those that normally take place within an organization. However, they serve to make
the point that preemptions based on authority
do not always stick and that one issue can
spread to other issues. In most of the reported
experimental groups, one can track and predict
structural changes using the behavioral constitution as a basis for analyzing behavior.

Data from these experiments do not invalidate
the analysis of the behavioral constitution,
and if one is employed, it has been possible
to make precise analyses of structural change.
The record of votes can also be used to analyze
other processes. Once the votes have been tabu-
lated for each issue, one can compare how each

person voted with the results of the election process. Votes that are consistent with the final outcome are called *favorable votes* and votes that are inconsistent with the final outcome are called *unfavorable votes*. The relative number of favorable and unfavorable votes can serve to analyze the influence of each member and the changes in the influence of its leaders. The relative intensity of the number of unfavorable and favorable votes can be used to predict the rate at which a structural change will occur. A model for this is presented in chapter 8.

Groups solving a series minimum list of symbols problem described earlier usually centralized into a wheel structure. The rate at which the groups centralized varied from group to group and varied for different milestones. A simple model based on the diffusion of innovation model (see Mackenzie, 1976b, chapters 12, 14) to explain the rate of adoption of a structure showed that the greater the number of favorable votes relative to the number of unfavorable votes, the faster the adoption of a structure. A favorable vote in this case meant a vote favoring the wheel structure that was eventually adopted. Unfavorable votes included votes for wheel structures with a different person as the hub or votes for other structural forms. A typical group would begin to solve the problems without any clear concept of how to organize. When one person had an idea to centralize, voting would begin. If there was a power struggle, either to get or to prevent oneself from getting the role of hub, there was a large number of votes cast. The arguments led to repeated recall votes and new elections. Often the person who made the initial suggestion lost out. These recalls and subsequent voting took time and delayed the adoption of the structure. If a suggestion to form a wheel about one person was made and the others concurred, the adoption process was quite swift. In this case, there was a very high incidence

of favorable votes relative to the number of
unfavorable votes. However, in other cases
where there was little agreement and long discussions, the relative number of unfavorable
votes was high and the adoption process took
much longer.

It must be noted that if one employs an approach such as that of a behavioral constitution, one is studying the manner whereby influence attempts are handled by a group. One is
not directly studying why these attempts are
made in the first place. The evidence for the
reason a person votes as he does is not inconsistent with the teleological notion that
structures represent need-satisfying interaction patterns and that persons vote in order to
get the structures that allow for these needs
to become satisfied. For examples, whenever a
group's structures work well, there is little
or no voting to change it.

It must be noted that behavioral constitutions are invented in order to describe structural change processes. There could be a difference between the way an analyst would view
the voting processes and the way a participant
would view them. To the author's knowledge, the
subjects in his experiments do not seem to have
any awareness that they are rule-following.
Many might even deny it. However, experimentally it has been found that when one deliberately
violates some of the rules, one can quickly
generate hostility that is directed towards the
violator (Mackenzie, 1976b, chapter 16). The
reaction by the group to a violation is similar
to what one would expect if a social norm is
violated. The testing process is analogous to
rubbing the fur of a cat the wrong way.

There are other behavioral constitutions that
are prevalent in North America. A trivial example includes the "rules of the road" when two
persons are walking down a hallway in opposite
directions. The rules are: Youth gives way to
age, lower status to higher status, healthy to

the infirm or handicapped, and males to females.
If you don't believe in such rules, a few violations of these rules will change your belief
quickly as you provoke quick reactions. If you
are a healthy young male undergraduate, see
what happens when you refuse to yield the
right of way to an elderly lady in a wheel-
chair. One can describe behavioral constitutions for two strangers to become intimate,
the formation of interpersonal hostility, bargaining with a shopkeeper, answering the telephone (see what happens when you answer the
telephone by preempting the "right" of the
person calling to control initially the content
of the conversation), greeting rituals, decorum
at meetings, etc. Often "rubbing the fur the
wrong way" is the best way to discover such
unwritten rules.

Behavioral constitutions are information- or
influence-processing rules that apply in
natural social settings. In social settings,
we are confronted with more stimuli than our
extremely small short-term memory can handle.
If someone gives you more than five nonsense
symbols or numbers in no obvious order, you
probably cannot remember them even if you are
asked to write them down immediately after
hearing them, unless you have developed some
mnemonic trick. If you can see information as
part of a pattern, you can develop methods to
cope with it. However, if you do not have such
a method, you simply cannot recall very much.
And, if the information requires a number of
comparisons, you will find the difficulty increasing very fast as you receive more information, unless this new information allows you to
perceive a pattern. To cope with the normal
complex stimuli from social settings, you need
devices to organize and process these stimuli.
Behavioral constitutions are one way of con-
verting information-dense situations to ones
that are informationally less complex.

Similar devices have been found in linguistics

(Chomsky, 1965) and socio-linguistics (Ervin-Tripp, 1969). One new line of research is to discover behavioral constitutions that seem to be operating in different social settings. As an exercise, the reader should try to infer the behavioral constitution for what happens at the beginning and the end of a date. Another is to work at a behavioral constitution for visiting your professor's office at other than office hours.

MAPPING FUNCTIONS

Adoption models for explaining the rate of change of a structure, based upon the relative number of favorable and unfavorable votes, do not specify exactly when a structure is adopted or what structure will be adopted. The behavioral constitution approach works for wheels, all-channels, and any other structure. Models that are derived for explaining the rate of change cannot be used for explaining when structural changes will occur because not all structural change processes start at the same time and not all of them involve the same sequence of votes, recalls, and elections. The model for the rate of adoption only tells us how fast the group adopted its structure in relation to when the change processes began. Because different groups begin at different times, we need other ideas to explain exactly when a structure will be adopted. Mackenzie (1976b, chapter 8) has described a new type of process model called a *mapping function* to make the analysis to explain the occurance of a structural change.

The occurrence of a structural change and what type of change it will be depends upon: (1) the milestone of the problem-solving process; (2) the current structure of the group for this milestone; (3) the existence of an ongoing voting process (has it started yet?); (4) the current electoral state of this process (is it elected or in recall?); (5) if it is in recall, whether the recall is one that would work if adopted; (6) the structural state of the milestone (is it centralized?), and (7) a capacity for change. This last variable refers to the span of control (see chapter 4) of the person who is or might become the hub. The idea of a mapping function is to put these variables together in such a way that for any given set of their values, one can predict the structural change that will take place on the next problem. The mapping function referred to earlier has been useful in tracking the structural changes taking place for both the minimum list of symbols and the network decomposition problems. It predicts well both the structural changes and absence of changes with regard to the centralization of the group for several milestones.

It is beyond the scope of this volume to go into the details of mapping functions for structural change. In the next chapter, you will see a mapping function for how a group of university administrators handle administrative problems for which their authority is in doubt. However, the author can impart some of the ideas for a mapping function by citing an example. Suppose you are in a group of five and are busily working on the solutions to a series of minimum list of symbols problems. Suppose further that the more you solve in two hours the more money you will make. There are a number of considerations that you might take into account in changing the hub of the wheel structure that you are in. As you gain experience, your "leader" can solve a problem in two minutes. You stick with him because that seems to be reasonable and you are not certain that a change would leave you better off. Now suppose another person in the group recalls the structure by attempting to replace the leader. You may cast votes against the suggestion explicitly or you may implicitly vote by continuing to send your data to the old leader.

82 *Organizational Structures*

Probably, the structure will not change. However, suppose at the same time the leader has
slowed down to ten minutes. His slowness is
costing you money. The joint event of unsatis-
factory delays by the old leader and the
willingness of someone else to take over may
trigger a structural change. A mapping function
considers such contingencies. It can be used
to track the "twists and turns" of a group
changing its structures as it confronts new
problems.

NOTES

[1]Not all groups solved all four network decomposition
problems and the number of groups at each channel charge
varied with the costs.

[2]"Clearly," we were young and foolish.

REFERENCES

Chomsky, N. *Aspects of the Theory of Syntax*. Cambridge,
    Mass: M.I.T. Press, 1965.

Ervin-Tripp, S. M. "Sociolinguistics." In *Advances in
    Experimental Social Psychology*, edited by L. Berko-
    witz, vol. 4, 91-166. New York: Academic Press, 1969.

Faucheux, C., and Mackenzie, K. D. "Task Dependency of
    Organizational Centrality: Its Behavioral Conse-
    quences." *Journal of Experimental Social Psychology* 2
    (1966), 361-75.

Jabes, J. *Individual Processes in Organizational Be-
    havior*. Arlington Heights, Ill.: AHM Publishing
    Corporation, 1978.

Mackenzie, K. D. *A Theory of Group Structures, Volume I:
    Basic Theory*. New York: Gordon & Breach Science Pubs.,
    1976a.

_____. *A Theory of Group Structures, Volume II:*

Empirical Tests. New York: Gordon & Breach Science Pubs., 1976b.

Simmons, R. "The Effects of Communication Errors on the Consistency of Functional Processes, and on Performance Times in Certain Communication Networks." Ph.D. dissertation, University of Pennsylvania, 1974.

3

Some Administrative Issues in Structural Changes

THEME AND PLAN OF CHAPTER

Chapter 2 contains a description of structural change and some processes of structural change that are the beginnings of a comprehensive theory of structures. That chapter emphasized theory and described a sequence of laboratory experiments. The first set of experiments tested a number of implications that would be consistent with the idea that a structure is a need-satisfying interaction pattern. We learned that the experiments yield reasonable conclusions about channel and structural preferences. Also discussed was the concept of a behavioral constitution and a mapping function. Behavioral constitutions describe how influence attempts are analyzed by those in a group. This analysis is essentially a system of rules for which observed behavior in changing structures is

consistent. Behavioral constitutional analysis
has been used to track the actual structural
change processes and to predict the rate of
adoption of group structures. Mapping functions
are more complex models that attempt to put
together relevant facts, which in varying combinations produce different outcomes. There
was a brief description of one of the mapping
functions used to predict the occurrence or
nonoccurrence of structural changes in actual
groups.

This analysis was limited in scope to little
laboratory organizations where the groups are
faced with a fixed set of problems and can
organize with only minor impediments to these
processes. Most organizations, on the other
hand, face more complex sets of factors and
events that lead to reevaluation of current
structures and processes and consideration of
alternative structures. These include exogenous
events—events taking place outside the organization—that can create needs for structural
change. They include changing technology.
There are also barriers to change and changes
in these barriers. Many times changes are
stopped, or at least the change process becomes
altered, because of the operation of influence
processes based upon authority, power, and
legal restrictions. It is the thesis of this
chapter that although these are very important
factors influencing structural change processes,
there are essentially different conditions for
applying the basic ideas introduced in chapters
1 and 2. Special structural problems for coping
with information-processing limitations and
changes in work load are presented in chapter
4. The structural issues of bureaucracy are
discussed in chapter 5. Chapter 6 discusses
issues of centralization and decentralization.
In chapter 7 there is a discussion of how, in
aggregate, organizational forms have been
shifting. The discussion in this chapter begins
with some general remarks about exogenous

influences. The main portion of this chapter, however, extends the ideas of chapters 1 and 2 to a study of methods used by administrators to cope with problems where their authority is unclear or their power to implement a decision is in doubt.

Exogenous Events

Exogenous events include those events taking place that are beyond the control of the group being studied. The relevant exogenous events of interest to us here are those that may lead to changes in membership, task and non-task processes, and interpersonal relationships. For example, if one is analyzing a suborganization, the relevant exogenous events may include decisions in other parts of the organization as well as those events occurring outside the larger organization. Changes in top level personnel, changes in key technical personnel, changes in market conditions, shifts in technology, availability and price of input factors, etc., can set off a sequence of changes to which the organization and its component suborganizations must react. The sudden action by the oil-producing countries in late 1973 to raise prices of crude oil fourfold set in motion many streams of events that upset even the largest enterprises and governments. Increases in crude oil prices affected the price of gasoline, which affected the demand for automobiles, which affected the demand for automotive parts, which affected employment, and which set off numerous and interlocking private, corporate, union, and governmental events. The rise in crude oil prices affected the retail clothing industry directly because many synthetic fibers are products of manufacturing processes that are dependent upon chemicals extracted from crude oil. The spreading inflation and unemployment traceable to the increase in crude oil prices altered the spending patterns of consumers. The ripple effects of many streams of changes traceable to crude oil price increases reached into many organizations that are only remotely connected to the oil industry. There were changes in school systems, churches, and unions, etc. Families were forced to alter life styles and standards of living.

It is impossible to overemphasize the dependencies of organizations on exogenous events, and very difficult to assess accurately the end results of so many exogenous factors. We should also mention changes in technology as prime exogenous events. A major technological change such as integrated miniaturized circuits in electronics has caused major changes in the type of product and in the method of manufacturing. These technological changes require new task processes and alter the mix and training of personnel, which in turn cause changes in structures. Heightened comprehension that there can be socially detrimental byproducts of socially desirable products (e.g., pollution caused by production of energy) can be followed by new governmetnal regulations and controls, by legal action, by lobbying and consumer interest groups, and can further cause exogenous events that may force changes in organizational structures.

Faced with so many possible exogenous changes that can set off processes to change structures, one could conclude that what is desperately needed is a more comprehensive systems model of the organization that includes environmental and other exogenous factors.[1] At our current state of technology for analyzing organizations it is possible to construct and apply models quickly to adapt to environmental, technological, and internal changes. This is being done on a practical basis using the ideas in this book with actual firms. Organizational design is seen as a continuing process, and one of the key issues is to enable firms to organize in order to adapt to change.

The discipline forced by attempting to understand which exogenous effects are important is
worthwhile. The processes of planning to meet
such contingencies are important, but the resulting plans are far less useful than the
process of planning.

LEARNING PROCESSES

Exogenous events, if they are relevant, cause
changes in the role matrix to occur. They can
affect the number and type of personnel required (changing X_n) and the task processes
used to complete the organization's tasks
(changing R). Thus, relevant exogenous events
set off changes in the structures of the
organization. An exogenous event leads to new
task processes. They learn the milestones, how
to reach them, in what order to reach them.
Given a goal, they learn from each other and
from experience how to organize themselves to
solve problems to attain their goals[2].
   Sometimes the effects of learning are summarized in a learning curve, which is a graph
of performance as a function of time. A commonly used learning curve compares the time to
solve a problem and the sequential number of
the problem. Usually the time taken to solve
the first problem exceeds the time to solve the
second, etc., until reaching some limit. This
limit represents the time it would take an experienced group to solve this type of problem.
For example, a simple negative exponential
curve of the form

$$X_T = Ae^{-\alpha T} + B \qquad (3.1)$$

where A, B, and α are positive, X_T represents
time per milestone of unit complexity, and B
represents this average time after a large number of problems, fits the data for network decomposition problems very well. This is shown
in Figure 3.1. The curve in Figure 3.1 is down-

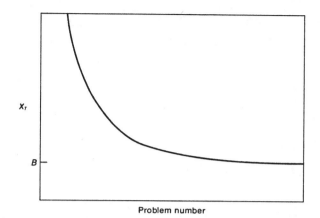

FIGURE 3.1 A typical learning curve for a performance measure as a function of problem number.

ward sloping because as the performance of the group improves, the dependent variable (X_T) decreases. If the performance measure were the type that got larger as performance improves, the curve would be upward sloping and, in terms of equation (3.1), the exponential coefficient α would be negative. Or, if P_T is the performance measure

$$P_T = Ae^{\alpha T} + B \qquad (3.2)$$

Equation (3.2) is illustrated in Figure 3.2. Productivity per man hour is one example of the performance measure P_T.

Task process learning resulting in new task processes and structures involves the organization's members. Managers may anticipate some changes and, by gaining a fuller understanding of the logical relationships of a task process, they can try to create task process changes. However, reliance on managers and engineers to do the work leading to task process changes may ignore the many intelligent workers who, by

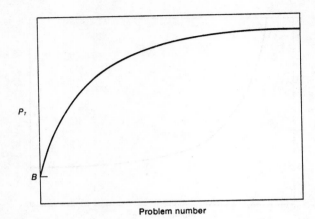

FIGURE 3.2 A typical learning curve for an increasing
measure of performance as a function of problem number.

their knowledge of the processes, can make suggestions and many little changes that can add
up to major changes in the task processes.
After all, no matter how clever the manager, he
usually has to work with people to adopt and
implement these changes. He and they have to
adjust to one another. Sometimes these adjustments improve the designed changes. Other
times, the many adjustments and interpretations
that take place as the basic idea percolates
down through the organization can radically
alter the original intent.

The author was peripherally involved in a
project to apply linear programming to a
multiple-plant lumber firm. Although a beautiful
model was specified, it had to be modified because
no one could figure out exactly how the sawyer
sized up a log when it came off the green chain
for its initial cuts. Another problem occurred
when the workers completed computer control
cards while they were on the job. The grease on
their hands caused malfunctions of the system.
As fast as the model could be specified to

cover a number of plants and products, top management merged and changed the problem, creating implementation problems. The point here is that the basic processes do not stand still while one is making a study.

Our experiments with laboratory organizations demonstrate the dynamics of change in task processes that result from experience in working with a problem. Members of these groups learn how to do the work as well as who can do what best. They actively discuss organizational changes and modify their behavior to fit current knowledge. As shown in the circle and chain channel-renting experiments, humans are quite capable of adjusting around an inadequate system of structures. They can, and do, alter task processes without supervision when there is an incentive and opportunity to do so. The capacity of groups to self-organize is a source of change in task processes that can lead to positive and negative changes in outputs. The conceit that these changes are the prerogative of a class of overseers is potentially dysfunctional, especially in industrial societies where the general level of education is high.

Simmons (1978) discusses how administrative, technical, personal, and interpersonal changes and events can affect productivity in an organization. The emphasis in this book has been on task-oriented behaviors, but the importance of non-task-oriented behavior is very important. Focusing only on task-oriented behaviors, we can also be led to view the task-oriented processes as the only important ones to understanding task processes. This is not unreasonable in the very short run. But the social relationships among the members of the organization can have major impact on the task processes. No one knows exactly how social relationships both on and off the job can affect task processes. However, there have been numerous studies in the last forty years begeinning with the old Hawthorne experiments

(Roethlisberger and Dickson, 1939) that demonstrate the effects. Interpersonal hostilities, for example, can result in reduced cooperation and effort and these may lead to replacements of members. Interpersonal hostility can also lead to greater productivity when one member works harder to spite another. We do not yet know enough to predict the effects of non-task-oriented behavior on task processes. We only know enough to assert that they can be an important factor in the type and rate of structural changes. Simmons' analysis is one of the most comprehensive statements on this problem.

INFORMATION-PROCESSING LIMITATIONS

A major but often overlooked factor in structural change is the limits each individual has to process information. It takes time to solve problems, carry out work, and to interact with others, and there are definite limits to each person's capacity. As the work load increases, as the organization grows, as the work becomes more complex, each person reaches a limit to how much he can do. The limit varies with the person, the norms of the group of persons with whom he interacts, and other factors. But when this limit is reached, to satisfy individual and group needs, the structures may begin to change. A theory for this problem in terms of span of control is developed in chapter 4. Implications for this theory are made for bureaucracies and the growth of hierarchies in chapter 5. The effects of overloading are also a key issue in the degree to which a multidivisional firm should decentralize its decision making. This is discussed in chapter 6.

Such work overloads are one source of information used by people to assess the instrumentality of existing structures. If we recall that structures are need-satisfying interaction patterns, it follows that as one set of structures is judged to be dysfunctional, pressures

will build up to change existing structures to
ones that are judged to be more need-satisfying.
A. C. Silcox and the author (Mackenzie, 1976b,
chapter 15) have caused major structural
changes in laboratory groups by simulating work
overload.

BARRIERS TO STRUCTURAL CHANGE

It takes time and effort to make structural
changes, and although members are dissatisfied
they may conclude that the benefits of any proposed change are simply not worth the effort.
For example, the new structure might not be
any better. There could be serious risks and
messy disputes involved in implementing a
profound change. However, in most cases there
is no precision in defining either the problem
or the solution. There is just a general feel-
ing ("poor climate," [Simmons, 1978]) that the
existing structures are not functioning well.
Not knowing what changes in task processes are
needed, or not having agreement that changes
will accomplish what proponents claim, can inhibit efforts to cause structural changes. Implicit in this argument is the notion of discounted expected net benefits. Any situation
involves some benefits and costs. Any change
involves future benefits and costs and the
costs and benefits associated with the change
process itself. There is more uncertainty about
the costs and benefits of the change process
and the results of the change process than
those of the current situation. In addition,
one is usually dealing with a sequence of
changes and not just a single change. Thus, one
could think about these problems as involving
a stream of future changes with varying degrees
of uncertainty. But the decision-makers (each
of the half-channel controllers) live now. So,
when structural changes are discussed, there
is a future stream of cost-benefit flows that
are considered from the point of view of the

current situation. Costs and benefits in the
far future probably do not count as much as
costs and benefits in the immediate future.
These are discounted much as future income is
discounted relative to money now. Thus, one
could consider the members who are thinking
about structural change as investors of time,
energy, and career who are going to decide to
work for, be apathetic to, or resist structural
changes according to whether their discounted
expected returns for the changes are positive,
neutral, or negative. Usually persons who gain
power support the changes, those who cannot
see any sizeable gain or loss of power tend to
be neutral (unless they become committed to a
crusade to benefit the larger mass), and those
who might lose power tend to resist structural
changes.

The existing organizational structures have
allocated authority, and there is a distribution of power. Often the distribution of power
is roughly parallel to the distribution of
authority and, hence, rank. Those having power
and authority can speed up or delay structural
changes. They can control resources and uncertainty, and these can be employed to influence the discounted expected net benefits associated with structural changes. If those
having the authority and power are against
changes (and they often are), structural
changes can be delayed and even stopped. Although each member has control over his half-
channels, he is often not in control of the
rewards and sanctions that can be affected by
his decision. He may decide not to "rock the
boat," even though the end result can be beneficial, because of the costs he associates
with change. In the case of a disliked supervisor, a subordinate may decide to wait until
the supervisor is changed. He may also believe
that despite the shortcomings of his supervisor, any likely replacements would be even
worse.

Problems involving changes in formal organizational structures are considered to be very

serious problems, because these decisions are
fraught with risk and uncertainty. At least
there is a redistribution of authority. Con-
comitant with authority changes are changes in
power, influence, and task processes. Access
to key persons is changed at more than one
level. Priorities for programs can get reset.
Mistakes can be made. There are problems with
any changeover and the organization's effectiveness can be temporarily but seriously reduced even though the end results may be excellent. These problems and uncertainties are part
of the process. Each person has to make his own
assessment and, for any objectively stated
structural change, there will be a variety of
assessments. Accordingly, members will vary in
the degree to which they support or resist the
organizational changes.

Informal changes appear more reversible than
formal changes. The authority basis does not
change in informal structural changes. But
when one is dealing with formal changes, these
processes result in redistributions of authority and power. Those with added authority and
power who favored the structural changes that
gave it to them may turn and resist changes in
this new status quo. They can also use their
new power and authority to affect future structural changes. In informal structural changes,
the authority system remains intact and can be
activated to influence a reversal of informal
structural changes. Of course, informal changes
can alter the distribution of power and this
can be used to resist reversing the structural
changes that gave rise to this new distribution
of power. The longer an informal change is allowed to operate, the more difficult it is to
change back to one that is more consistent
with the formal system. Still, formal changes
in organizational structures tend to be less
reversible than informal changes. Accordingly,
the stakes are higher and there is more uncertainty. Consequently, the actual task process
system is more dynamic than the formal authority system. As a direct result, the two systems

are often out of synchronization with each
other.

Some of these administrative procedures are
relatively straightforward, such as reassign-
ments, promotions, demotions, and transfers.
Some of the problems have already been worked
out and the purpose of the structural change
is to recognize and legitimize the *de facto*
changes. A problem could be recognized and
solved by delegating the required authority or
changing a policy or a number of standard operating procedures. Unfortunately, the solution
to a structural problem may be the cause of a
number of other problems that lead to other,
often only remotely related, structural problems.

The greater the number of role matrix or task
process changes involved with an administrat-
ively planned structural change, the greater
the possible risks in implementing the solution. For organizations having supervisors with
low power and circumscribed authority, even
minor structural adjustments can cause serious
problems and so are treated with caution. And
even in cases where the position of an administrator to make a change is strong, there are
always two related problems with any change.
The first is coming up with a change suggestion
that should work to solve the problem. The
second, and at least as important, is the political acceptability of the suggested change
to those who are affected by it. A brilliant
idea that is stubbornly resisted and sabotaged
because it is unacceptable is not a feasible
solution in most organizations. Even if the
person wanting the change gets away with his
suggestion, the resistance to these ideas can
generate many new problems and make his life
miserable. The original issue can spread to
other issues. Taking the time to gain acceptance *before* implementation is usually desirable
because it limits issue-spreading and other
conflicts.

Outside Interventions to Change Task Processes

A recurring problem in studying organizations
is the definition of a boundary separating
their external and internal components. The
author does not know of any definitive criteria
for making such a definition. There are legal
definitions, such as those involving ownership,
but when one studies any given organization,
legal definitions often are too fuzzy. Although
it is not very satisfactory, one method of describing the organization's boundary is defining it with respect to the processes and behaviors that are of interest to the analyst.
He should include the persons whose behaviors
are relevant to the study. For example, if one
is asked to study an organization such as a
wholesale lumber yard, one might include the
producing mills and major customers if the interest is selling and buying. For another purpose, one might include the banks with which
financial arrangements are made. Conceivably,
if there is a customer service requiring exchange of technical information, one might include those parts of the U.S. Forest Service
providing such data. For another purpose, the
focus of the analysis may be a small group of
company officers. Increasingly, one might want
to include various city, state, and federal
agencies if their decision, policies, and procedures for enforcement can vitally determine
company activities.

The definition of who is inside or who is
outside this organizational boundary is unclear, but there are actions and actors from
outside that can have significant impact on
structural change policies. The author has already mentioned the intrusion and supervision
by various governmental agencies. There are
also trade associations and unions whose actions can set change processes in motion. Pressure groups and law suits can also force
changes, and higher authorities can often reach

in and pluck out key personnel. They can uni-
laterally force task-process changes. For example, a parent organization may order a subsidiary to change its product line.

Sometimes outside experts such as consultants
are brought into the organization temporarily
to alter attitudes and task processes, and to
provide expertise. A consultant having expert
knowledge of technical processes, legal problems, or administrative problems may be hired
temporarily for his knowledge. The costs of
his services, even if he is on a retainer, may
be less expensive than having him included
within the boundary on a full-time basis.

There is another, more subtle use for which
consultants are employed. An organization may
hire a consultant to resolve internal disputes.
The professional knowledge of a consultant
can be used to legitimate administrative actions which, without this legitimacy, could
lead to many organizational problems. If there
is a strong difference of opinion about a decision, a consultant may be used as an informal
arbitrator. Suppose there is a need for a new
computing facility and different groups within
the organization are strongly divided about the
decision. An expert on computing systems may be
hired to make a study and offer an opinion. If
he is judged to be neutral with respect to the
opposing groups, his opinion and how it is
reached can be used to resolve the dispute.
However, the persons who hire him may have some
indirect influence on how he reaches his opinion. This is especially true if the consultant
needs continuing business. He who pays the
piper often calls the tune. Lippitt and Mackenzie (1976,1977) describe a decision process by
which a person in authority having an organization decision problem in an authority-task gap
will decide to hire a consultant. This issue
is taken up in the next section.

INDIRECT ADMINISTRATIVE METHODS

Up to this point, direct administrative methods
for gaining acceptance of structural changes
have been stressed. There are also indirect
methods that can be used when the political aspects of the solution become important. If we
can agree that: (1) groups can self-organize,
and (2) structures represent need-satisfying
patterns of interactions, then we can agree
that a group would reorganize itself to a desired task-process system if the members believed that by such changes, their needs would
be satisfied with the newer system. Hence, the
main idea behind indirect administrative control is to create incentives and conditions
such that it is to the advantage of the members
to structure themselves in the desired way.
Probably this could be done, in some cases, by
cynical manipulation. However, most structural
changes require time and involve social influence processes. Too heavy a hand or suspicion
can upset a too detailed plan. Most people in
a democracy object to being asked to contribute
to a structural change only to find out that
they lose whenever their opinions differ from
those of a person with authority. After all,
why should they go through such processes when
the only outcome is that which has already been
decided?

However, when there is time, it might be
wiser to set objectives that guide the change
process but do not dictate too many details.
There is more than a single task process that
could solve a problem. There are a number of
different acceptable structures for these task
processes. There is more than one center of
knowledge about personnel and how to solve problems. Groups are capable of organizing themselves and, if they are allowed to do so and
and are given proper incentives, they will do

it. They know each other and can often work
out relationships among themselves to get the
job done that are at least as good as the one
a supervisor might be tempted to enforce. By
controlling the controls rather than the people
directly, a workable task-process system can
evolve that is satisfactory to both the supervisors and the other group members. A structural solution that evolves to satisfy the
needs of all parties is preferred. Group members can impose social sanctions and controls
on each other that are often much more subtle
and powerful than those a supervisor could employ. If the task-process system works, and if
it is acceptable to the members, it will be
stable.

Of course, there are often conflicting goals
and personal frictions among members that inhibit the formation of a workable task process
system. It is sometimes necessary for a person
with authority to intercede to resolve conflicts. There can be emergencies that dictate
fast action by a responsible person. A self-
organized system may need changing because it
is dysfunctional to the organization. Cliques
and other subgroups can interfere with the
liberties of other members. It may be necessary
to step in from time to time to effect changes.
Nevertheless, it does not follow that direction
from the "top" is always necessary. Furthermore, there is more than one way to assert this
direction. Groups can be given statements of
policy and incentives that can set in motion
structural change processes that result in a
solution to its structural problems. It is not
necessary always to make specific and direct
control attempts to accomplish a desired result. As we have seen form our discussions of
structural change processes in the experiments
of chapter two, desired changes can be made by
indirectly controlling incentives and task conditions that can channel these processes of
structural change to acceptable end results.

In the next section, we take up the problem
of how administrators handle problems for which
the authority system is inconsistent with the
task process system. A theory and a mapping
function to describe the choices in terms of
the theory are presented. The theory was developed with M. Lippitt and has been tested
with administrators at a major state university. M. Lippitt conducted the field study. We
call this a theory of committee formation.

A Theory of Committee Formation

The theory of committee formation contained in
this section examines the way an administrator
selects a strategy for solving a structural
change problem in which his authority is unclear. Such problems arise because the task
processes are out of synchronization with the
authority system or because there has been an
outside intervention (e.g.. new governmental
rulings and regulations), which alters the
legitimacy of the authority system. The administrator has a twofold problem: (1) determining a reasonable solution to the problem
that is technically sound and (2) worrying
about how to get the solution implemented,
which is often a political process. As we see
it, he has essentially seven choices: Do
nothing, solve the problem, give it to some
standing committee, appoint a task force, appoint a committee, pass the problem up to his
superior, and hire a consultant.

Building from the ideas expressed in chapters
1 and 2, a theory with a model is developed,
which allows one to predict which of the seven
choices is made for these types of problems.
This model type, called a mapping function,
will illustrate the ideas about mapping functions expressed in chapter 2. The theory and
model are descriptive. We make no explicit assumptions that the administrator is "rational,"

has some special utility function, is thinking much beyond his immediate situation, has some great concern for the betterment of mankind, etc. Despite this, this mapping function has successfully predicted the choices of nineteen senior administrators at a state university.

AUTHORITY-TASK GAPS AND OTHER PRINCIPAL CONCEPTS

Changes in authority occur more slowly than changes in organizational structures. The authority system usually lags behind the changes in structures but it, too, is subject to change. In many cases the changes in authority reflect the *de facto* structural changes that have already occurred. Changes that have already occurred are often merely legitimized by changes in authority. Authority changes can, by themselves, set in motion more structural changes. In either case, the planned "ideal" represented by the authority system is always partially inconsistent with the actual task-process system. The degree to which the authority system is inconsistent with the task-process system varies considerably. In some cases the authority systems act as a rudder to maintain order and continuity in the behaviors of the organization's members. However, it can also act as a brake and a constraint that impedes necessary change.

The reader inexperienced in organizational decision-making may be bewildered by the necessity for all of this organizational "tiptoeing." To him, someone should just give an order and it should be carried out. Of course, there are cases where one can do this. The main reason for the care and indirection is that in most organizations the system of authority is to some degree out of touch or inconsistent with the functioning task-process system. Wherever there is a gap between the authority system and the task-process system, it is unclear who has the authority to make the changes. Also unclear

are which changes to make and how to implement
or install them. The source of many structural
problems may be in this *authority-task gap*.

When one considers that in 1974 there were
over 6,000 different agencies in New York City
providing "social services" and that city,
county, state, and federal programs were involved, there are many authority-task gaps.
There are also conflicting statutes and policies for these many programs. An attempt by
one official to "straighten out the mess" could
cause major upheavals in the city. In a firm,
the president may lack the authority to make
personnel decisions because of the terms of a
negotiated labor contract. An accountant may
be asked to make certain changes in his reporting by his "boss" which conflict with the current state of generally accepted accounting
practices. The president of a university may
want to ask the economics department to separate its operations from those of the school
of business, but cannot do it because of the
resistance by the students and faculty. One
result of a system of checks and balances is
the existence of substantial authority-task
gaps.

Organizations have three role systems, which
can be depicted in three role matrices, R_T,
R_A, and R_C. There is the task-process system
which can be described by the timely task role
matrix, R_T. The entries in R_T describe who
performs or takes responsibility for performing
an activity. The entries in R_A, on the other
hand, describe who has the *right* to preempt the
activities. The reader will recall that, from
our discussion of a behavioral constitution in
chapter 2, preemptions are a special type of
vote wherein the action of preemption determines the state of an entry in a role matrix.
A third role system is the organization chart,
describing which persons are subordinate or
superior to others. We label this third role
system as R_C. In most cases, the three systems

are not fully consistent. For example, the actual task processes may involve one set of persons and their relationships, which differ from those in the formal authority structure. The organization chart is often misleading, because it neither reflects the authority system accurately nor the actual task process system. One example is an administrator who is responsible for the conduct of certain activities but does not have the right to preempt all of these activities, and thus does not have the authority to carry out his responsibilities.

The person whose decision we are describing is in the organizational chart-role system. He has a title and faces an organizational chart of other persons with whom he interacts. He may or may not have the authority to carry out his activities. Hence, there can be a gap between R_C and R_A. But the actual task process system can be different, in practice, from both his position in the organizational chart (R_C) and the authority-role system (R_A).

These gaps between the person's role in the three systems are commonplace in organizations. Persons are aware of these gaps but they are easily tolerated. We argue that most organization members act as if there is a tacit agreement, called a *behavioral treaty*, which sets the range of permissible behaviors and allowable departures from normal behavior in the gray areas of authority-task gaps. Behavioral treaties are important to understanding the stability of organizational processes. At one university, the eight departments teaching organizational behavior are separated from each other and do not attempt to intrude on the teaching or research activities of the others. For example, if the department of psychology says that the school of business should not teach certain courses in organizational behavior, the school of business could always counter by claiming the psychology department should not teach other courses.

An exogenous event such as a sudden drop in enrollments could create a problem in this authority-task gap because of the method for academic departmental funding. Suppose, for example, enrollments in psychology dropped 25%. The department should cut back on its staff. To prevent such losses, they could conceivably demand that students in the school of business take more psychology courses. Financial exigency may set off a number of "inreach" programs, which could trigger violations in the behavioral treaty which had previously stabilized relationships in this gap and thereby create a need for task process or structural changes.

Whenever an issue arises that forces a problem lying within the authority-task gap to come up for resolution by an administrator, it becomes an *authority-task problem*, denoted as ATP. Authority task problems, ATP's, may involve a rupture of a behavioral treaty. The existence of a gap may make the reallocation in R_A a part of an issue. The parties to the resolution of an ATP are usually involved with the redistribution of the authority role matrix, R_A. A resolution of an ATP results in new entries and new values of the entries in R_T and possibly in R_A for the persons involved. Naturally, they are concerned with both the process and the outcome of the resolution of an ATP. An issue is said to be raised when there is a recall of one or more activities in the groups' task role matrix, R_T. (Check back to the behavioral constitution for a description of a recall.) Issues may arise from both exogenous and endogenous events. The responsibility for resolving the issue, which recalls some of the activities in R_T, rests with the administrator who lies in the organizational chart at the lowest common level above those involved in the dispute. For example, if the issue involves two subunits in a branch of an organization, the administrator is the immediate supervisor. If it involves subunits from two separate branches, the administrator may be the administrator who is the boss of both branches' bosses. This administrator, found in the R_C, is called the *lowest common ancestor* or LCA. It is the responsibility of the LCA to resolve the issue. Looking to R_A now, if the LCA does not have the right to preempt all of the activities recalled in the issue, that is, if some lie in an authority-task gap, the issue is an ATP.

For any ATP there exist a minimum number of controllers, among whom agreement on the value of the entries in the part of R_T involved in the ATP constitutes a preemption and, thereby, resolves the issue. An authority-task gap is said to exist in a structural hierarchy when the immediate superior does not have the authority to preempt all of the activities performed by his immediate subordinates. An issue which recalls activities in R_T for which the LCA does not have corresponding authority (in R_A) is said to be an authority-task problem or ATP.

In resolving an ATP, the lowest common ancestor, the LCA, acts as if he faces a two stage solution process: (1) finding a technically feasible allocation of the disputed activities and (2) gaining acceptance of this allocation. We identify seven strategies for resolving ATP's. These were listed earlier. They include do nothing, solve the problem, give it to a standing committee, appoint a task force, appoint a committee, pass the buck, and hire a consultant. These strategies represent means for directing the resolution process. Subordinates generally have some expectations as to the resolution process to be followed for a given issue and set of conditions. Thus the choice of strategy by an LCA for resolving an ATP affects the form of the solution and its stability. We assume that LCA's act as if they evaluate a set of conditions on the problem and on the organization in deciding which strategy to choose for attempting to resolve the issue.

We assume that each member who is involved in an ATP acts as if he has a preference function for the performance of each activity in R_T. The stakes of an issue are proportional to the opportunity costs of how he evaluates these activities. Each member is assumed to attempt to *enhance* his role. He does this by adding positively evaluated activities to his role set and deleting negatively valued activities. Detractions from his role set occur when positively evaluated activities are deleted or negatively evaluated activities are added. In voting to resolve an issue, the group acts as if each member desires to enhance his role set as much as possible and to detract from it as little as possible. These evaluations can change during the resolution process.

When a preemption of an activity results in an enhancement of one member's role set and a detraction from another, a *preclusion* is said to have occurred. Preclusions can occur during the resolution process, especially when the authority role system is unclear. Those involved with the LCA act as if they hold expectations about the LCA's choice of strategy during a resolution sequence. The LCA's choice is affected by his perception of the influence processes. The group acts as if there is a behavioral treaty whose terms reflect the participants' expectations as to the proper resolution process to be followed. When the entries in R_A for an issue are unclear, the group acts as if the terms of the behavioral treaty contain the conditions under which preemptions may be case without being considered as preclusions in R_A.

This theory contains a number of propositions about what happens when a preemption fails or when one member or group of members attempts to block a preemption. Attempts to block are themselves preemptions, because they are votes to prevent the consummation of activity changes in a previous system.

An LCA's decision as to his choice of one of

the seven strategies for resolving an ATP can
be represented in terms of a mapping function.
The arguments for our choice of eleven variables and the logical ordering of them in the
mapping function are beyond the scope of this
book. However, the eleven variables will be described, the mapping function presented, and
examples given of how it works in practice.

THE 11 VARIABLES OF A MAPPING FUNCTION FOR LCA's CHOICE OF RESOLVING AN ATP

There are 11 variables in our mapping function.
Each will be described in turn.

X_1 Does an ATP exist or will one arise in this
issue? X_1 is 1 if the answer is yes and 0
if no.

X_2 Does the issue need to be resolved? X_2 is
1 if yes and 0 if no. Variable X_2 reflects
the LCA's estimate of whether or not the
issue will go away if he ignores it. However, if he misjudges, he may have a new
ATP.

X_3 Does the LCA know a technically feasible
solution? X_3 is 1 if yes and 0 if no. At
X_3, the LCA asks whether or not he knows
of a solution that would remove the ATP if
it were implemented. X_3 does not include
his assessments of the acceptability of the
solution to his subordinates.

X_4 Does the LCA have the capacity to solve the
ATP? X_4 is 1 if yes and 0 if no. The problem in X_4 is whether or not the LCA believes he has the time to find a solution.

X_5 Does the LCA have authority to solve the
ATP? X_5 is 1 if yes and 0 if no. The issue
in X_5 is whether or not the LCA believes
he has the right to preempt solution activities. This is not the same as having the
right to determine a technically feasible
solution.

X_6 Is the problem recurring? X_6 is 1 if yes
and 0 if no.

X_7 Would the solution be accepted, or could an acceptable solution be negotiated by the LCA? X_7 is 1 if yes and 0 if no. Sometimes the LCA feels that either his solution would be accepted or that he could call the parties together for a meeting to negotiate a settlement. His ability to negotiate depends in part upon his ability to identify the participants in an issue. This is not always easy, especially in a campus protest issue. It also depends upon the size of the group with which he expects to negotiate. If it is too large, negotiation may not be feasible. Persons who are viewed as inflexible may preclude negotiations. Sometimes a part of the process for assessing X_7 is the LCA's talking the situation over with his close friends and allies.

X_8 Can the LCA pass the buck? X_8 is 1 if yes and 0 if no. Passing the buck means giving the ATP to the LCA's LCA. This involves both the willingness of the LCA to give it to him and the willingness of the LCA's LCA to receive it. One special form of buck-passing occurs when the LCA agrees with subordinates on an issue and wants to serve as an advocate for their solution to an ATP. If he cannot resolve the issue in their favor himself, he becomes one of the parties to the ATP, and advocates their position to his superior.

X_9 Does an appropriate standing committee exist and have time to solve the problem? X_9 is 1 if yes and 0 otherwise. Many organizations will already have standing committees whose charge covers the activities in the ATP. The importance of the issue will cause the LCA to consider the legitimacy of this standing committee when assigning the issue to it. If it is legitimate (e.g., it is an elected, representative body), it will be a new ATP to bypass it unless there is not enough time for it to make a decision. Bypassing a legitimate standing committee can create new issues and, hence, more ATP's.

X_{10} Is it feasible to have a consultant? X_{10} is 1 if yes and 0 if no. A consultant here comes from outside the organization and requires an expenditures of funds. Essentially, feasibility refers to the availability of both a consultant and budgeted funds to pay for him. It should be noted that committees may be formed when there is no such budget because the committee is seen as a free good—just spreading fixed costs of salaries.

X_{11} Is there a severe time constraint or a deadlock. The value of X_{11} is 1 if the answer to either or both parts of the question is yes and 0 if both are no. A severe time constraint makes certain strategies impossible to pursue. When a deadlock occurs and the LCA believes that no more bargaining, discussions, compromises, and education will result in any one of the parties' changing his mind, he may have to intervene and impose a solution. Furthermore, if other strategies have been tried and failed, he may impose a solution. By evaluating $X_{11} = 1$, the LCA preempts the issue by imposing a solution. The willingness to impose a solution may be a personality variable.

THE SEVEN STRATEGIES AVAILABLE TO THE LCA

The seven are not listed in order of frequency of occurrence or importance. They are described so that the reader can understand the mapping function.

1. Solve. This means that the LCA will implement his solution without further discussion or negotiate a solution directly. He can meet with them, admit a previous mistake, and reverse a previous decision. He can also meet and communicate a solution.

2. Pass the buck. This means that the LCA will give the ATP to his LCA. It can also mean that he has become an advocate and so his LCA is the true LCA after he has taken this position.
3. Do nothing. This is self-explanatory.
4. Hire a consultant. This is described in X_{10}.
5. Appoint a committee. The LCA appoints members to this committee and charges them with proposing solutions to the ATP. The committee is not directly responsible for implementing the activity changes identified in the solution.
6. Form a task force. The LCA appoints its members. A task force is charged with both proposing solutions and implementing them. Implementation may require the delegation of some authority to the task force. Task forces are temporary organizations or *ad hoc* operating groups.
7. Send the problem to a standing committee for recommendations. This is described in X_9.

The reader may realize that there are now so many committees in most organizations, that the word committee has almost become an epithet. Consequently, the committees are often re-labeled as task forces, panels, advisory groups, etc. One has to examine their charge and method of functioning to see whether these are, in fact, what they are labeled or just committees under a new name.

A MAPPING FUNCTION FOR THE DECISION OF THE LCA FOR CHOICE OF STRATEGY TO RESOLVE AN ATP

The mapping function connecting the 11 variables and the 7 strategies for the LCA to resolve an ATP are given in Figure 3.3. An ATP is assumed to involve each of the 11 questions that define the variables, X_1, X_2, . . ., X_{11}. Because each variable, X_i, has only two values, there are 2^{11} or 2,048 values of these 11

variables. There are only 24 endpoints in
Figure 3.3. Thus, the theory behind the mapping
function has placed order on the sequence of
values of the X_i and has organized them into
24 distinct chains of values. If one begins
with X_1 on the left and proceeds to the extreme right hand side of Figure 3.3, one can
see how each combination of variables works
together to explain the LCA's choice of strategy. The most simple path occurs at the bottom
of Figure 3.3 when the value of X_1 = 0. This
is the case where there is no ATP. A simple
path occurs when X_1 = 1 and X_2 = 0. The strategy chosen in this case when there is an ATP but
it does not need to be resolved is to "do
nothing." More complex cases occur in the upper
portions of Figure 3.3. Consider the vector of
X = (1, 1, 1, -, 0, -, 1, -, -, -, -). The
blanks mean that the variable of the corresponding value of X_i is not important. The
vector X above means that

X_1 = 1. There is an ATP
X_2 = 1. It needs to be resolved.
X_3 = 1. The LCA knows a technically feasible
       solution.
X_5 = 0. The LCA does not have the authority.
X_7 = 1. The solution would be accepted.

The resulting choice of strategy is to *solve*
the problem directly.
  Let us try another vector. Suppose X = (1, 1,
1, -, 1, 1, 0, -, 0, 0, 0). In this case we
have

X_1 = 1. There is an ATP.
X_2 = 1. It needs to be resolved.
X_3 = 1. The LCA knows a technically feasible
       solution.
X_5 = 1. The LCA does have the authority.
X_6 = 1. The problem is recurring.
X_7 = 0. The solution would not be acceptable.
X_9 = 0. There is no appropriate standing com-
       mittee.
X_{10}= 0. It is not feasible to hire a consultant.

$X_{11} = 0$. There is no severe time constraint or deadlock.

In this example, the choice of strategy of the LCA to resolve the ATP is to appoint a committee.

The reader will note that there are 10 endpoints in Figure 3.1 for solving, 2 for passing the buck, 1 for doing nothing, 3 for hiring a consultant, 3 for appointing a committee, 2 for appointing a task force, and 3 for giving the ATP to a standing committee. Thus, there is usually more than one combination of values of the X_i that can lead to the same choice of strategy. The question of which of these strategies is the more common or preferred depends, therefore, on what conditions obtain. It can be seen, however, that even though there are only three endpoints ending as committees, the spread of committees in modern organizations would suggest that these three conditions are at least prominent.

The mapping function converts a vector of 11 contingent conditions $X = (X_1, X_2, \ldots, X_{11})$ to a choice of $Y = (y_1, y_2, \ldots, y_7)$ from the 7 choices of strategies. Figure 3.3 is a network connecting the values of X to determine the value of Y. Thus, the network of Figure 3.3 is a function. We can say that

$$Y = F(X) \tag{3.3}$$

where the function F is the network in Figure 3.3. Other mapping functions have been developed by this author. This is a new type of mathematical function and one that is expected to become more prevalent in the future. Its advantage is that it allows predictions on strings of contingent variables. It orders and places the variables in sequence. These sequences reflect the logical contingencies among the variables. It does not assume the usual independence that is found in so many models. Organizational behavior is contingent on a

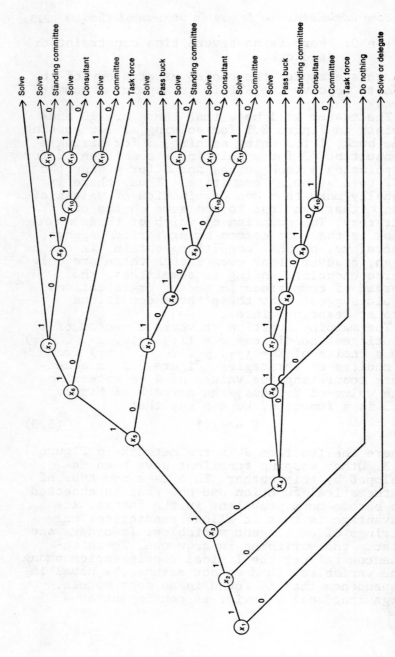

FIGURE 3.3 A mapping function for the choice of strategy of the LCA to resolve an ATP.

number of functions and, perhaps, a new form of function such as a mapping function will be used more and more in the future. The mapping function also permits clear predictions. One can evaluate the variables, make a prediction, and then check the predicted choice against the actual choice.

NOTES

[1]The article by R. Jurkovich (1974) describes a core typology of organizational environments which gives an idea of how complex the relationships really are.

[2]Two other books in this series (Jabes, 1978, chapter one for individual learning) and Tuggle (1978, chapters 4 and 5 for organizational learning) delve into learning. This book has a concern with learning task processes.

REFERENCES

Jabes, J. *Individual Processes in Organizational Behavior*. Arlington Heights, Ill.: AHM Publishing Corporation, 1978.

Jurkovich, R. "Core Typology of Organizational Environments." *Administrative Science Quarterly* 19 (1974): 380-94.

Lippitt, M. E., and Mackenzie, K. D. "Authority-Task Problems." *Administrative Science Quarterly* 21 (1976): 643-60.

_____. "A Theory of Committee Formation." In *Communication and Control in Social Processes,* edited by K. Krippendorf (in press), 1977.

Mackenzie, K. D. *A Theory of Group Structures, Volume II: Empirical Tests*. New York: Gordon & Breach Science Pubs., 1976b.

Roethlisberger, F. J., and Dickenson, W. J. *Management*

and the Worker. Cambridge, Mass.: Harvard University Press, 1939.

Simmons, R. E. *Managing Behavioral Processes: Applications of Theory and Research.* Arlington Heights, Ill.: AHM Publishing Corporation, 1978.

Tuggle, F. D. *Organizational Processes.* Arlington Heights, Ill.: AHM Publishing Corporation, 1978.

Span of Control

THE BASIC PROBLEM

Imagine a desk covered by a large glass pitcher
standing partially empty amid many different-
sized glasses filled with water. Also on the
table are a stack of towels and an opened
attaché case. On a signal the glasses are emptied into the pitcher. As each glass is emptied
into the pitcher, the water level rises until
it is full to the brim. There are still some
glasses yet to be emptied. As these are poured
into the full pitcher, water splashes over the
top of the desk. When the last glass has been
emptied, the desk is a watery mess. The towels
are then used to soak up the excess water,
and the soggy towels are then stuffed into the
attaché case. The attaché case is closed and
taken home where the towels are dried.
  This little story contains most of the

ingredients needed to understand the main concepts in determining the span of control of
a supervisor. Span of control is the number of
subordinates with whom a supervisor interacts.
There are many scarce resources in an organization, such as money, space, customers, raw materials, and so on. One of the most scarce of
all resources, however, is time, especially
the time of competent managers. Time, its allocation and scarcity, is the key to understanding the issues of span of control. The pitcher's
capacity represents the time available to the
supervisor to carry out his functions. It is
partially filled because a supervisor must
spend some time writing reports, thinking, and
so forth, that does not involve direct interactions with other people. The remaining capacity in the pitcher represents the time he
has available for interaction with others. The
glasses full of water stand for his subordinates. The amount of water in each glass represents the amount of the supervisor's time that
is taken up by the subordinate. As each subordinate uses up a portion of the supervisor's
capacity to interact, the pitcher becomes fuller. The supervisor reaches his limit when the
pitcher is full. But, just because the pitcher
is full, that is no reason for the demands on
his time to decrease. Problems requiring his
attention keep coming and the excess load,
which is analogous to the overflow that gets
mopped up by the towels and stuffed into the
attaché case, means that the supervisor takes
this work home with him or works on weekends.
The work done on the commuter train and at home
in the evenings, weekends, and holidays is
analogous to drying the soaked towels. The
supervisor can look forward to returning to
work and facing a new cycle of demands on his
time.

When the total time requirements exceed his
capacity, the supervisor is *overloaded*. When the
total time requirements equal his capacity he

is at *maximum span of control* and when the total
time requirements are less than his capacity,
he has *excess capacity*. This limit on time is,
within broad limits, dependent upon the supervisor's abilities, performance, experience,
the task process, and the expectations of
others about how much time he needs for his
task process. The manner in which he interacts
and the problems that he works on can be
changed. He can set priorities, delegate, ignore some problems, and even flee from the
problems. Furthermore, his subordinates are not
passive. They adjust to each other and
to the task-process demands. Consequently,
an analysis of span of control involves
active social processes. These processes
are contingent on the factors that take up his
time. These factors and their impact on behavior are different when he is overloaded than
when he has excess capacity.

The analysis of span of control in this chapter builds upon ideas presented in chapters 1,
2, and 3. The emphasis is on understanding how
span of control is dependent upon the person's
capacity. Accordingly, we are interested in
how time is spent and the factors that make up
the determinants of the time spent. These considerations will be compared to his time capacity. When the total demands on his time reach
his time capacity, he is at his maximum span of
control. The factors determining the amounts of
time are relatively simple. The main ideas for
combining and synthesizing these factors are
also simple. However, interpreting these factors to solve a span of control problem can
be subtle because of the contingencies and
contingent processes that may occur. The analysis of these problems in this chapter is a bit
more complex than arguing for or against different possible spans of control. The issues
lie deeper than whether or not the average
supervisor should have a span of control of 5,
6, 10, 20, and so on. But what we invest in

time to dig more deeply is rewarded by a newer
set of concepts and ideas for studying the use
of a number of management techniques. It will
become clear that these techniques increase
capacity and thereby the maximum span of control.

A Brief Survey of Span of Control Problem-Analysis

Before presenting a more modern analysis of
span of control problems, we should briefly
examine some of the issues that are directly
or indirectly part of span of control problems.
The oldest issue concerns the average span of
each official in a structural hierarchy. The
basic shape of the structural hierarchy depends
upon this number. Consider the structural hierarchy with every person having a span of control of 2. There is one person at the top
having two immediate subordinates. Each of
these has two more, each of these has two, and
so on. There would be 11 levels to have an
organization of just over 1,000 persons. Con-
trast this with a structural hierarchy whose
average span of control is 10. If the span of
control were 10, it would only require 4 levels
to have an organization of just over 1,110
persons. Clearly, the larger the average span
of control, the "flatter" the structural hierarchy. In addition, if one considers all levels
above the bottom level to be supervisors, then
in the structural hierarchy whose span is 2,
there are 511 supervisors and 512 "workers."
Thus, when the span is only 2, the ratio of
the number of supervisors to the number of
workers is approximately 1. But when the span
of control is 10, the number of supervisors for
a 4-level structural hierarchy is 111 and the
number of workers is 1,000. The ratio of supervisors to workers is approximately a tenth of the
the size. As span of control becomes larger,

the ratio of supervisors to workers becomes
smaller in a structural hierarchy of constant
span of control.

Thus, if one has a structural hierarchy of
constant span, one immediately sees that the
span of control is a critical number. What
this means, in practice, depends upon what assumptions one makes about the advantages and
disadvantages of having small or larger spans
of control. One could argue that with larger
spans, the costs of supervision would tend to
be reduced, because a smaller percentage of the
members of the organization are supervisors.
On the other hand, if the span of control is
too large, the supervisor may not have the capacity to supervise effectively such large
numbers of immediate subordinates. Thus, there
is a possible trade-off to be made in an attempt to balance these possibly opposing tendencies.

However, such an analysis ignores the resources the group's members bring to the organization, the types of task processes, the frequency, direction, and content of interactions,
the role and capacity of each person, information-processing costs, the possibility that
different persons on the same level and across
levels might have different jobs, the social
relationships among the members, and the effects of incentives and sanctions. Furthermore,
there is no obvious reason why these members
could not be staff persons or persons above
the bottom level who have no immediate subordinates (e.g., the company lawyer).

Consequently, an attempt to optimize span of
control by balancing the presumed control of
smaller spans against the lower supervisory
costs of larger spans is not realistic. Because
the task demands vary with the job and, hence,
between levels and even on a level, the problem
of determining the optimal span of control with
these ideas is pointless. One might as well try
to calculate the optimum size wheel for a

vehicle. Since vehicles come in all sizes and are designed for a variety of tasks, there can be no optimum size wheel for all vehicles. Just as it makes sense to determine the best wheel size for a vehicle having a specific purpose, it also makes sense to consider the best span for a particular person in a specific job. But it makes sense neither to calculate the best-sized wheel for all vehicles nor to calculate the best sized span of control for all people. It does not even make much sense to calculate the optimum span of control for a single person if his job demands change. For example, a professor might be able to supervise actively four Ph.D. dissertations, a lecture class of 75, a seminar of 15, and some of his own research. But the same professor might be overloaded with five Ph.D. dissertations and two lecture classes of 25 students.

The meaning of *optimum* is unclear in such formulations. Usually one says that x is optimum for y under conditions w for purpose z. To say that $x = 5$ is the optimum span of control without specifying the problem, y, the conditions, w, and the purpose, z, is meaningless. Consequently, the basic formulation of "optimum" span of control, even if one can incorporate some of the factors described in the preceding paragraph, is hopelessly inadequate for practical use.

There is another, more interesting, set of issues related to span of control. What is the effect of the size of a group on individual and group behavior? Usually the problem is examined in the context of the group with whom one interacts. Most persons, even in very large organizations, only interact with a small fraction of the total. A structural hierarchy serves to define the primary groups with whom one works. Thus, the problem is of practical interest here even though most of it comes from studies of small groups. Group size can affect productivity, creativity, social relationships, and types of conflict. There are a number of studies relevant to this type of problem.[1] For example, we know that the resources brought into the group increase with the size of the group. On the other hand, many studies have shown that the tendency for members to inter-act[2] (the "interaction potential" in the social psychology literature[3]) decreases with group size[4]. Bales and Borgatta (1955) report studies indicating that actual expression of tension and conflict decrease as the size of the group increases, whereas disagreement and antagonism show, if anything, an increase with size. Perhaps the smaller groups tend to smother expressions of conflict, and such activities that are felt to lead to overt expressions of conflict. For example, Slater (1958) reports that groups of size 2, 3, and 4 are more prone to inhibit disagreement than groups of size 5, 6, and 7. Thomas (1965) also reports studies concerning the effect of group size on such variables as propinquity and cohesiveness. Bass and Norton (1951), Frye, Sprvill, and Stritch (1964), Hare (1952), and Hauron and McGrath (1961) examine the ability to obtain consensus as the size of the group varies. Davis and Restle (1963) present interesting models for problem solving and group structure of different *sized groups*. Entwistle and Walton (1961) and Hare (1952) remark on the tendency of groups to form cliques as the group size increases. The hard evidence from laboratory experiments is not strong, but it is an often reported and discussed finding. Warner and Hilander (1964) report a study on the relationship between group size and membership participation.

The problem of group size is often the focus of ideological disputes in terms of the amount of control a supervisor should be allowed to exert on a subordinate with the underlying assumptions that: (1) the smaller the group, the more control the supervisor gains over his subordinates, and (2) this control affects the

morale and autonomy of the worker in an emotionally unsatisfying way. This dispute is
proto-scientific in that unscientific questions are discussed in a scientific style.
Considerations of situation, personality,
problem, content of interaction, and type of
task process are usually not made explicit.

The position taken in this book is that although group size may be an important variable
in the study of group behavior, it acts more
as an intervening variable that moderates group
behavioral processes. Its easy manipulation
and measurement has made it an obvious "independent" variable in examining the more gross
features of group behavior. Given many problems
and the plethora of different task processes a
group can follow to solve problems, the size
of a group, *per se*, is only one of the many determinants of group behavior. It has probably
been over-emphasized as a "variable" because
it is easy to measure.

The notion of the "optimal" span of control,
as it has been described, is not very useful
for diagnosing management problems. We can
see no consideration of how to allocate the
scarce and expensive resource of time. There
is no analysis of the factors that take up
this time. There is no allowance for the type
of task processes engaged in by the supervisor
and his work force. There is no allowance for
the effects of colleagues and supervisors on
the time resources of a supervisor. There are
no analyses of the effects of informational
overload. The determination of the optimal span
of control is not related to any explicitly
stated theory of organizational behavior. For
example, if a supervisor's span of control is
too large, what does a group do about it? Too
large a span of control or too small a span of
control can set off numerous social processes
that may have been unanticipated. As we shall
see, one result of too large a span of control is the starting up of structural change

processes that can result in a replacement of the supervisor.

Clearly, there is a need to reformulate span of control problems to include structures, task processes, and time. The reformulation offered in this chapter emphasizes time and how it is used. It incorporates a number of ideas about structures and task processes. In fact, the formulation of span of control, when combined with knowledge of task processes and the mapping function of chapter 2, has been used directly to cause structural changes in laboratory groups. The unresolved questions of what constitutes control and what is meant by *optimum* are sidestepped. The question becomes: What is the maximum span of control for a specific person under specified combinations of task processes and for the purpose of obtaining some goal? The emphasis has shifted from the aggregate and average to the individual in a specific instance. The following presentation of the new formulation is followed by a discussion of its practical and managerial implications.

DETERMINANTS OF THE MAXIMUM SPAN OF CONTROL

The span of control is not a constant for all members in an organization. Nor should it be. It varies with the person, his task processes, the time he has available for these task processes, and the expectations of those with whom he works. An analysis of the maximum span of control is presented in terms of the total time available to a group member for interacting with others. The basic idea is that each person has a capacity constraint measured in time and that each activity uses up some of this capacity. The maximum span of control occurs at the point when all of the time demands for his activities add up to this capacity.

This reformulation offers a new approach that emphasizes a person's capacity for interaction

rather than his "control" and is consistent
with our more modern concepts of group structures and task processes. *Span of control* is used
here as the number of persons with whom a person can interact. If the person is a supervisor having supervisors and colleagues, we
can split these out to find the maximum number
of subordinates. This is a special case of this
formulation. By stressing span as the number
with whom he interacts, we can apply the analysis to cases where there are not clear-cut
divisions between supervisor and subordinate
such as in a small group or a family. For example, consider a family with a mother, a
father, and four daughters. The father faces
five channels—one to his wife and one to each
of the four daughters. The mothers faces five
channels—one to her husband and one to each of
the daughters. The daughters face five channels—one to each of her parents and to her
three sisters. It is hard to know which person
is a boss and which is a subordinate. The
task demands on the mother vary with the time
of day, with peak periods of interaction just
before the daughters go off to school and at
dinner time. With the new formulation, it is
possible to do an analysis of the span of control of each family member without having to
worry about arbitrary classifications into
categories of superior and subordinate. Each
family member can be thought of as a hub of a
wheel for the purposes of interactions if he
or she is not the designated "leader." The
situation of the six-person family is shown in
Figure 4.1a and Figure 4.1b.

It is often difficult to know which person
or persons are supervisors and which are subordinates. There are job descriptions and
organizational rules and policies that help
make these distinctions in some organizations.
In others, the division of members into two
categories, supervisors and subordinates, is

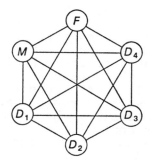

FIGURE 4.1a All-channel 6-member family with father, mother, and four daughters.

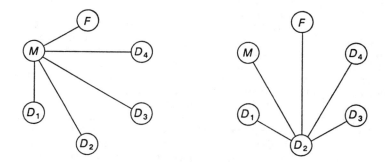

FIGURE 4.1b The family viewed from points of view (for interaction) by the mother and one of the daughters (D_2).

much less clear. In the analysis presented here, it is not necessary to make this classification. The analysis can be made for each member. The clues offered by the authority system may be used in picking candidates for applying this analysis.

The word *control* in the phrase *span of control* has never been clearly defined. One can lose control if the numbers with whom one interacts

become too large without changes in the task
process. This problem is discussed in chapter
6. If one has excess capacity, he could "do"
more and this excess capacity represents a form
of opportunity costs to the organization. The
persons with whom the supervisor interacts
also exert controls on the supervisor. If control is used a a verb it roughly means power,
and power is bilateral. If he is overloaded he
will tend to lose control, and if he has excess
capacity he could exert more control. He is
neither overloaded nor does he have excess
capacity when he is working at full capacity.
But this is the point at which he has maximum
span of control. The notion of maximum span of
control may be a reasonable surrogate for the
elusive optimal span of control. One can demonstrate, as is done below, that changes in the
factors making up the maximum span of control
can result in structural changes. Changes in
structure and task processes occur, and one
major factor in explaining these changes is the
maximum span of control of an individual relative to the demands on his time.

There are no explicit assumptions about power
or the "formal" organizational structures implied by the definition of span of control in
terms of the number of persons with whom one
can interact. The analysis depends upon the
time available to interact and the determinants
of how this time is used. Clearly power,
authority, and task processes are major determinants of who interacts with whom, how often,
and for what reason. But, instead of making
them our theoretical centerpiece, they are seen
as important aspects that are reflected in the
values and variables that go into calculating
the maximum span of control. This analysis
adopts the strategy of studying the problem of
maximum span of control in terms of a set of
determinants whose values vary with the person,
the group, and the task processes.

TOTAL TIME AVAILABLE

Let us assume for the sake of exposition that, from the point of view of the person we are studying, there are three types of persons with whom he interacts: supervisors, colleagues, and subordinates. Supervisors are those on a higher level within the organization with whom he interacts. Colleagues are those who are neither his supervisors nor his subordinates in the organization with whom he interacts. Usually colleages are cousin relationship persons, on the same level. Colleagues can also include "buddy" groups, protégés and patrons with whom our person has an uncle-nephew relationship.[5] Colleagues may also include friends in other parts of the organization. Subordinates are those on a lower level in the organization with respect to whom our person is a superior. Staff members can be in any of the three types depending upon where they are located and the nature of his involvement with the staff. The key here is that a person often has to interact with others who are not subordinates and that such additional interactions can take up time and thereby reduce the maximum span of control.

Many persons have more than one responsibility, work on more than one type of problem, and hold several jobs. The relevant persons with whom one interacts depend upon the task processes in which one is engaged. Let us assume that we have in mind a particular task process and a particular set of people. We have to determine the amount of total time that can be allotted to this task process. In some cases this may be a work day, such as eight hours. In other cases the time may be less than an hour. There are limits to this time because of the *discretion* allowed. The maximum period of time that a person has during which he is authorized and expected to exercise discretion in dis-

charging the responsibilities allocated to him
without review has been used as a measure of
status by Jacques (1956). This maximum time
span of discretion could be used to estimate
the allowable time to complete a task process.
The total time allowable will be longer, the
more complex and novel the task process. The
total time allowable will tend to decrease
with repeated experience in the task process
and with his experience in interacting with
the same persons. Changes in personnel and
alterations in task processes tend to increase
the maximum allowable time. Previous experience in similar task processes with others may
have set a norm for the maximum allowable time.
There is a tempo associated with most jobs and
conforming to it places severe limits on the
maximum allowable time to complete certain
task processes.

Mackenzie (1976b, chapter 12) reports an experiment with the minimum list of symbols and
network problems wherein he had to estimate
this maximum allowable time. His results are
consistent with an assumption of "no-worsening"
wherein the best time to complete a phase of
a task process was the basis of the norm for
maximum allowable time. The person was allowed
to improve but ran into difficulties if his
time became slower. In fact, in a number of
cases, when the maximum allowable time was violated, the group often replaced a hub with a
new person whom the group believed could meet
the standard. These data are consistent with
allowing departures from this norm when errors
were made. Errors called for a repeat of portions of the task process. This phenomenon was
so pronounced and regular that in two other
experiments one could cause a group to restruc-
ture itself merely by violating the time taken
by an experienced confederate to do his work.

The maximum allowable time is set partially
by the nature of the task process and partially
by experience with the group. It is not a uni-

versal constant but depends very much upon past experience. These experiences jell into a norm for how long the person can have to do his job without notice and comment. This is why the maximum allowable time should be related to the maximum span of discretion of Jacques. In our problem, the review can come from anyone and not just supervisors. The maximum allowable time reflects the norms of those involved in the task process and is not just an objective number set by industrial engineers. Persons can feel the pressure of this norm and seek to relieve the pressure by conforming to the norm.

One interesting aspect is that the norm cuts both ways. It puts pressure on one who is too fast to slow down whenever the excess speed can cause dislocations in the task processes. It should come as no surprise, then, to see output norms for workers with pressures to conform within acceptable limits. Too slow persons can become ostracized because they can create extra work for the others, and persons who work too quickly can be criticized because they "show up" the others. The fear that the work standard set by management could be increased because at least one person can easily beat it is genuine. Output norms are a surrogate for the maximum allowable time to complete a task process.

The author once delivered mail during the Christmas season and found that he could deliver all of the mail on a route in less than half the time it took the regular carrier. The first day when he started to report in for more work after completing deliveries by 11:30, he was met by the regular postman and told to stay away until 2:00. Although he was only 20 years old, he had the distinct impression of imminent bodily harm if he had insisted on checking in at 11:30. He remembers discussing this with other college students working at the same station and learning that almost all of the able-bodied ones had the same problem.

Factors Tending to Use Up Allowable Time

Let us assume that the person for whom we are studying span of control must: (1) spend time whenever he interacts and whenever he solves problems between interactions, and (2) spend time whenever others interact with him. We can examine the interactions on each half-channel for the time used up on that half-channel. Then by summing over all of the half-channels involving our person, we can determine the total time in interacting. This approach will hold for subordinates, supervisors, and colleagues.

The basic idea behind this calculation is that the time taken to interact with another is directly proportional to the product of the average amount of content of the interactions and the number of interactions within the time period. This means that a complex interaction rich in content will, on the average, take more time than a simple interaction. Furthermore, holding the content constant, the greater the number of interactions with a person, the greater the amount of time spent. A large number of simple interactions may take as much time with one person as a smaller number of infrequent but more complex interactions with another. The proportionality factor relating time to interact with a person and the product of the measure of content and frequency is called the *interaction ineffectiveness*. The interaction ineffectiveness is the unit of time it takes to transmit a given *volume* of content (content times frequency of contact). When two persons have experience in interacting on a specific issue, the interaction ineffectiveness tends to decrease. The reciprocal of interaction ineffectiveness is called *interaction effectiveness*. Interaction effectiveness tends to increase with experience unless severe interpersonal problems between the two have arisen.

The time taken for one person to interact

with another increases with the interaction
ineffectiveness, the amount of content of the
average interaction, and the frequency of interactions. The time for one person to interact
with another may differ when considered from
the other person's point of view. The time for
one person to interact with subordinates, colleagues, and supervisors is the sum of the
times that are taken to interact with each. The
time taken to interact with one person is
analogous to the amount of water in a glass in
the opening story of this chapter.

There is another factor that influences the
maximum allowable time usage. Although many
executives spend the bulk of their time in
direct interactions, they also spend time in
problem-solving, planning, setting procedures,
scheming, report-writing, and so forth, which
do not involve direct interactions. The time
taken for these private activities, called
internal calculations, is assumed to be directly
proportional to the amount of content of these
internal calculations. The proportionality coefficient represents the *information-processing
ineffectiveness* of the person. The information-
processing effectiveness is the reciprocal of
the information-processing ineffectiveness.
The more quickly a person can perform these internal calculations, the greater his information-processing effectiveness. On the average,
experienced, competent, and talented persons
are more effective in performing these internal
calculations.

The requirements for internal calculations
depend upon the task processes. For example,
the mere collation of a list of symbols in the
minimum list of symbols problem requires far
fewer internal calculations than finding the
network and making its interpretation in the
network decomposition problems described in
chapter 2. New problems, altering task processes, working out operating procedures, and
planning tend to increase the requirements for

internal calculations. These internal calculations take up time. The amount of time taken by them is analogous to the amount of water in the pitcher before the water in the glasses was poured in. The greater the time spent on internal calculations, the less time to interact; hence, the less the maximum span of control for the individual. Included in the internal calculations is a quantity called *slack time*.

Slack time is an amount of time allowed that is in excess of the normal loads. This slack time acts as a buffer to meet contingencies. Not every person will want to interact each period. But sometimes the volume of interactions will become very large. A person needs a buffer to be able to cope with fluctuating demands on his time. Slack time is a special case of organizational slack discussed in Tuggle (1978). Some jobs include in the job description a percentage of time that is allocated to keeping up with recent developments in one's field. Examples include some engineering jobs and faculty positions at university that seek to foster research.

The actual time spent by the person on his job may be different from the maximum time allowable. Now let us assemble the various pieces of this development of the determinants of maximum span of control. Maximum allowable time represents the capacity of the pitcher. It is used up by: (1) interacting with subordinates, (2) interacting with colleagues and supervisors, and (3) internal calculations. Hence, the sum of these three times should be less than or equal to the maximum time allowed[6].

The member has *excess capacity* when the sum of these three times is less than the maximum allowable time. The member is at maximum span of control when the sum of these three times equals the maximum allowable time. When the sum of the times is greater than the maximum allowable time, the person has *insufficient capacity* and is *overloaded*. When there is excess capacity, the person could increase his span of control, and when there is insufficient capacity, he has too large a span of control.

The person with insufficient capacity will be taking home some of his work in order to cope with the overflow. He may try to reduce the total time taken by altering structures and task processes that can reduce the span of control, the times that he spends with supervisors and colleagues, interaction time with subordinates, and time for internal calculations. In addition the maximum allowable time may also change.

The discussion of the factors that determine the various quantities allows us to frame a discussion of numerous management techniques. Let us now use these ideas about the maximum span of control to diagnose and solve various managerial problems qualitatively. The precise estimate of the quantities and the precise use of formulae connecting them is far less useful than the ability to juggle the ideas to attack managerial problems. The theoretical development provides a framework for conducting such analyses. Most managerial situations are too fluid for precise estimates of the quantities. However, if one can understand how the various factors go together, one can perform "quick and dirty" diagnoses which can lead to better practice.

The effects of structures on the maximum span of control and how the maximum span of control affects structure are discussed below. Then, applications of the ideas of this analysis of the maximum span of control are used in order to analyze and to diagnose a number of managerial problems.

MAXIMUM SPAN OF CONTROL AND ORGANIZATIONAL STRUCTURES

MAXIMUM SPAN OF CONTROL CAN DETERMINE THE BASIC SHAPE OF AN ORGANIZATION

If the basic structural configuration is a hierarchy, the maximum span of control determines the number of subordinates to each supervisor on every level. As is evident, the maximum span of control varies from person to person because of varying abilities of the persons involved and varying task processes. It is clear that everything else being equal, the larger the maximum span of control, the fewer the number of supervisors required to do the same work and the smaller the number of organizational levels. The larger the average span of control, everything else being equal, the "flatter" the organizations.

Because supervisors tend to be more expensive (salaries, fringe benefits, space requirements, perquisites, and overhead) than nonsupervisors, increasing each supervisor's actual span to his maximum span of control can result in direct cost savings. Flatter organizations provide more direct access to those at higher levels. And if R. Simmons' work (Simmons, 1974) is applicable, reducing the length of the chain of command can lower the number of transmission and clerical errors, thereby promoting efficiency and lowering administrative costs.

The two types of advantages, lower supervisory costs and reduction of probable occurrence of transmission and clerical errors that could accrue as a result of adjusting actual spans of control to the maximum spans of control, are reasonably clear and direct. There are a number of less direct advantages. If one recalls that in the discussion of hierarchy, cousin and uncle relationships reduced the degree of hierarchy, one can reorient this an-

alysis. For example, interactions with colleagues are usually cousin or uncle-nephew relationships, and if there are a number of
supervisors, cousin relationships among them
and numerous uncle-nephew relationships
between them and our person occur. These interactions tend to *decrease* the maximum span of control
(by raising the interaction time for superiors
and colleagues and increasing the volume of internal calculations and thereby the internal
calculation time) and decrease the degree of
hierarchy. The close link between the degree of
hierarchy and efficiency ($H \leq E$), suggests that
such interactions would tend to depress the
level of efficiency for the task processes.
Thus, if an organization is seriously interested in performance, one would expect to see
adjustment in structure that would tend to increase the maximum span of control of each
supervisor. (One should not assume, however,
that all organizations and supervisors within
an organization are primarily concerned with
efficiency. Many are more concerned with other
goals—personal advancement, organizational
survival, and avoidance of conflict.)

Reducing the number of transmission and
clerical errors can reduce the number of untimely and redundant behaviors. This reduction
of untimely and redundant behaviors will increase both the degree of hierarchy and the
degree of efficiency. But if there is a reduction of untimely and redundant behaviors, the
volume of interactions will tend to decrease.
Thus, there is a reduction of interaction
times, and because the task processes would be
simpler, there might also be a reduction in the
volume of internal calculations. Hence, the
maximum span of control would tend to rise. The
dependence of maximum span of control on the
factors mentioned earlier leads to processes to
alter both structures and task processes, and
these alterations change the maximum spans of
control. Working against such natural processes

are personal and organizational goals that are
often inconsistent with greater efficiency.

CHANGES IN CAPACITY CAN RESULT IN STRUCTURAL CHANGE

The discussion in the previous section focused
on the cases where the maximum span of control
was greater than or equal to the actual span of
control. There we mentioned some direct and
indirect effects of enlarging the actual span
to meet the maximum span of control. The main
effect of changing capacity was to promote efficiency by altering structures and task processes. There are, however, a number of powerful processes that can occur when the actual
span of control is larger than the maximum
span of control, or when there is the case of
overload. The obvious one is for our person to
work longer hours. Another is for our person to
take steps to reduce the factors that take up
his time. These maneuvers are discussed in detail in the next section.

Let us examine some other processes resulting
in structural change when overload occurs.
Specifically, one can describes some processes
of structural change that occur in this case.
This analysis takes place within the context
of a little laboratory organization where the
absence of authority and resource controls
(such as promotion and salary adjustments)
allows us to observe structural changes in
less inhibited circumstances that exist in
most organizations having traditions and legal
authority. Overload is simulated by first
allowing a norm for maximum allowable time
to be set and then causing delays that violate
this norm. The minimum list of symbols problem
and the network decomposition problem were
described in chapters 1 and 2. You will
recall that groups of five tended to form
hierarchies for the simpler minimum list of
symbols and tended to remain relatively

decentralized for the more complex and infer-
ential network of decomposition problems.
Mackenzie (1976b, chapter 12) has shown how
the span of control calculations in conjunc-
tion with a series of contingent conditions
could be put together in mapping function
and successfully used to predict the occurrence of certain major structural changes. For
example, it is possible to predict the problem on which the groups will centralize about
a hub person and when previously centralized
groups will decentralize. Subsequent experiments provided further validation to
this line of reasoning and for the calculation of maximum span of control in particular.

Having an understanding of the voting
processes and the calculation of maximum span
of control, it is possible to control these
processes of structural change in the minimum list of symbols problems with the aid
of two confederates and three naive subjects
(Silcox and the author ran this experiment).
The two confederates, labeled Blue and
Orange, and the three subjects, labeled Black,
Red, and Green, began to work on the minimum
list of symbols problems. After receiving
instructions about how to solve this problem,
the group met for two hours and were each
paid $0.20 for every problem solved within a
two-hour period. Thus, the more problems they
solved, the more money they would earn. These
groups were motivated to solve as many problems as possible. Their behavior was very consistent with the assumption that they were
efficiency-minded.

By prearrangement the confederates, Blue and
Orange, would both seek leadership (the hub
position in a wheel) at the beginning of the
second problem. It was further arranged that
Blue would win and become the hub of a wheel
network for both the data-sharing and the
answer-forming phases of the task process. Confederate Blue would keep the hub position for

four problems and set a norm for the maximum
allowable time, which was between 0.5 and 3.0
min. depending upon the problem complexity. By
the end of problem six, the groups were solving
the problems quickly within the maximum allowable time and were content. There were no votes
to alter the structures. At the beginning
of the next problem, say problem seven, Confederate Blue would violate the norm by delay-
ing from three to nine minutes. This delay
would set off voting processes to change the
structures. Confederate Orange would jump in
to bid for the hub position. Within the next
problem, Confederate Orange would be elected
the new hub. We then repeated the cycle, allowing Orange to set a new norm, which was the
same as that set by Confederate Blue. After
being the hub for four problems, Confederate
Orange was instructed to delay as Blue did
earlier. The delay stimulated voting and soon
Confederate Blue became the new hub. Thus the
group went from an all-channel to a wheel, back
to an all-channel, then to a wheel about a
second person, then to an all-channel, and
finally back to the original wheel structure.

We ran a number of control experiments to remove the possibilities that the changes were
due to the type of persuasion rather than the
violation of the maximum allowable time. The
first control involved no delay on the part of
the Confederate Blue who was the hub. But,
Confederate Orange sent the exact messages as
in the main experiment. Without the delay, she
could not get elected hub and Blue kept the
job until the experiment was terminated. We
also had one control condition in which Blue
was introduced as a person of higher status
than Orange. We determined that it was the delay and not the status that resulted in structural change. Despite Blue's greater initial
status, Orange was able to wrest the hub position away when Blue caused a delay. There is
some evidence, too, that the groups reevaluated

Blue's relative status downward after he was
"unsuccessful."

There are several lessons in this experiment.
The first is that because structures represent
need-satisfying interaction patterns, the group
would keep a structure as long as Blue was able
to satisfy its needs for efficiency. When he
gave evidence of not being able to satisfy
these needs, structural change processes were
started up to remove him. The second is the
fleeting and process-dependent nature of status.
When Blue did not perform he lost some of his
status. This loss is consistent with a theory
of leadership by E. P. Hollander (1964; see
Simmons, 1978, for a discussion). Third, the
theories of structural change described in
chapter 2 seem to hold up well in making predictions. Fourth, the theory and procedures for
determining maximum span of control appear to
be useful. Fifth, and this is hard to describe
without reproducing the actual written messages,
is the outright duplicity of the subjects. For
example, in trying to get rid of Confederate
Blue another subject would brutally assess the
performance of Blue to Orange and at the same
time send a conciliatory message to Blue.

AN EXPLANATION OF THE FORMATION OF HIERARCHIES

In 1973, H. Pattee edited a book entitled *Hierarchy Theory: The Challenge of Complex Systems,* wherein
five authors from widely different backgrounds
argue for the necessity of hierarchies for
complex systems. The arguments by H. Simon
(1973, pp. 1-28) are compelling because they
relate the information economy of a hierarchy
with our current understanding about the limits
of human information-processing capability and
theories about human memory and problem-solving.
A. Tannenbaum *et al.* (1974) report a series of
cross-cultural studies relating the distribu-

tion of control and the widespread existence
of hierarchy even where there is collective
ownership of a factory. Organizational hier-
arches are needed to coordinate the efforts of
many persons who perform a wide variety of
tasks in an organization. However, the divisions that arise because of rank and allocation
of resources are often unwanted side-effects
of hierarchy. Tannenbaum *et al.* argue that a high
degree of formal participativeness and equali-
tarianism among members can reduce the unin-
tended and perhaps dysfunctional effects of
hierarchy.

Many social scientists are emotionally and
professionally committed to eradicate hierarchy
in organizations. It probably is neither possible nor even necessary. The author thinks
that most of the criticisms stem from a concept of hierarchy that is a pyramid of offices
rather than a coherent amalgamation of multiple
structures and task processes which is embodied in the concept of hierarchy presented
in chapter 1. The arguments in the Pattee
volume show reasons for the necessity, and the
studies by Tannenbaum *et al.* show how humans can
adjust systems of control and task processes
to vary the degree to which an organization is
structurally hierarchical. The hierarchy of any
complex system is a matter of degree, and humans can make adjustments to form viable
organizations for any degree of hierarchy.

We know from the laboratory studies reported
in chapter 1 that there is a strong linkage
between the degree of hierarchy and measures
of efficiency. However, it is not always the
purpose of participation in an organization to
foster efficiency. Hence, pure hierarchies are
not always the actual or even the desired state
of an organization. In fact, many organizations
evolve systems of checks and balances that
build into the structures a degree of hierarchy that is less than 1.0. For example, at
the national level in the United States, the

judicial and legislative branches of government
provide controls on the executive branch that
limit the maximum degree of hierarchy. It is
pointless to argue that an organization should
ever have some specified level of hierarchy
without carefully considering the situation
facing the organization. However, if we can
understand why and under what conditions a
hierarchy would emerge, we can better understand our choices for organizational design.
Consequently, a short discussion based upon our
knowledge of group structure and the maximum
span of control is presented to argue why,
under conditions of scarce resources and a compelling drive towards efficiency, hierarchies
would tend to evolve.

Let us assume that we start with a little
organization in which every member is necessary, there are scarce resources, and each member wishes to control as many of these resources as possible, which creates competition
for these resources. In addition, each member
and his activities are evaluated in order to
judge the net contribution to the organization.
A member's activities will be allowed to grow
and new members will be added whenever there
are net positive advantages to the organization
for such growth. A member's activities will be
allowed to shrink if it is to the organization's net advantage and members will be
dropped from the organization when the net advantages to having their participation are
negative. Now suppose, further, that the
organization starts with a small number and
then proceeds to grow.

What will the initial structure look like? We
have assumed that each member is necessary, and
that each member wishes to maximize his share
of the resources. These imply that the organization will seek to minimize the number of
channels and will prefer the most centralized,
minimum number of channel structures.[7] Two
simple structures, the wheel and the chain,

have the minimum number of channels. The chain
presents some difficulty in controlling its
resource-maximizing members because members in
the middle of the chain could take resources
from others and distort information flow to
their own advantage. Some procedure for control
is necessary to insure proper allocation. The
wheel structure, the most centralized, has a
hub person who can make the allocation and
exert control and thereby some coordination.
He, too, is a resource-maximizer but if he
takes too much, the others will form a new
structure with another as hub. If he fails to
allocate properly, some may get too many resources at the expense of others. This could
cause a failure and/or a reorganization. He is
thereby constrained to allocate resources
fairly.

Suppose that the little organization is successful and begins to grow. As it grows it
will eventually reach the capacity of the hub
to handle the demands. When this happens his
span of control becomes greater than his
maximum span of control. There are a series of
exchanges and if he becomes overloaded he may
no longer be able to make proper allocations
that satisfy the members. They may start opening new channels to get around him; but this
will distort the allocations and some may not
get enough to maintain membership. However, if
every member is necessary for survival, this
will not work for very long. A new leader may
emerge but even if he does and the organization
keeps growing, there will come a time when
there will be an excess load and another breakdown. Rather than have a breakdown, the hub can
give up some direct control in order to maintain overall control. He can do this by reducing the number who report directly to him by
having some report to others who in turn report
to him.

Thus the old two-level hierarchy can split
into three or more levels. The old hub of the

old wheel is now the hub of a wheel and each
of his spokes may become the hub of a subsidiary wheel. The logic for the wheel is still
strong at each level and will tend to form under
the assumed conditions. However, now that there
are several levels, the control by which he
allocates resources becomes less direct. He
will be forced to allocate control over sub-
functions to his subordinates. These allocations, to work, must be capable of satisfying
needs of each of the maximizing members, or
else the organization will die or at least subdivide into a number of separate organizations.
Rules and division of labor will evolve and
tend to be maintained by a number of control
devices. Thus, what started out as a little
organization would evolve into a hierarchy and
would be maintained as long as the resource-
maximizing members could benefit. The decision
to grow and how to grow would depend upon comparing the marginal benefits of adding new
units and the marginal costs of the new units.
One would expect growth to increase to the
point at which the marginal costs become equal
to the marginal benefits. The option of forming
more levels and a hierarchy keeps moving the
marginal costs downward in a series of shifts.
What would be too costly in an overloaded system can be less costly in a reorganized system.

The arguments presented here are heuristic
but they do show a possible chain of reasoning
for how structural hierarchies would tend to
form. This discussion complements those of
chapter 1 and those of H. Simon (1973). The
significant feature of this argument is how
considerations of maximum span of control lead
to multiple levels. By carefully considering
the assumptions underlying this argument, one
has a basis for analyzing conditions when a
hierarchy will not form. For example, if one
relaxes the need of each member for the survival of the organization (a case when public
organizations can grow independent of demon-

strated capability of delivering needed services), one can see how the all too frequent
"bloated" governmental agencies can prosper
even when the additions provide no new and
useful services. In such systems, the sources
of resources may not match the flow of services. This is not to say that all governmental
organizations are insensitive to need and can
grow without providing services, but it is
theoretically possible to explain the continued
expansion of certain agencies even when they
have discharged their original purpose.

Organizations with a strong ideological basis
can avoid the constraints imposed by assuming
each member seeks to maximize resources. Thus,
there are numerous instances when organizations
will not evolve into hierarchies. However, external audits and reviews of any system may
force its members to justify personnel changes
and policies. Competition among organizations
may enforce some of the "market" discipline.
There are strong tendencies to form structural
hierarchies as the system becomes more complex.
This seems true even for systems where the
participants lack legal mobility. A real problem for an organization lacking the discipline
of competition and having external controls on
processes is that its members, to protect themselves, tend to create structural hierarchies
with multitudinous rules. The task processes
can get distorted until the structural hierarchy has a low degree of hierarchy because of
the many redundant and untimely task behaviors.
Such organizations are referred to as bureaucracies. Chapter 5 is devoted to a discussion
of bureaucracies.

RELATIONSHIPS BETWEEN INCREASING MAXIMUM SPAN OF CONTROL AND MANAGEMENT TECHNIQUES

MANAGEMENT TECHNIQUES VIEWED AS DEVICES TO INCREASE MAXIMUM SPAN OF CONTROL

The basis for this analysis of span of control is the use of the limited resource time for members of an organization. Persons, especially supervisors and executives, are expensive. Figuring out methods for making better use of this expensive resource has always been an important managerial problem. Over the centuries, numerous managerial techniques have evolved to consume and make better use of time. The formation of hierarchies with an authority system, division of labor, and rules has been one means. The use of staff personnel, standard operating proceudres, delegation of responsibility, and the setting of priorities are also capable, in some cases, of reducing the time required to perform the activities. More recently, schemes have evolved to focus attention on problems by setting up a system of controls which generates reports and requires supervisory time only when reports from the control system lie outside a range of acceptable values. These are referred to as *management by exception schemes*. Systems of governance are set up to reduce the time spent on conflicts. Many involved with human relations strive for attitudes and interpersonal competence that could result in more open (and possibly more efficient) interactions and more creative problem-solving. System designers and specialists in management information systems try to rationalize the collection, filtering, and distribution of necessary information. In some cases, this more rapid and planned flow of information can save time in gathering, analyzing, and exchanging information.

There is a myriad of possible managerial techniques that, when working properly, tend to

increase the maximum span of control of each
member in the organization. However, because
the connection between these techniques and the
saving of time, which increases the capacity
to interact, is often not understood, it is
possible that a technique becomes abused. Knowing how to put together the many factors that
determine the maximum span of control allows
one to diagnose and construct managerial reme-
dies to managerial problems. In the next section, we discuss a few managerial techniques
in terms of the maximum span of control. One
of the findings is that a good solution that
can save time when first installed can actually
come to worsen a situation, because inherent
factors to increase time requirements have
been allowed to more than offset early advantages.

EXAMPLES OF SEVERAL MANAGERIAL TECHNIQUES AND THEIR EFFECT ON MAXIMUM SPANS OF CONTROL

STAFF Many managerial problems require the
mixing and coordination of specialized knowledge. Policies must be formulated to insure
that the task processes are sensible and to
make proper integration of the many aspects of
a problem. From these deliberations flow plans
and procedures for implementing these policies.
Conceivably, an executive can solve these problems himself. However, as the organization
grows and its many task processes and legal
obligations become more complex, the time taken
for these internal calculations and interactions increases to the point where the maximum
span of control becomes too small for the job.

One method for coping is to create a group of
staff members who are assigned to a supervisor.
The staff group can perform many of the internal calculations for the executive, and thereby,
increase his maximum span of control by decreasing the time for internal calculations.

Staff members can also cut down on the number
of interactions with both the set of subordinates and with the supervisors and colleagues. Consequently, a staff group can greatly enhance the capabilities of an executive.
But, and this is often ignored, the existence
of a staff can also have the reverse effect.
First, the staff group members are usually additional subordinates and thereby directly increase the actual span of control. Second, the
staff groups may create new problems that are
now necessary to solve. For example, they can
cause numerous authority problems for the executive, because they may intervene in the task
processes of the regular subordinates. Their
solutions, which appear well-grounded on paper,
may not work so well when implemented. This
can create more staff problems and more interactions. Third, there is exhaustive documenta-
tion that demonstrates how staff groups tend to
grow even when the volume of production shrinks.
These staff members, who are often professionals, bring to the organization both task processes and professional responsibilities that
can be inconsistent with the regular task processes. Resolving these differences can increase the internal calculations and the volume
of interactions and thereby decrease the maximum span of control.

Thus, what was originally a good idea can
turn out to be a nightmare for the executive.
Keeping the labor-saving advantages of a staff
in mind, along with the time-consuming disadvantages of a staff, the executive is better
equipped to strike a favorable balance. Staff
assistants and clerical workers can reduce the
time for internal calculations and thereby allow for an increase in the maximum span of
control. To the extent that the time saved by
having a staff exceeds the extra time required
to control, direct, and interact with the staff,
the presence of a staff can increase the
maximum span of control. But when the trade-off

becomes negative, steps should be taken to re-think the usefulness of one's staff.

STANDARD OPERATING PROCEDURES Tuggle (1978, chapter 4) presents a description and analysis of standard operating procedures. They are a learned set of behavior rules that "are the focus for control within the firm; they are the result of a long run adaptive process by which the firm learns; they are the short run focus for decision making within the firm (Cyert and March, 1963, p. 113)." SOP's describe the task processes, the control and continuing reports, the procedures for the flow of information, and may constitute a plan. Having SOP's reduces the number of problems to be solved. They can have the effect of reducing the volume of internal calculations by decreasing both the problem-solving ineffectiveness and the content of the problems to be solved. They can cut down on the volume of interactions, because they specify how a task is to be accomplished and the conditions for interacting about the problems covered by the SOP's. They tend to decrease the volume of interactions by reducing the interaction ineffectiveness and the content of these interactions. Thus, SOP's tend to increase the maximum span of control.

But they can also cause side effects that work against these advantages. The very existence of the SOP focuses attention on certain information and problems. This focus could be directed to gathering information and solving problems that are actually inappropriate to the real problems. A company that stresses rules for production of a chemical may not have paid attention to pollution or the changes in factor inputs such as oil. Following old SOP's could be dysfunctional. SOP's do change but they change more in response to short range and local problems than to longer range strategic problems. The methods for adjusting standard

operating procedures may impede problem-solving.
The tendency is to tinker with the details of
an existing SOP rather than to create a whole
new set appropriate to the actual problems. It
is very time-consuming and difficult (and may
involve numerous staff conferences and committees) to adjust a complex set of SOP's designed
for one situation when faced with a novel set
of problems. The SOP's can evolve into an
ad hoc common law that constrains the organization. Previous commitments and existing distribution of power and resources are often reflected in the SOP's. Attempts to alter SOP's
can, therefore, be intensely political. Political infighting to alter them can result in new
SOP's that have not solved the newer problems.
The inconsistency between the old ones and
those that might be necessary to solve newer
problems can eat up time because they create
more, and more complicated, problems. These
side effects can serve to decrease the maximum
span of control. The arousal of vested interests that often occurs in such disputes can
lead to issue-spreading and thereby to more
problems that contribute further to overloading
supervisors and staff.

Dornbusch and Scott (1975) argue that procedures for evaluating personnel or programs
that are considered invalid can result in a
serious loss of authority and power for the
manager who uses the invalid procedures. However, even though the manager realized that
the SOP for making evaluations is incorrect, he
may not have the time and energy to correct
them. Thus, the SOP's that were designed to
help may actually hurt.

MANAGEMENT BY EXCEPTION Pounds (1969) and Kepner and Tregoe (1965) associate a problem with
a discrepancy between what one desires and
what one has. Pounds argues that in established
organizations most problems arise out of deviations from a historical standard. For example,

if the cost of manufacturing a unit was $1.75 and the new report shows that it is now $2.35, the increase of $0.60 is signaling a problem. Efforts will be made to study reasons for the $0.60 increase and to figure out what to do about it. If the costs are industry-wide, the effect may be to raise prices. If the costs are due to a production problem, efforts will be made to solve it.

Practically speaking there will be numerous fluctuations in levels of production, costs of production, accident rates, delays, sales, accounts receivable, absenteeism, and so on. If every fluctuation created a new set of interactions, the executive would have an increased volume of interactions, and thus a reduced maximum span of control. In order to keep on top of fluctuations but to limit the number of interactions necessary to analyze and report these fluctuations, schemes are evolved to specify what level of and type of fluctuation should warrant managerial action. These techniques are called *management-by-exception* schemes. That is, when the fluctuation falls outside of some acceptable range, it is an exception that signals the need for a manager to work on the source of the discrepancy. For example, if the costs were $1.75 to produce a unit, a manager might set limits of $1.65—$1.90. Numbers falling into this range would not be reported but numbers outside of this range (above $1.90 or below $1.65) could signal the need for action. If the costs fall below $1.65, the production would be analyzed to find out why, in the hope that reasons could be exploited in other parts of the firm. The tolerable range for exceptions will tend to be smaller whenever the production quantities are large, the gross profit margins are small, and when management is aggressively pursuing its profit goals.

Management-by-exception schemes tend to reduce the volume of interactions and thereby increase the maximum span of control. They are a special type of standard operating procedure. They can have the same sort of problems as other SOP's and improper or invalid management-by-exception schemes can sometimes create time-consuming side effects that offset the advantage.

DELEGATION The general topic of delegation is discussed in chapter 6 in the context of de-centralization of a firm. For our purposes here, delegating responsibility means to in-crease the functional autonomy of subordinates. By increasing the responsibilities of his sub-ordinates, the supervisor can decrease the range of task processes for which it is neces-sary to interact. For example, if a manager allows his subordinate manager to hire three more persons and delegates the choice to his subordinate, he will not have to become di-rectly involved in the hiring processes. Dele-gating responsibility for the performance of portions of overall task processes reduces the number of topics for discussion between organi-zational levels. Delegating can increase the maximum span of control by reducing the volume of interactions and hence the time taken for these interactions. Delegations may also in-crease subordinate initiative, which could further reduce the volume of interactions and the need for internal calculations. Thus, suc-cessful delegation could increase the maximum span of control.

However, delegation can result in organiza-tional disasters and setbacks in the personal career of a manager. Trust in the subordinate's judgment and character is part of the decision to delegate, because by delegating some of his responsibility he reduces his control and may be more vulnerable to political moves by those whose interests would not suffer if he were to get into trouble. Confidence in his ability to weather possible short-run setbacks that could occur with mistakes by a subordinate is also part of the decision.

PRIORITY-SETTING Each of us has only so much money to spend on housing, transportation, education, insurance, food, social life, charities, and so on. If we purchased everything that we wanted, we would go rapidly into debt. In our personal lives we learn to set goals and establish priorities. Food and shelter may be the highest priority item for most of us. That new Mercedes might have to wait; we could get by on a bicycle. The swimming pool might have to be put off to pay life insurance if one is financially responsible for a family. Most prudent persons set personal goals in light of current assets, income, borrowing capacity, anticipated income flows and needs. One cannot have everything, and so one sets aside money for essentials, and the excess is allocated to less essential purposes. These other purposes can be ranked and taken care of in order of priority.

Similarly, a manager has many competing demands on his time budget. Some tasks are essential and must be taken care of immediately. Some can be put off until the essential ones are taken care of. By planning, deciding which demands are the most important and which are of lesser importance, a manager budgets his time in much the same manner as he would budget his personal expenses. Time, like money, is a precious resource.

A manager might be able to get along without setting priorities to allocate his time. But if the requirements on his time for internal calculations and interactions increase too much, he can fall into a situation where his maximum span of control is too small for his job. By setting priorities, he can cut down on the immediate volume of work. This can allow him to maintain his current span of control and in some cases even increase it, especially when he can delegate lower priority problems to subordinates. However, there are limits to

how far this can be done without creating dele-
terious side effects that can offset the
short-run savings.

NORM FOR ALLOWABLE TIME A central feature in
our analysis of span of control is the amount
of time which the group allows a person to complete his duties. Establishiment of work norms,
using good managers to set the norms, can
create strong pressures on the new person to
meet these standard. A manager might want to
do what he can to help set realistic norms for
performing jobs. The expectations of the subordinates from below, the manager from above,
and his colleagues can provide incentives to
produce that can be far greater than the manager could impose by himself. The informal
norms may even take precedence over the formal
ones such as those included in a job description.
   Many of us are raised with an ethic that encourages hard work and personal sacrifice in a
job. We may, therefore, overlook the possibility that someone might be working to keep
the norm for maximum allowable time higher than
is necessary. The manager's work and the relationship with subordinates sets the time norm.
Once set, it is difficult to change. Many have
vested interests in setting the time norm
higher than it needs to be. This creates slack
time and helps stabilize the task processes
(see Tuggle, 1978, chapter 6, for a discussion
of organizational slack). The manager may not
want to work faster because this would result
in a norm of lower time. Once set, this lower
norm becomes the standard. So, if one were
able to do the work much faster than before,
one would be expected to maintain the pace.
Failure in the future to meet the standard
could result in unfavorable evaluations. Too
much efficiency could also make others in the
group and former occupants of the job look

bad. No one wants to be shown up or made to re-
evaluate himself because of some super-energetic
colleague or boss. Showing them up could result
in many unanticipated personal problems.
Having demonstrated superiority, not maintaining it could result in negative assessments of
one's judgment and intentions.

Restriction of output is a managerial technique for survival. In organizations where
such practices are widespread, there is not
much lower-level persons can do. Such practices, instead of being condemned, should be
examined from the point of view that their existence provides significant clues about the
levels of trust and commitment to the purposes
of the organizations. The first questions
should ask why such norms exist. Maybe, given
past practices, they make a lot of sense. Maybe, because of the erratic nature of the demands on time, they are necessary because they
provide slack. Maybe, there are a couple of
key persons who are setting such norms and
encouraging such behavior who should be replaced. About all that one can advise in the
absence of some specific case is to be very
cautious about trying to change such norms.

NOTES

[1]Three useful review articles of the results of some
of these studies are McKeachie (1963), Starbuck (1965),
and Thomas (1965). These three articles contain extensive bibliographies for educational problems, organization studies, and social psychological studies, respectively. A new book edited by Starbuck (1971), extends
his earlier work.

[2]See, for example, Dodd (1953, 1955), Fischer (1953),
Gibb (1954), and Thalen (1949), Bales (1951) and Stephan
and Mischler (1952).

[3]See, for example, Bass (1960).

[4]Stephan (1952), Keller (1951), Gustafson (1955), and Coleman (1960) argue that various simple statistical models can explain the relative participation rates.

[5]See chapter 1 for a discussion of cousin and uncle-nephew relations. A protégé is someone on a lower level whose interests are advanced by a patron on a higher level. For our purposes here we include those patron-protégé pairs which are not immediate superior-subordinate relationships.

[6]Details of the algebraic developments for these calculations can be found in Mackenzie (1974; 1976a, chapter 6).

[7]See chapter 6 for a discussion of the concept of structural centrality.

REFERENCES

Bales, R. F. *Interaction Process Analysis*. Cambridge, Mass.: Addison-Wesley, 1951.

Bales, R. F., and Borgatta, E. F. "Size of Group as a Factor in the Interaction Profile." In *Small Groups*, edited by Hare, Borgatta, and Bales, pp. 396-413. New York: Knopf, 1955.

Bass; B. M. *Leadership, Psychology, and Organizational Behavior*. New York: Harper and Row, 1960, chaps. 17-21.

Bass, B. M., and Norton, F. T. M. "Group Size and Leaderless Discussions." *Journal of Applied Psychology* 6 (1951): 397-400.

Coleman, J. S. "The Mathematical Study of Small Groups." In *Mathematical Thinking in the Measurement of Behavior*, edited by H. Solomon, Part I. Glencoe, Ill.: The Free Press, 1960.

Cyert, R. M., and March, J. G. *A Behavioral Theory of the Firm*. Englewood Cliffs, N.J.: Prentice-Hall, 1963.

Davis, J. H., and Restle, F. "The Analysis of Problems and Prediction of Group Problem Solving." *Journal of Abnormal and Social Psychology* 66 (1963): 103-16.

Dodd, S. C. "Testing Message Diffusion in Controlled Experiment: Charting the Distance and Time Factors in the Interactance Hypothesis." *American Sociological Review* 18 (1953): 410-16.

_____. "Diffusion is Predictable: Testing Probability Models for Laws of Interaction." *American Sociological Review* 20 (1955): 329-401.

Dornbusch, S. M., and Scott, W. R. *Evaluation and the Exercise of Authority*. San Francisco, Calif.: Jossey-Bass, 1975.

Entwistle, D. R., and Walton, J. "Observation on the Span of Control." *Administrative Science Quarterly* 5 (1961): 522-33.

Fischer, P. H. "An Analysis of Primary Groups." *Sociometry* 16 (1953): 272-76.

Frye, R. L.; Sprvill, J.; and Stritch, R. M. "Effect of Group Size on Public and Private Coalescence, Efficiency, and Change." *Journal of Social Psychology* 62 (1964): 131-37.

Gibb, C. A. "An Interactional View of the Emergence of Leadership." *American Psychologist* 9 (1954): 502 (abstract).

Gustafson, H. W. "On the Frequency Distribution of Participation in Small Group Discussions." Ph.D. dissertation, University of Utah, 1955.

Hare, A. P. "Interaction and Consensus in Different Sized Groups." *American Sociological Review* 17 (1952): 261-67.

Hauron, M. D., and McGrath, J. E. "The Contribution of the Leader to the Effectiveness of Small Military Groups." In *Leadership and Interpersonal Behavior*, edited by B. M. Bass and L. Petrillo. New York: Holt, Rinehart, and Winston, 1961.

Hollander, E. P. *Leaders, Groups, and Influence*. New York: Oxford University Press, 1964.

Jacques, E. *Measurement of Responsibility*. London: Tavistock Pub., 1956.

Keller, J. "Comment on 'Channels of Communications in Small Groups.'" *American Sociological Review* 16 (1951): 842–43.

Kepner, C. H., and Tregoe, B. B. *The Rational Manager.* New York: McGraw-Hill, 1965.

Mackenzie, K. D. "Measuring a Person's Capacity of Interaction in a Problem Solving Group." *Organizational Behavior and Human Performance* 12 (1974): 149–69.

_____. *A Theory of Group Structures, Volume I: Basic Theory.* New York: Gordon and Breach Science Pubs., 1976a.

_____. *A Theory of Group Structures, Volume II: Empirical Tests.* New York: Gordon and Breach Science Pubs., 1976b.

McKeachie, W. J. "Research on Teaching at the College and University Level." In *Handbook of Research on Teaching,* edited by N. Gage, pp. 1118–72. Chicago: Rand McNally, 1963.

Pattee, H. H., ed. *Hierarchy Theory: The Challenge of Complex Systems.* New York: Braziller, 1973.

Pounds, W. F. "The Process of Problem Finding." *Industrial Management Review,* Fall 1969, pp. 1–19.

Simmons, R. E. "The Effects of Communication Errors on the Consistency of Functional Processes, and on Performance Times in Certain Communication Networks." Ph.D. dissertation, University of Pennsylvania, 1974.

_____. *Managing Behavioral Processes: Applications of Theory and Research.* Arlington Heights, Ill.: AHM Publishing Corporation, 1978.

Simon, H. A. "The Organization of Complex Systems." In *Hierarchy Theory: The Challenge of Complex Systems,* edited by H. Pattee. New York: Braziller, 1973.

Slater, P. E. "Contrasting Correlates of Group Size." *Sociometry* 21 (1958): 129–39.

Starbuck, W. H. "Organizational Growth and Development."

In *Handbook of Organizations,* edited by J. G. March, pp. 451–533. Chicago: Rand McNally, 1965.

Starbuck, W. H., ed. *Organizational Growth and Development.* Baltimore: Penguin Books, 1971.

Stephan, F. "The Relative Rate of Communication between Members of Small Groups." *American Sociological Review* 17 (1952): 482–86.

Stephan, F., and Mischler, E. G. "The Distribution of Participation in Small Groups: An Exponential Approximation." *American Sociological Review* 17 (1952): 598–608.

Tannenbaum, A. S.; Kavcic, B.; Rosner, M.; Vianello, M.; and Wieser, G. *Hierarchy in Organizations.* San Francisco, Calif.: Jossey-Bass, 1974.

Thalen, H. A. "Group Dynamics in Instructions: Principles of Least Group Size." *Scholastic Review* 57 (1949): 139–48.

Thomas, E. J. Effects of Group Size." *Psychological Bulletin* 60 (1965): 371–84.

Tuggle, F. D. *Organizational Processes.* Arlington Heights, Ill.: AHM Publishing Corporation, 1978.

Warner, W. K., and Hilander, J. S. "The Relationships between Size of Organization and Membership Participation." *Rural Sociology* 29 (1964): 30–39.

5

Theory of
Bureaucracy

Arguments are made in chapters 1 and 4 for the
existence and possible advantages of hierarchy
in organized systems. Hierarchy is linked to
widespread use of bureaucratic organizations.
The technical meaning of bureaucracy will be explained in the next section. Bureaucracy also
has a common "street" usage. In everyday
language, bureaucracy implies large, rigid, insensitive, and even inhuman organizations. To
describe an organization as a bureaucracy is
to damn it. When, for example, one's telephone
bill is messed up and one is harassed by
letters threatening to shut off service, one
has unkind thoughts about bureaucracies and
hurls insults at its servants—the bureaucrats.
We mutter, "That damned bureaucracy!" or
"Stuffed shirt bureaucrat!" In everyday life,
the word bureaucrat or bureaucracy is almost an
epithet.

In this chapter bureaucracy is discussed
technically, but it is difficult to surmount
its pejorative connotations. These negative
feelings make it hard to evaluate patiently
the technical meaning and the conceptual advantages of a bureaucracy. Each of us has been
exposed to antibureaucratic sentiments so
consistently and for so many years that it
takes an open mind to consider even its theoretical meaning. It will be helpful to follow
a few suggestions.

1. Technically, the definition of a bureaucracy describes an "ideal-typical" organization. In its ideal form, there is a type of
   organization called bureaucracy. Any real
   life counterpart is, at best, only an approximation to the "ideal." Many theories
   employ idealized abstractions. For example,
   in the economic theory of the firm there is
   a notion called perfect competition. In
   physics there are smooth, frictionless
   particles, whose effective mass is concen-
   trated at a single point, as well as
   vacuums, atoms, and so on. In geometry there
   are things called points, lines, planes,
   and geodesics. These idealizations are used
   to simplify the complexities and allow ex-
   amination of basic properties with a minimum
   of encumbrances. We know that perfect competition is probably nonexistent, that no one
   has ever found a vacuum, and that geometric
   planes cannot exist physically. Try to think
   of a bureaucracy as just such an ideal-
   typical abstraction.
2. Words of a language change with usage. Meanings can be altered or altogether discarded.
   Thirty years ago any pair of laughing gentle-
   men having a good time might have been described as a *gay couple*. Today, at least in
   North America, this label implies homosexu-
   ality. Some words just stretch over more
   constructs and slowly lose their meaning.

Chauvinist once referred to a fanatical patriot, after the French patriot, Chauvin. Today it is widely used in the phrase *male chauvinist* to describe decreasingly specific attitudes towards women. The slang phrase *male chauvinist pig* is an extension both of chauvinist and pig. The word *bureaucracy* has undergone similar changes. Most individuals would have difficulty defining bureaucracy without using strings of "red-tape monster" examples and nonspecific connotations. It is necessary to have a clearer definition.

3. In order to recognize the gap between the technical meaning and its "street" usage, we use two words, *bureaucracy* and *buroid,* for these two different meanings respectively. The term *bureaucracy* refers to the ideal-typical case, *buroid* to an actual organization approximating some of the properties of a bureaucracy. The science fiction fan is familiar with humanoids and androids, who resemble humans. Similarly, buroids *resemble* bureaucracies, but they are not the same.

4. Only the ideal-typical case is a pure bureaucracy. All other organizations can only approximate its properties. Consequently, you can consider each organization in terms of the extent to which it succeeds in approximating a pure bureaucracy. Classifying an organization as either a bureaucracy or not a bureaucracy does not make sense. It is more useful to locate organizations on a continuum with pure bureaucracy as one extreme and a crowd milling about in an airport as the other.

Experience gained in class after class has taught the author that these suggestions are hard to follow. It takes conscious effort for the student to make new categories and to manipulate a value-laden word such as bureaucracy. Using the two terms, bureaucracy and

buroid, does help, but it is still a difficult
concept to grasp. Your patience and diligence
are solicited as you study this chapter.

THE CONCEPT OF A BUREAUCRACY

The German sociologist Max Weber is usually
credited with developing the concept of a
bureaucracy. His work on bureaucracy was
written before World War I and published
posthumously in 1921 in a volume called
Wirtschaft und Gesellschaft. The English transla-
tions by Gerth and Mills (Max Weber: *Essays
in Sociology*, 1946), and by Henderson and
Parsons (*The Theory of Social and Economic Organizations*, 1947) are especially relevant to the
topic of this chapter. His description of a
bureaucracy is embedded in a stunningly
erudite collage of history, personal knowl-
ege, cross-cultural gleanings, sociology,
economics, politics, psychology, and religion.
For example, in one paragraph (see Gerth and
Mills, 1946, pp. 226-27) Weber brings together Russia, China, France, Egypt, and
Roman rule. He wrote in an era preceding
quantification and deliberate field study.
The study of bureaucracy and its implications
is a common theme in modern sociology and
organizational behavior. Blau (1956) and
later Blau and Meyer (1971) provide an excellent discussion of bureaucracy and its
implications for modern society. They
discuss the results of numerous studies
in reference to bureaucracy theory. The
writings of Bennis (see Bennis, 1966) and
the collection of studies edited by Merton
et al. (1952) offer other points of view.
    The recent progress in understanding group
structures and, in particular, the concept and
measure for the degree of hierarchy (see chapter 1) give new perspectives from which to

study bureaucracies and buroids. These newer ideas allow us to link task processes and structures. Weber argued that when a leader was able to rationalize tasks and strove to be efficient, a bureaucracy would result. His description of the properties of a bureaucracy concerns what the organization should be in order to implement organizational task processes. Although over half a century has passed, the ideas and concerns are remarkably fresh and up to date, especially if viewed with our newer ideas about group structures.

Weber was conscious of the needs for efficiency and work realizations. Gerth and Mills (1946, p. 214) quote Weber:

> This decisive reason for the advance of bureaucratic organization has always been its purely technical superiority over any other form of organization. The fully developed bureaucratic mechanism compares with other organizations exactly as does a machine with the non-mechanical modes of production.
>
> Precision, speed, unambiguity, knowledge of the files, continuity, discretion, unity, strict subordination, reduction of friction and of material and personal costs—these are raised to the optimum point in the strictly bureaucratic administration, and especially in its monocratic form. As compared with all collegiate, honorific, and avocational forms of administration, trained bureaucracy is superior on all these points. And as far as complicated tasks are concerned, paid bureaucratic work is not only more precise, but in the last analysis, it is often cheaper than even formally unremunerated honorific service.

There is no question that Weber believed in the advantages of a properly run bureaucracy. He was also aware of how "the disintegration of the Roman Empire was partly conditioned by the very bureaucratization of its army and official apparatus" (Gerth and Mills, p. 210). He criticized the spread of the bureaucracy in Germany.

He was careful not to describe a system as bureaucratic unless it met his many conditions. His implicit notion of degrees of bureaucracy reflects the distinction that should be made between the idea of a pure bureaucracy and those buroids that resemble them.

In attempting to describe a bureaucracy one should distinguish between *antecedent conditions* and *implementation properties* of a bureaucracy. The main antecedent conditions (provided that tax revenues or other sources of stable income are available to support the bureaucracy) are the rationalization of the tasks and a concept of efficiency. Rationalizing tasks means to determine what needs to be done, calculating precisely how it can be done, and how to insure that the tasks are performed. This rationalization of the work is made with respect to a concept of efficiency. Once the antecedent conditions are met, it is necessary to plan and design an organization to implement the solutions arising from the fulfillment of the antecedent conditions. The implementation conditions describe the main features or properties of a bureaucracy. These include a division of labor, a high degree of specialization, a hierarchy of authority, a system of rules and procedures, a spirit of formalistic impersonality, and a system of promotions and hiring based on seniority and/or achievement.

These conditions for implementation follow logically from planning to achieve the antecedent conditions. Ideally, one first rationalizes the administrative tasks with respect to a goal of efficiency, and then sets up a real organization with the features of a bureaucracy. When there are budget and personnel constraints, the straightforward process of meeting first the antecedent conditions and then the implementation conditions becomes more complex. Time and political pressures also influence this process and meeting the antecedent conditions takes time and resources. The exigencies and pressures giving rise to the new organization may not allow one the luxury of spending this time. The usual result is an organization that, on paper, has a hierarchy of authority, some rules, and some division of labor, but which is a buroid and not a bureaucracy. The task is usually not well defined and the goal of efficiency is often replaced by one of expediency. The relationships between the new organization and previously existing ones are unclear and left to be worked out as one proceeds. It is easier to proceed by first getting resources, hiring personnel, and then, through experience, to muddle through. In some cases, such organizations may resemble a bureaucracy as they mature. The compromises about purpose and policy, and the needs to recruit staff, however, can often inhibit the development of a bureaucracy. These early commitments can severely constrain the way the organization evolves.

There are many levels of detail which need consideration. The organizational entrepreneur who can attract the funds and do the necessary promotion to obtain enabling legislation and personnel is often unsuited to deal with the mundane problems of meeting the antecedent conditions. He is often too busy to spend the time and he may believe (with good justification in many cases) that if he spent more time on this planning his likelihood of being successful in other areas would lessen. Because he may believe that the tasks are so urgent, he chooses to get the organization going rather than to invest time in more careful planning. He may hope that as the new organization evolves it will tackle the antecedent conditions. In fact, he may be using this new program to foster his rise in a larger organization. That is, after being a successful midwife to one organization, he can use it to launch another or to climb to a hierarchically higher level, where he can help resolve some of its problems in a larger context.

One of the results of reversing the logical process of meeting the antecedent conditions

before working on the implementation conditions
is the widespread existence of buroids. These
buroids are usually riddled with special task
forces, standing committees, and committees
appointed to meet special problems. Wasted
time, resources, and personnel are inevitable
when the antecedent conditions are derived
from the implementation conditions rather than
having the implementation conditions derived
from the antecedent conditions.

While it is inevitable that some degree of
waste occurs in the creation of a new organization, probably more waste occurs when the logic
of first rationalizing the task with respect to
a goal of efficiency and then meeting the implementation conditions is reversed. Years ago
when the economy was more competitive and the
role of government more restricted, an economic
entrepreneur whose new organization was wasteful would, in a competitive market, tend to
have higher costs and hence higher prices. The
discipline of competing in a competitive market
encouraged the reduction of such waste. Today,
however, many organizations, such as public
universities and governmental agencies, are
almost immune from such continuous discipline.
The discipline provided by legislation is usually insufficiently precise, up-to-date, relevant, or persistent to eliminate waste. Previous legislation and prior commitments may even
inhibit the necessary adjustments that allow
bureaucracy to evolve from a buroid.

Furthermore, a bureaucracy may not be the
proper organizational form for some organizational functions. Many organizations, like universities, are almost fully bureaucratic for
housekeeping functions such as payroll, parking, registration, class-scheduling, janitorial
and maintenance services. These same organizations are simultaneously unbureaucratic about
research and the teaching of courses. Thus, a
university can be both bureaucratic and non-
bureaucratic. Being able to see an organization
in terms of its component structures is helpful

in discussing buroids. This difference in the
degree of bureaucratization for different substructures is proper because the expertise for
doing research, the decision for what research
is to be done, and the changing theoretical
bases for what should be taught lie more in
the hands of those actually doing the work than
those charged with its administration. It is
difficult to understand how a philosopher who
is a vice-chancellor can know enough to tell
the economists, physicists, biochemists, and
other professionals how to carry out their research and teaching responsibilities.

In short, when there is insufficient knowledge to state and work out the antecedent conditions, it is probably inefficient to attempt
to create a bureaucracy to implement them. Of
course, this creates heavy burdens on an administrator who is both responsible for activities and unable to exert direct control over
how they are to be performed. These pressures
set off attempts to obtain such control and to
eliminate the inconsistency of being in charge
of activities without the necessary knowledge
to guide them. If the actual research and
teaching activities were static, bureaucracies
would form around them. This could be accomplished by recruiting experts into administration. However, at present the work is still
too dynamic to permit the effective development
of rationalized tasks. Instead, those responsible for academic programs must. rely on budgeting procedures and consensus in order to
govern. But as sources of research funding dry
up or if the labor market for qualified personnel decreases in its mobility, the shift away
from the *laissez faire* conduct of teaching and
research and toward more buroidal administra-
tions can become more pronounced. This occurs
simply by an increase of those activities that
can be bureaucratized relative to the others.

Hospitals and research agencies for various
governmental units have problems similar to
those of a university. For example, if a

hospital performs heart surgery, its heart surgeons determine how the surgery is to be performed. A committee of professionals may oversee these operations to insure conformity with what are judged to be professional and ethical standards. The hospital administrator, who is concerned with financing, personnel problems, lawsuits, compliance with legislation, working his board of governors, and many other duties, simply does not have the time to worry about detailed procedures in the operating room. Even if he had been a heart surgeon years ago, he may no longer be up to current professional standards. He can, however, work with his professionals to insure that the proper environment is present to facilitate their work. He serves them and they, in turn, serve their patients. Having the responsibility to run the hospital places him in the awkward position of being responsible without direct control. He is additionally hampered because the professionals may have ethics and standards that conflict with his authority.

Volunteer organizations have problems being bureaucratic because of the need to keep members participating without direct control of them through financial incentives for membership. Policies can be established by vote and efforts made to train personnel, but if a policy conflicts with the needs of a member, he can quit and spend his free time in other pursuits or even create a rival organization. The basis for achieving compliance with the system of rules may be lacking. Hence, it is difficult to create a bureaucracy in a volunteer organization.

We have seen several cases where a bureaucracy may not form. There is the case of the multiple-structured university where a portion is bureaucratic and another portion (e.g., the research and teaching) is much less so. Hospitals and research groups exhibit the same characteristics. The main points are: (1) when there is insufficient knowledge to satisfy the

antecedent conditions, it is probably inefficient to bureaucratize them; and (2) organizations involve multiple structures, and some
substructures involve activities for which the
antecedent conditions can be met and some for
which they cannot. Substructures that can be
bureaucratized tend to become bureaucratized.
Those substructures that cannot be bureaucratized offer a continuing challenge and source
of problems for work rationalization leading to
more bureaucratization over more dimensions of
an organization. The author knows one tireless
memo-writer who even would consider drafting a
"policy" for the content and range of acceptable results for doctoral dissertations.

There is another case where bureaucracies may
tend not to form. Organizations or organizational parts experiencing rapid shifts in technology have a difficult time rationalizing
their tasks, making it hard to form a bureaucracy. What they can do, though, is to form
special units for handling such changes. These
function to solve complex novel problems (see
chapter 7 on the discussion of organizational
joint problem-solving) by buffering the functioning organization from many of the changes.
This way the problems of rationalizing the
changes are kept partially separate from the
rest of the organization. The many false
starts, organizational learning, and problem-
solving that mark work rationalization are
kept from disrupting the ongoing system. Thus
specialized and even *ad hoc* subunits function
as the innovative tip of an advancing organization. As they do their job, the regular organization can usually absorb the changes with only
minor further changes that are more easily
understood and integrated than if the whole
system had to rationalize the new work while
functioning simultaneously. By the time the
special groups have rationalized the new work,
they have reduced the maximum possible changes.
As the work is rationalized it can be removed
from active problem-solving and becomes a part

of the mechanized or routine operations of an organization. In some of these cases, a computer or device is used to relieve humans of tedious tasks.

The case of volunteer organizations involves a different principle. One condition for the formation of a bureaucracy is the existence of sufficient resources to maintain member participation even when the work itself may not be intrinsically rewarding. Volunteer organizations such as Parent Teacher Organizations in public schools in the United States have to encourage participation without offering direct compensation. In fact, they have to get their members to *pay* money to belong. Attempts to enforce bureaucratic rules and structural hierarchy, in the absence of offsetting compensation, lead to reduced participation and to organizational changes. These groups can provide ideological compensation by building commitment to the ideals of the organization, or offer status by having lots of officers and committee chairmanships, and so on. But their lack of control over continuing financial rewards for participating inhibits bureaucratization. Volunteer groups may also be less interested in efficiency than more formal organizations. Members may join and participate just *because* there is no relentless pursuit of efficiency. The author is a member of numerous organizations for bicycling, which strive to be unorganized while bicycling. One group does not even pick its destination in advance. The group assembles at a point, judges the wind direction, and then rides into it in order to finish with a tail wind. This unorganized procedure results in little adventures and is fun as well as good exercise. If the group became bureaucratic, most of the members simply would go their own individual way. However, if the bicycle club sponsors a race or special touring event, the group functions bureaucratically for a short time to meet its obligations. Thus, the group

not only has a *partial* bureaucracy according
to type of function but also has a *temporary*
bureaucracy which is tolerated only for a
short time for a specific problem.

Despite the cited cases of no bureaucracy,
partial bureaucracy, and temporary bureaucracy,
and the difficulty of rationalizing work with
respect to a goal of efficiency before worrying about implementation, the dominant organizational form today is the buroid. Many
buroids form because the attempt to create
the implementation properties is made before
satisfying the antecedent conditions. Thus,
it is argued that the reason for so many
buroids is the process of systematic muddling
through, whereby the hierarchy of authority
and other implementation conditions are created before anyone seriously plans how to
rationalize the task or decides upon a goal
or criteria for efficiency. Furthermore,
most of the criticisms leveled (and justly
in most cases) at buroids are aimed at the
very fact that they are not behaving as
bureaucracies.

PROPERTIES OF A BUREAUCRACY: IMPLEMENTATION CONDITIONS

1. DIVISION OF LABOR AND A HIGH DEGREE OF SPECIALIZATION

Once the work has been rationalized, the
regular activities required for the purposes
of the organization can be distributed in a
fixed way as official duties. Different people
do different things and full advantage is taken
of specialized functions. Division of labor
means that the work is subdivided into mostly
disjoint clusters and that different people
perform different activities. This can lead to
reasonably high levels of performance and ac-
curacy, because each person knows what he is to

do and how to do it. The subdivided tasks can
be grouped at a higher level and these, in
turn, grouped at an even higher level. It takes
time to plan and to implement the division of
labor. This is done to take advantage of time
and resource savings involved in the performance and learning of tasks. For example, sol-
diers with little education can be used for
some basic electrical tasks. If each man is
trained in a specialty, and different speciali-
ties are offered, very complex equipment can be
operated and maintained with little formal education in physics or electronics. However, if
the specialized skills are not to be used very
many times, it may not be advantageous to push
the specialization and division of labor very
far, since the costs of setting the system up
and maintaining it may not be offset by the
benefits. In a manufacturing plant, for example, if one type of product is to be made
thousands of times, it is probably worthwhile to
incur the set-up costs in order to take advantage of the savings in production. But if
only a very small number are to be made, the
hours needed to set up the system may not be
offset in the minutes saved. Thus, level of
production is a major determinant for the degree of division of labor and specialization.
Another limitation is the acceptability of
overly routinized tasks by the members of the
organization. With at least subsistence levels
of public support for living expenses, many
members may choose to forego work or to change
jobs in order to avoid the boredom that characterize overly subdivided work. Thus, while
division of labor can lead to greater productivity, there is nothing inherent in the concept to tell one how far to go in subdividing
the work.

2. HIERARCHY OF AUTHORITY

In a bureaucracy, positions are called *offices*.
Each lower office is under the supervision and

control of a higher one. Related and supposed-
ly identical to the hierarchy of offices is a
hierarchy of authority. This hierarchy of
authority defines relevant official activities
and limits the range of permissible behavior.
It, for example, does not generalize to activities lying outside the organization.

We learned in chapter 1 that hierarchy can
attain high levels of efficiency. The definition of hierarchy included both structures and
task processes. The hierarchy of authority in
a pure bureaucracy does not include task processes. By definition, the hierarchy of authority in a bureaucracy is a structural hierarchy.
There are no cousin or uncle relationships.
Because task processes are not included in a
structural hierarchy, the degree of hierarchy
is unity. There is some doubt that all behaviors are timely and that a hierarchy of authority is sufficient to insure a high degree of
hierarchy in our task process sense. The discussion of authority-task gaps in chapter 3
illustrates this problem.

We discussed the possibility of an authority
task-gap in chapter 3. Authority-task gaps occurred whenever the structure implied by the
authority system was inconsistent with the
actual task-role system. A weak point in a
hierarchy of authority is that in many organizations the authority system is out of synchronization with the task-role system. If the
division of labor and task-role system no
longer fit the authority system, it is very
possible for the authority hierarchy to interfere with the operations of the organization
and, thereby, to reduce efficiency, which is a
violation of the main ideal feature of a
bureaucracy. Therefore, in order to insure efficiency of operations, it is necessary to say
something about the task processes as well as
the hierarchy of authority.

3. CONSISTENT RULES AND REGULATIONS

Weber (1947, p. 330) states that a function

or operation is governed "by a consistent system of abstract rules . . . [and] consists of
the application of these rules to particular
cases." Explicit rules and regulations define
each member's set of activities and his relationships with other members. If such a system of abstract rules and regulations could be
devised, it would go far in reducing the authority-task gap. Ideally, the addition of this
system of consistent rules and regulations
closes the gap between a hierarchy of authority
and the concept of hierarchy involving both
structures and task processes introduced in
chapter 1. Thus, this third property is essential to achieving high levels of efficiency.

These are the first three implementation
properties: (1) division of labor, (2) hierarchy of authority, and (3) a consistent system
of rules and regulations. When functioning,
they should result in a degree of hierarchy
that is close to unity. Because the degree of
hierarchy is less than or equal to the degree
of efficiency, it is clear that these three
implementation conditions should also result
in a high degree of efficiency. The measure
for the degree of hierarchy approximates closely the first three implementation properties of
a bureaucracy.

The measure for the degree of hierarchy,
which was developed for relatively short-lived,
little laboratory organizations, needs to be
augmented in order to insure stability and
maintenance of the organization when the group
is larger, and when the time span of operations
is longer. Weber gives two other conditions
that serve to provide consistency and continuity.

4. FORMALISTIC IMPERSONALITY

"The ideal official conducts his office . . .
[in] a spirit of formalistic impersonality,
sine ira et studio, without hatred or passion,
and hence without affection or enthusiasm"

(Weber, 1947, p. 340). Each official attempts to keep his private personal feelings and opinions out of his official duties. This helps to insure equitable treatment of all persons and may tend to foster democracy. This statement by Weber has provoked strongly negative reactions from many scholars in organizational behavior because, in Weber's own words, the impersonality of the ideal official makes him seem like an organizational automaton. Such an official appears to be inhuman and contrary to what we would hope to be as persons. Each of us might object to having such a person for a boss. But many would find this much less objectionable in a subordinate.

It may be true that if every member in a bureaucracy exhibited this spirit of formalistic impersonality, the other three implementation conditions could be maintained. However, it is hard to think that such persons are sufficiently common in our well-educated, hedonistic, and affluent society to man the offices of our many buroids. Weber may have overstated this point and many have been misled by his statements. His work, taken as a whole, suggests that he meant that persons of every sex, race, and creed would be treated equitably, that there would be due process for hiring, promoting, discharge, allocation of rewards, and the handling of grievances. The duties of the office and compliance with the organizational roles would take strict precedence over personal desires. For example, the relatives or lovers of an official would not receive special treatment and privilege.

5. CAREER: EMPLOYMENT IN A BUREAUCRACY IS A CAREER

"There is a system of 'promotions' according to seniority or to achievement, or both" (Weber, 1947, p. 334). Employment is based on technical qualifications and the system for promotions provides some guarantee for due process against arbitrary decisions that are inconsistent with the rules and regulations.

This feature of a bureaucracy provides for qualified personnel with a stake in the organization. The emphasis on employment as a career helps to attract and retain qualified personnel. This feature is reasonable and consistent with what many people expect in industrialized societies. However, in too many cases promotions based on seniority can conflict with promotions based on merit, unless there is some system for training personnel for higher positions. Recently, many buroids with financial contracts with the U.S. Government and buroids within the government have been faced with "affirmative action" programs wherein members of stipulated minorities, such as blacks or women, are to be given preferential treatment in hiring and promotion. For many reasons, such as prejudice, custom, and lack of qualified members in the various minority groups, many buroids employing old rules were seen to act as if they were inhibiting employment opportunities. Thus, the old system of hiring and promoting was judged to be working against what many considered to be fair. The promulgation and enforcement of laws to correct past abuses has resulted in a new set of ground rules for operating a buroid. In some cases, the affirmative action program has been in conflict with older, established organizational personnel policies. In other cases, these rules have eased tensions by bringing in and promoting qualified minority members who were frustrated at being underemployed.

There are numerous issues to be resolved in affirmative action programs. There are always issues of fairness and efficiency in hiring and promotion decisions. Many buroids react to such new legislation by adopting and implementing a new set of rules to govern hiring and promotion. These new rules and regulations redefine the process and the buroid keeps functioning. One dominant characteristic of a

buroid is the ability to modify itself by
changing its rules and regulations in order to
adapt to changing conditions.

6. SIZE OF BUREAUCRACIES

Many writers suggest that it is necessary for
an organization to be large in order to be a
bureaucracy. Although we usually associate
buroids with bigness, it is not a logical conclusion to draw from either the antecedent or
implementation conditions describing a bureaucracy. There is no reason for limiting the
size of a bureaucracy to more than a specified
number. A little group of five could function
as a bureaucracy and a large institution of
60,000 could have a low degree of bureaucracy.
Experience suggests, however, that as organizations become large there is a need to perform
many of its functions in a manner approximating
that of a bureaucracy. Little groups, precisely
because they are little, can avoid more mecha-
nistic systems of coordination and control,
since their continuing face-to-face interactions allow the quiet operation of social and
task controls directly. But as the group size
increases, it becomes more and more difficult
to receive and transmit information directly
and continuously. Thus, as the organization
grows, the group tends to use formal procedures
more often. Consequently, larger groups tend
to have more properties of a bureaucracy than
little groups. Thus, the tendency of groups to
appear more bureaucratic with increased size
becomes apparent. However, it is still very
possible for small groups to be bureaucracies.

CRITIQUES OF BUREAUCRACY

There are numerous criticisms of a bureaucracy
in professional journals and books on organizational behavior and sociology. Functionally,
the two most serious are: (1) a bureaucracy is
static and incapable of change; and (2) a

bureaucracy is too machine-like or inhuman.
Logically, we may conclude: (3) its terms are
not well defined, and (4) there may or may not
be a close correspondence between a given administrative problem and a specific bureaucratic structure. And methodologically, (5) because bureaucracy is an ideal-typical abstraction, it may be inherently incapable of empirical testing.

Out of these basic criticisms flow many specific complaints, queries, and judgments about
bureaucracies. Almost any textbook on organizations will serve to provide examples. Probably,
the best come from W. Bennis (1966). The flow
of criticisms contains many truths about
buroids. These are serious enough to cause
doubt about the basic concept of a bureaucracy.
What is the value of an idealization if
every example of it in the real world is judged
to have defects? It is not necessary for humans
to use only one form of organization. Perhaps,
as Bennis urges, we can evolve a new form of
organization that is preferred to a bureaucracy. We can certainly do better than buroids.

The first two criticisms are the most prevalent and serious. An organizational form that
is static and inhuman in our current society is
simply unacceptalbe if only on the grounds that
it would be dysfunctional. Organizations are
continually changing in response to changing
conditions. Products change, markets change,
personnel change, technology changes, and there
are many social, environmental, and governmental changes. These all impinge on an organization, and the organization has to adjust. An
organization that is incapable of change because it is static is simply unworkable in such
a milieu. It is certainly easy to see how one
could take the first three implementation conditions of division of labor and specialization, a hierarchy of authority, and a consistent set of rules and regulations, and conclude
that such a system would be static and hard to
change. What is overlooked, however, is the

possibility that because of the stability of the organization, it is easier to implement changes. What is needed is a mechanism for spotting areas that need changing, a staff to work out the necessary accommodations, and some willingness to implement the changes. Once the organization has determined what is to be done and how to do it within the present organization, then the three implementation conditions make it easier to carry out the change. After a new set of rules and regulations is set up, the jobs realigned, and authority adjusted, the implementation can be swift. When the rules and regulations are vague, the division of labor obscure, and the authority fuzzy, it is harder to determine what is to be done and how to do it.

The adjustments to changes occur continually. The organization is always adjusting towards becoming more bureaucratic. But as soon as it gets close, a change occurs and the pursuit starts up again. This process of adjustment reminds one of a greyhound race. The dogs can get close, but the mechanical rabbit always keeps out in front. No matter how swiftly the dogs run, they never get the rabbit. But if they do not run fast, they cannot even get close. They have to run hard just to stay in the race. Administrators in companies, universities and government work hard pursuing the elusive goal of becoming bureaucratic. Like the greyhounds, they never reach the goal, because as soon as they begin to close in some new change occurs and they have to keep going. It is a race against organizational chaos and towards self-respect.

They keep running because the race is never quite hopeless. Many activities in the organization have been rationalized and there is a suborganization to handle these. Other, newer activities have not yet been rationalized and made routine. Managers pursue these. They can often call upon staff for help. Specialists such as top management, boards of directors,

research and development groups, management
scientists, economists, and consultants help
identify, solve, and implement solutions to
the changes. The existence of such groups, if
the organization is alert and willing to adapt,
makes a buroid more adaptable. That is, these
specialists help routinize the nonroutine. The
use of econometric forecasting, operations research, marketing surveys, opinion polls,
standard operating procedures, management-by-
exception schemes, and so forth, all aid in the
rationalization of an organization functioning
in adaptation to change. There is not a strong
a priori case that a bureaucracy is incapable of
change. There is the continuing pursuit towards
the goal of becoming bureaucratic. It is probably better to assert that while a pure bureaucracy never exists, except perhaps for a brief
moment, most large systems continually adjust
themselves in pursuit of this goal.

Technically, if changes were necessary but
not made, the organization would be violating
the two antecedent conditions of work rationalization and efficiency; it then could not be a
bureaucracy. Thus, it is contradictory to argue
that a bureaucracy is static and incapable of
change. For if changes occur, it must change
to insure the antecedent conditions. This leads
to a dynamic evolutionary conception of a bureaucracy. Over time, a buroid is actually a
succession of buroids, each step of which is
contingent on the previous state and new problems. The successive evolutions are not always
smooth and linear. Temporary moves away from
bureaucracy can also occur, but the relentless
logic of managing with scarce resources and
dealing with information overload brings an efficiency-minded group back towards the pursuit
of a bureaucracy.

One problem affecting adoption is the failure
of information to reach the decision-makers.
Problems can be ignored and information distorted and lost as it passes throughout the

buroid. It is not rare for buroids to maintain
separate organizational units to maintain contact with outside information and issues. For
example, if governmental decisions are vital,
the buroid may maintain a staff (often just a
lobbyist) at the seat of government or working
with the agency of government whose actions are
vital. A large contractor may work closely with
local governmental planning groups. If technological changes are important, the buroid may
maintain close contacts with those scientific
communities whose work is important to the
company. It often has its own "in-house" scientific staff. Another way to keep information
flowing is to encourage suggestions, giving
bonuses for useful new ideas. Auditing and
other control systems can also be useful to insure that the actual system is functioning as
it is designed to operate. No method is fool-
proof, and errors, distortions, and even fraud
may occur.

Often, persons in an organization may be un-
willing to voice complaints. They can be un-
willing because they do not believe that they
can effect changes whose benefits exceed the
time and personal costs invested in seeking a
change. A private in the infantry may fear the
consequences if he complains about his sergeant. A citizen may feel that he has been
treated unfairly by an official, but it would
cost him too much time, money, and energy to
fight back. Another might be given "the run-
around" by a buroid and feel powerless to receive what he thinks is fair treatment. Officials at one level may try only to pass information that is favorable to their position or
which is what they hope their superiors want to
hear. To offset these problems, organizations
may set up "inspector generals" or "ombudsmen"
(Gellhorn, 1966). Some enterprising television
stations and newspapers maintain "action
reporters" who intervene on behalf of
a person. Historically, a free press has been

a safeguard against governmental caprice and corruption.

It is probably impossible to avoid information distortion and loss even in small groups. While some of the loss is necessary to prevent overloading the officials in the buroid, it is essential to the maintenance of the organization that deliberate steps be taken to keep them informed. Otherwise, in a changing environment, the buroid will be unable to keep the work rationalized and to pursue efficiency.

Bureaucracies are judged to be machine-like and inhuman. Weber (1946, p. 214) states: "The fully developed bureaucratic mechanism compares with other organizations exactly as does the machine with nonmechanical modes of production." It is the purpose and the design of a bureaucracy to function as a human machine to complete its tasks. That does not mean that a bureaucracy must, therefore, be inhuman. The word inhuman refers to a lack of the qualities of mercy, pity, kindness, tenderness, warmth, or geniality. The fourth implementation condition, that an ideal official should attempt to keep his private opinions from interfering with his official function, does not mean that the official need be excessively aloof, have a ritualistic attachment to routine and procedures, resist change, and insist upon petty differentiations of authority and status. V. A. Thompson (1961, pp. 152-53 and 170) describes such petty tyrants as *bureaupathic*, with a social disease he calls *bureausis*. There is no reason why an official need not be cordial, courteous, kind, genial, and fair about the application of the rules and regulations. He can be courteous and fair in order to induce persons to perform better. If a rule creates excessive hardship, there is no reason why exceptional cases could not be referred to special officials having more discretion.

The indictment that buroids are inhuman is a social judgment. The judgment may be made by an observer who is piqued because he lacks power, cannot achieve his ends, or is reacting to his own or others' inconsiderate behavior. Let us accept the judgment that buroids often act insensitively and unfairly. Nevertheless, the main reason for our complaints is that we most often deal with officials of minimum discretion, whose ability to use the rules or to get around the rules is severely constrained. Another reason is that many large-scale buroids are inefficient, and this inefficiency causes defensiveness which in turn encourages persons to hide behind their concept of the rules. Too fine a division of labor and over-specialization can engender feelings of personal powerlessness and anomie, which can lead to efforts to extract a minimum of prestige out of one's limited role. It can also result in buck-passing of those problems which involve several highly specialized officials. A student of mine went to get a library card at a university she was visiting and fit into *two* categories. The low official did not know how to file her application because he lacked discretion to punch two holes. She either had to be an x or a y. Being both an x and a y caused her to have her application for a card denied. It was necessary to see one of the library's directors to obtain a card.

Another reason for poor treatment by officials in a buroid is that it is often unpleasant to work with the public. Many of the clients are abusive, aggressive, and quick to complain about actions even when the problem objectively does not warrant such strong reactions. So the officials react to the clients, clients react to the officials, the officials react to each other and to reactions by the clients, etc.

It is obvious, but one should remember that officials in buroid A are clients of buroid B, C, and D. They are people with the usual wide range of personal needs and idiosyncrancies. Consequently, there will be a wide range of emotional and behavioral responses. It is

questionable that persons behaving consistently
in their official duties can act in a completely detached manner. Thus, Weber's ideal official cannot exist for very long before the
personal and job pressures take their toll.
They are humans and will respond as humans.
What one hopes, however, is that an official
will make his decisions based upon the pur-
puses, rules, and regulations of the buroid,
and will not be unfair and capricious in his
actions. If you are in a buroid and are more
competent than the lover or relative of the
supervisor, you would like to receive the promotion based on merit. If the supervisor ignores merit, allowing his personal feelings to
affect the decision, then the goal of efficiency is being violated and the rules are being broken.

Another feature of bureaucracies is that they
tend to exhibit procedural consistenty in
making decisions. Due process under previously
established rules and regulations constitutes
the usual concept of *fairness*. Employment or
promotions are supposed to be based on technical qualifications and not the peculiarities
of race, creed, sex, hair length, and costume.
A person having the qualifications seeks fairness, because if the official is fair to him,
he has a better chance for success. Persons
holding a job desire fairness in keeping it.
Trice, Belasco, and Alutto (1969) argue that
the ceremonies associated with personnel procedures may even be integrative and the very
impersonality of these processes may make the
organization seem more personal. Rogow (1968)
and Alford (1969) offer some scant evidence
that fairness and centralization are associated
with greater participation.

But if you lack the technical qualifications,
you may question whether consistency is necessarily fair. For example, in the United States
it is common for members of minority groups to
seek employment at all organizational levels in
proportion to their fraction of the population

and use "affirmative action" to seek acceler-
ated promotions for these minority group members if their proportion in top-level jobs is
lower than their fraction in the population
from which the organization draws its members.
This cannot be done "fairly" unless qualified
persons exist in the right proportions, non-
minority members are willing to move aside, or
there are sufficient growth rates to make
enough "slots" available to the newcomers.

A bureaucracy can be fair, but in behaving
fairly some members or clients will not achieve
their goals. Assuming people are goal-oriented,
if they can reach their goals by the rules they
prefer fairness, and if they cannot, they naturally prefer to have the rules and regulations
broken in their favor. This is mercy, not fairness in the sense of procedural consistency.
Thus, the bureaucratic quality of fairness will
be attacked by those seeking mercy and not attacked by those who can do well within the
rules. Those achieving goals within the system
will voice fewer complaints than the less successful. It is obvious that the question of the
relevance of a rule system to a situation is
always present and is a constant source of
problems within any buroid. Many times the
rules are altered, albeit only through the
force of law in some cases. Considerable quantities of time go into the establishment and
modification of a system of rules and regulations as the bureaucracy operates.

The terms and language used to describe a
bureaucracy are poorly defined. Terms like
division of labor, high degree of specialization, hierarchy, supervision, control, authority, functions, impersonality, career, promotion, and efficiency are all unclear in the
context of a large-scale organization. We have
described a concept of hierarchy and efficiency, but the other concepts are vague. This
vagueness makes it very difficult for two ob-
servers to agree on descriptions of a buroid.
A checklist or descriptive analysis of a buroid

creates difficulties, because even if the concepts are clear for the study, in actual cases
the buroid exhibits features related to the
concepts that vary in degree from case to case.
For example, one real buroid may be 82% hierarchical and another 57%. Is it fair to assert that one is hierarchical and the other is
not? The degree to which a buroid is a bureaucracy may be a latter-day Rorschach inkblot
where what one sees is more a matter of what
one wants or needs to see than a separate objective reality. The looseness and vagueness
of the concepts used to describe a bureaucracy
restrict the usefulness of any analysis of a
buroid. Furthermore, the vagueness makes it
difficult to compare separate studies involving
the operations of a buroid.

Another criticism of the concept of a bureaucracy is that there is a lack of uniqueness between a bureaucratic structure and an administrative problem. For any given problem, there
are a large number of task-role systems that
would work equally well. There are many possible divisions of labor, authority systems,
hierarchies, task processes, measures of efficiency and effectiveness, role and promotion
systems, and concepts of what constitutes "a
spirit of formalistic impersonality." Clearly,
more than one bureaucratic structure is possible for any given problem. The managerial
question of developing an *a priori* theory allowing one to pick the best of a set of alterna-
has not been solved. If the goal is efficiency,
then once one has a pure hierarchy there is no
way (yet) of selecting from among possible
hierarchies. However, if other goals are allowed (such as minimum cost for the organization), then choices can be made. In some organizations a pure hierarchy is impossible because of the rules and regulations governing
its operation. It is usually necessary to make
economic trade-offs between the degree of hierarchy and measures of effectiveness subject to
a series of legal and ethical constraints.

Thus, this criticism of a bureaucracy seems valid. However, the way to resolve this criticism is to employ far more sophisticated techniques than are currently available. A form of mathematical programming could be useful in solving such problems.

In the meantime, because there is a lack of uniqueness between a bureaucracy and the administrative problems it is designed to solve, the mechanisms for deciding how to design a bureaucracy involve more than concepts of efficiency. Reorganizations and administrative changes involve political issues, too. This leads to conflict, because it is difficult to accept a solution which does not benefit one personally when there is another, equally as good, that does. These conflicts will involve self-interest and competing values. They get resolved by muddling through by a sequence of incremental changes, and by political processes wherein one set of persons with a set of values tries to gain ascendency over another. The lack of uniqueness almost guarantees some degree of politics, as Pfeffer (1978) discusses in his book. Consequently, a key problem in organizational behavior is how to select (on a more comprehensive basis than efficiency) one organizational form over a large set of alternative forms. Solutions can be quantitative and/or behavioral. For example, it is possible to let subgroups work out their own structures within a succession of tightening constraints. This way the natural leaders can emerge and the subtleties of interpersonal relations can work themselves out without direct intervention. If the group is not doing well, constraints and incentives can be imposed gradually to achieve a joint solution to the problems of technical efficiency and interpersonal relations. It is doubtful that one will be able to impose a mathematical solution in one step and still maintain efficiency. But if the technical solution and behavioral solutions adjust mutually, it may be possible to implement

organizational designs that promote both efficiency and satisfaction. Such a procedure for
accommodating the technical and the behavioral
systems is well within the limits of current
technology.

The criticism that a bureaucracy is an ideal-
typical case and therefore incapable of empirical test involves methodological issues that
are not trivial. For example, if one accepts
the criticisms that the very terms describing
a bureaucracy are vague and represent a range
of values, then a procedure that assumes only
the extremes (e.g., either a hierarchy or not
a hierarchy, etc.) cannot lead to a test of
propositions derived from bureaucracy theory.
Empirical studies involving ill-defined concepts can suggest hypotheses and generate new
ideas, but it is difficult to see how one could
design a crucial experiment to refute the theory.

The laboratory experiments reported in chapter 2, relating hierarchy and efficiency, involve a deficient concept of a bureaucracy because the measure for the degree of hierarchy
does not include the implementation properties
of formalistic impersonality and employment as
a career. They suggest that there is a close
relationship between hierarchy and efficiency.
However, because of the deficiencies, these are
not tests of the hypothesis that bureaucracies
lead to more efficiency. Laboratory groups may
not be accurate surrogates for testing a theory
of bureaucracy.

The paper by Weick (1965) discusses some of
the methodological problems in using laboratory
experiments to study organizations. The first
46 pages of the book edited by Evan (1971) discuss these issues for both laboratory and field
experiments. Clearly such issues are beyond the
range of this book, but it will help if the
reader can recognize that: (1) it is possible
to study a theory of bureaucracy scientifical-
ly, (2) there is not an *a priori* "best" method
or location for research in bureaucracy theory,

(3) most studies of bureaucracy do not really study bureaucracy but only some aspect of it, and (4) this is a wide open field in which scholars can accomplish socially significant research.

Field studies by Gouldner (1954), Hall (1963), Hall, Johnson, and Haas (1967), Merton (1957), Selznick (1948), Udy (1959), and many others report theoretical and empirical findings that question the validity of the Weberian concept of bureaucracy. However, these studies are deficient because they study buroids, each providing different answers to the definition of concepts and method of analyzing such impressionistic data. There is a "straw man" flavor to some of these analyses. Collectively they demonstrate that many large-scale organizations or buroids do not always exhibit desirable properties. Despite the methodological shortcomings of such studies and conflicting results, one is persuaded that many large-scale organizations tend to be dysfunctional. To be fair, though, investigating buroids is not the same as testing a theory of bureaucracy. "It hardly seems fair, for example, to blame a cocker spaniel for not being a wolf. Or to say wolves are bad because a particular unhouse-broken cocker spaniel exhibits a few unpleasant behaviors" (Mackenzie, 1974, p. 6).

There have been some laboratory studies (e.g., Miller, 1970, and Sengupta, 1969) that report empirical relationships in close agreement with those of Weber. However, the interpretations of any analysis, whether logical, laboratory, or field, depend upon how one defines his terms, how the study is conducted, and which aspect of bureaucracy theory one is testing.

The widespread existence of buroids across a number of industries, governments, periods, and cultures does suggest that the logic for forming a hierarchy presented in chapter 4 is persuasive. One can think of every organization as a type of experiment wherein, as the

organization gets formed, grows, and matures,
the persons in that organization are empirically adjusting the functioning of their organization. That so many organizations tend to resemble at least the form of a bureaucracy is
strong evidence that the basic formulation of
Weber's bureaucracy is sound. Although a lot
of social science research tends to emphasize
anomalies and extreme cases, we should not ignore the apparently massive regularities shown
by large-scale organizations. We should try to
understand the regularities in order to learn
more about why they exist. This knowledge would
then give us a more secure basis for judging
the necessity of such organizations. Someday
we may be able to work out a range of possible
organizational forms and have the knowledge to
pick and choose, knowing the consequences and
conditions of how we live and operate in organizations. This work is being done in many
countries and some is discussed in chapter 7.
In the meantime, if one is involved in an organization faced with scarce resources and the
goal of efficiency, it would be wise to consider the bureaucracy as a solution. And in
doing so, one should try first to examine the
tasks. Try to rationalize the work with respect to a goal of efficiency before going into
the implementation conditions. Keep in mind the
logical necessity of working on the antecedent
conditions before setting up a pyramid of offices, promulgating rules and regulations, and
so forth. In fact, if someone brings you a plan
for reorganization that has lots of charts,
budgets, and rhetoric, be suspicious. Ask what
are the jobs to be done and how is the work to
be rationalized. Ask what the efficiency goals
are. If he can answer these questions, consider
his proposal. If he cannot the antecedent conditions have not been worked out. The conclusions embodied in his charts, budgets, and
diagrams will be suspect. Ask him to try again.
Otherwise, you may only have the form, and not
the substance of a bureaucracy--and you will
have to live with it.

NOTES

[1]The measure for the degree of hierarchy has been augmented and adapted for use in larger, complex organizations. It is currently being used as the basis for evaluating the efficiency of actual organizational systems.

REFERENCES

Alford, R. R. "Bureaucracy and Participation in Four Wisconsin Cities." *Urban Affairs Quarterly* 5 (1969): 5-30.

Bennis, W. *Beyond Bureaucracy.* New York: McGraw-Hill, 1974. Also published as *Changing Organizations* by McGraw-Hill, 1966.

Blau, P. M. *Bureaucracy in Modern Society.* New York: Random House, 1956.

Blau, P. M., and Meyer, M. W. *Bureaucracy in Modern Society*, 2nd Ed. New York: Random House, 1971.

Blau, P. M., and Scott, R. *Formal Organizations.* San Francisco: Chandler, 1962.

Evan, W. M. *Organizational Experiments: Laboratory and Field Research.* New York: Harper and Row, 1971.

Gellhorn, W. *Ombudsmen and Others: Citizens' Protectors in Nine Countries.* Cambridge, Mass.: Harvard University Press, 1966.

Gouldner, A. W. *Patterns of Industrial Bureaucracy.* Glencoe, Ill.: Free Press, 1954.

Hall, R. H. "The Concept of Bureaucracy: An Empirical Assessment." *American Journal of Sociology* 69 (1963): 32-40.

Hall, R. J.; Johnson, N. J.; and Haas, J. E. "Organizational Size, Complexity and Formalization." *American Sociological Review* 32 (1967): 903-12.

Mackenzie, K. D. "Organizational Theories: State of the Art for the Problem of Bureaucracies." In *Manpower Planning Models*, edited by Clough, Lewis, and Oliver, pp. 3-24. London: The English Universities Press, 1974.

Merton, R. K. "Bureaucratic Structure and Personality." In *Social Theory and Social Structure*, edited by R. K. Merton. Glencoe, Ill.: Free Press, 1957.

Merton, R. K.; Gray, A. P.; Hockey, B.; and Selvin, H. C., eds. *Reader in Bureaucracy*. New York: The Free Press, 1952.

Miller, J. P. "Social-Psychological Implications of Weber's Model of Bureaucracy: Relations Among Expertise, Control, Authority, and Legitimacy." *Social Forces* 49 (1970): 91-101.

Pfeffer, J. *Organizational Design*. Arlington Heights, Ill.: AHM Publishing Corporation, 1978.

Rogow, R. "Membership Participation and Centralized Control." *Industrial Relations* 7 (1968): 132-45.

Selznick, P. "Foundations of the Theory of Organization." *American Sociological Review* 13 (1948): 25-35.

Sengupta, A. K. "Some Features of Malfunction of an Industrial Organization." *Sociological Bulletin* 18 (1969): 122-37.

Thompson, V. A. *Modern Organization*. New York: Knopf, 1961.

Trice, H. M.; Belasco, J.; and Alutto, J. A. "The Role Ceremonials in Organizational Behavior." *Industrial and Labor Relations Review* (1969): 40-51.

Udy, S. H., Jr. "'Bureaucracy' and 'Rationality' in Weber's Organizational Theory: An Empirical Study." *American Sociological Review* 24 (1959): 791-95.

Weber, M. *From Max Weber: Essays in Sociology*. Translated by H. H. Gerth and C. W. Mills. New York: Oxford University Press, 1946.

_____. *The Theory of Social and Economic Organization*. Translated by A. M. Henderson and T. Parsons. Glencoe, Ill.: The Free Press, 1947.

Weick, K. E. "Laboratory Experimentation with Organizations." In *Handbook of Organizations*, edited by J. G. March, pp. 194-260. Chicago: Rand McNally, 1965.

6

Centralization and Decentralization

CONCEPTS OF CENTRALIZATION AND DECENTRALIZATION

STRUCTURAL CONCEPT OF CENTRALITY

There is more than one meaning for the word *centralization* and its opposite, *decentralization*. In graph theory and in the study of communications networks, a fully decentralized structure is given by an all-channel as in Figure 6.1a. The all-channel is characterized by the property that each node or vertex has a channel or edge to every other vertex. The all-channel graph was used in experiments described in chapters 1-4. Its opposite, in terms of being the most centralized, is the wheel structure, shown in Figure 6.1a, which was also used in experiments described in chapters 1-4. The concept of centrality used in this context is

called *structural centrality*. Numerous papers
exist describing several measures of structural
centrality (see Beauchamp, 1965; Leavitt, 1951;
Lewin and Tapiaro, 1973; Mackenzie, 1966, 1967,
1976a; and Sabidussi, 1966). The seminal paper
on the concept of structural centrality is that
of Sabidussi (1966).

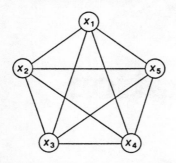 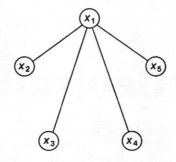

FIGURE 6.1a A fully decen-   FIGURE 6.1b A fully centralized structure.   tralized structure.

The main idea behind structural centrality
can be illustrated by examining a sequence of
alterations in a structure by which an all-
channel is successively transformed into a
wheel.

In Figure 6.2, the set of vertices is x_1, x_2
x_3, and x_4. The edges connecting pairs of vertices are labeled e_1, e_2, . . . , e_6. Starting
with structure (a), we go to (b) by *deleting*
edge e_6. We move from (b) to (c) and from (c)
to (d) by deleting edges e_5 and e_4 respectively. The structure at (b) is reffered to as a
slash, the one at (c) as a *circle*, and the one at
(d) as a *chain*. With each of these deletions,
the structural centrality has increased. When
we move from (d) to (e), we simultaneously de-
lete e_3 and add e_6. This is called a *switch*. So
the switch of the edge from x_3 to x_2 converts
the chain in (d) to a wheel with x_2 as the hub.
Not all switches are permissible. The switches

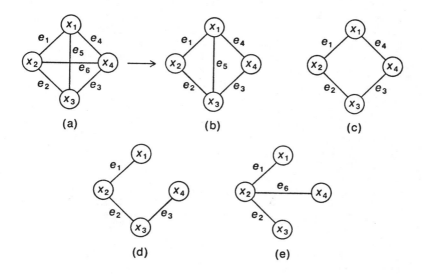

FIGURE 6.2

must be from a noncenter to a center. For example, in (d), x_1 and x_4 are peripheral and not centers. So a switch of the edge from x_1 to x_2 to an edge between x_1 and x_4 would not increase structural centrality because the result would be a new *chain*. Thus, deletions and permissible switches increase structural centrality. There are a few subtle conditions on deletions and switches which are described by Sabidussi. But, setting these details aside, it is clear that one can describe structural centrality as being increased or decreased by simple operations on the edges. The opposite of a deletion is an addition. One can see that going backwards from (d) to (a), the successive steps are additions. Working from (a) to (d), the successive steps are deletions.

The measure of structural centrality one

chooses to use varies with the purpose. However, if one wishes to include direction, intensity, or frequency, and incorporate actual
data, a measure of structural centrality with
these capabilities that is consistent with the
concept of structural centrality is given by
Mackenzie (1966). Lewin and Tapiaro (1973) also
provide a useful measure.

Sabidussi's contribution was to remove the
problem of defining structural centrality from
clumsy and misleading words to clear and simple
manipulations of the structure. His approach
has cleared up numerous technical problems in
defining structural centrality. One immediate
consequence of his formulation is that it allows one to see quickly that a structural hierarchy is a different concept from a structurally centralized structure. For example, in Figure 6.3(a) the hierarchy of three levels is not
fully centralized because edge e_3 can be
switched to edge e_7 (moving from an edge between x_2 and x_4 to the edge between x_4 and x_1).

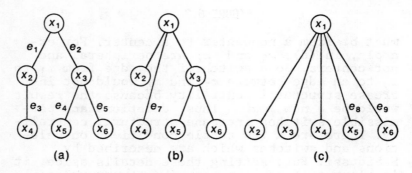

(a)   (b)   (c)

FIGURE 6.3

This switch increases structural centrality.
The result of this switch is (b). Likewise,
edges e_4 and e_5 can be switched to create edges
e_8 and e_9. This structure (c) is more structurally centralized than the structural hierarchy (b), which is more centralized than the

structural hierarchy (a). If there are only
two levels, a structural hierarchy is also
structurally centralized. But as the number of
levels in a structural hierarchy increases, the
degree of structural centrality decreases. This
nonobvious result is a direct consequence of
Sabidussi's formulation. The increasing (with
number of levels) discrepancy between structural centrality and structural hierarchy is the
reason why it was necessary to create a separate measure for the degree of hierarchy, presented in chapter 1.

When a group is fully centralized structurally, there is a *hub* position with an edge or
channel to every other position, called a *spoke*.
There are no links (cousin and uncle relationships described in chapter 1) between pairs of
spokes. A hub can be thought of as a "boss" and
the spokes as his immediate subordinates. Recalling that most groups have more than one
structure, it is possible to derive indices of
structural centrality combining the separate
structures. One fascinating result is that if
one does combine substructures, the structural
centrality of the whole is always less than or
equal to the sum of the structural centralities
of its parts. This is illustrated in Figure
6.4. The wheel in 6.4(a) and the wheel in 6.4
(b) are both structurally centralized but the
combined structure is much less structurally
centralized. This follows from the simple notion that one can go from (c) to (a) by deleting each of the edges contained in (b).
Note that the edge from x_1 to x_2 in (a) is also
contained in (b). An algebra for combining and
decomposing graphs on the basis of edges is
given in Mackenzie (1967). Most books on graph
theory contain procedures for decomposing by
sets of vertices. (For analyses of graphs, see
Berge, 1962; or Harary, Norman, and Cartwright,
1965.)

In terms of structural centrality, groups become decentralized as more channels of edges
are opened and permissible switches are

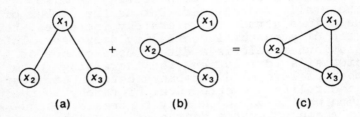

FIGURE 6.4

reversed. Therefore, when one says that a decentralized group has become more centralized or a
centralized group has become more decentralized, the concept can be easily understood in
terms of the changes in arrangement of used
channels. That is, the actual configuration of
the used channels is altered. However, in the
management literature on centralization and decentralization the basic structural configuration is often unaltered in form but changed in
content. The word *delegation* is used as a synonym
for decentralization. Thus, the very concept of
centrality is different for these two literatures. This makes it very difficult to apply
theories developed in, say, the small group
communication network literature to managerial
literature on decentralization and vice versa.

Managerial Concept of Centrality

It is probably best to conceive of a multidivisional organization, such as a university
with its schools and departments or a corporation such as General Motors, to place the managerial concepts of decentralization and centralization into perspective. In such organizations each division has a capability of carrying out most of those functions necessary to
produce a given line of products or to serve a
selected market. For example, a school of business could contain departments of management,

organizational behavior, accounting, finance,
marketing, operations research and statistics,
industrial relations, and various others such
as health administration, real estate, life
insurance, and so on. Each of these runs a
program for teaching and its members engage in
some form of research or consulting. However,
because of common core requirements for degrees
such as the M.B.A., there is some need for
coordination. The department may share computers, libraries, secretarial pools, and even
faculty members. To provide coordination and
control, there is often a "headquarters" unit
called the office of the dean, subordinate to
higher levels within the university.

There are advantages and disadvantages in
having headquarters provide this coordination
and control. The choice of which functions or
activities are to be performed and controlled
by a "headquarters" unit is the essence of the
decentralization-centralization problem. Allocation of classroom and laboratory space,
changes in personnel (hiring, promoting, separation), budget preparation, admission and
graduation, changes in programs and course requirements, travel and research expenses, and
many other problems arise that may involve
many subunits. The more these activities are
allocated to each subunit, the greater its
autonomy, and the more decentralized the organization. For example, the person above the
dean, who might be a vice president or vice
chancellor for academic affairs, could let the
business school run independently and the dean
of the school of business could allow each of
his departments to run independently. Such an
organization would be considered highly decentralized. Conversely, the vice president for
academic affairs could try to control and coordinate every aspect of the school of business, and the dean in turn could run the departments the same way. In this event, the organization would be considered highly centralized.

At both extremes, there is the same basic structural hierarchy, but the allocation of functions has been delegated to lower levels in the decentralized versions and has not been delegated in the centralized version. In the case of a multidivisionsal corporation, each could take care of its own production, marketing, accounting, finance, research, personnel, and so forth. In fact, the separate divisions could compete with each other in the market, and for resources. Such divisional autonomy would be considered highly decentralized. The converse, wherein headquarters makes most of the decisions and controls the functions tightly, would be considered highly centralized.

There is no hard and fast answer for determining the best degree of centralization. Most companies and organizations adjust the allocation of activities to meet changing market conditions, personnel changes, and adjustments in the distribution of intraorganizational power. Furthermore, most well-run organizations fall in between extreme centralization and decentralization. W. T. Morris (1968) presents a comprehensive view of the substantive technical issues for determining degrees of centralization in an organization. He demonstrates how to formulate a number of technical problems, such as capital budgeting, to illustrate the types of considerations needed for determining the degree and activities of centralization. Although he presents interesting models, he is very careful to point out the limitations of making such determinations by formulae. Each issue is considered on a case-by-case basis. For example, if a company such as a coal or steel company uses standardized technology for production, produces a relatively homogeneous product, services a small number of large customers, and is very capital intensive, it will usually be relatively highly centralized. But if it has a wide range of products, technologies, customers, and relatively low capitalization, it will probably be managed in a decentralized fashion. Faced with great diversity of actual organizations, it is unsound to argue for or against extremes of centralization or decentralization in the absence of the types of specific issues and conditions that are considered important.

Ideally, a highly decentralized organization can respond quickly and effectively to changes in each division's requirements because it does not have to seek successive approvals from higher levels. Each division knows its own markets and conditions better than headquarters. It allows headquarters to judge the efforts of its divisions and division managers because each has control over its own activities. Each division operates as an independent company. Morris lists eleven advantages for decentralized decision-making (Morris, 1968, pp. 176-77):

1. reducing the need for coordination and the communication of specialized knowledge
2. increasing incentives for subordinate decision-making
3. permitting decisions to be made by those best equipped to provide the necessary intuitive or judgmental inputs, and reducing the need to base decisions on readily communicable data
4. achieving a more effective distribution of decision-making work load throughout the organization
5. reducing delays in decision-making and implementation
6. providing a better basis for the necessary trial-and-error process of management
7. quickening the organization's reactions to changes in its environment
8. widening the experience and training of executives coming up through the organization
9. facilitating the comparison of subunits' effectiveness with other organizations having similar products or processes
10. providing a basis for allocating capital and other resources controlled by headquarters among the subunits

11. encouraging one subunit to share its specialized knowledge and skills with the other.

The ideal of fully decentralized decision-making in an organization could operate if each division acted as a separate organization in a perfectly competitive market and, in fact, if the conditions of perfect competition were present. However, these conditions are rare and organizations have to adjust themselves to take advantage of complementarities while keeping each division self-contained to some degree. Basically, each organization has the problem of breaking down the total activities and assigning them to units. This is the problem of forming the group role matrix described in chapter 1. Then, once the initial assignment has been made, the problem is to coordinate the resulting subunits. The real problem here is how to distribute authority and power in order to achieve the goals of the organization.[1] To economists this problem is roughly the technical one of developing a system of transfer prices for exchanges among the divisions and to find a method of defining and measuring divisional profit so that: (1) if each division maximizes its profits, the profits of the whole organization will be maximized; (2) each division acts independently in that it need not concern itself with the action of other divisions and even act without knowledge of the activities of other divisions; and (3) the headquarters group needs to devote little time to coordinating divisional activities because it has motivated the divisions to maximize individual profits.

This task, for most firms, is very difficult —and almost impossible for organizations in the public sector which lack the incessant discipline of being forced to operate in a competitive market. Usually, there exist compelling reasons for some degree of interdependence, as in the case of a school of business or university. Whenever this interdependence exists, the

attainment of complete decentralization of the
above ideal becomes difficult. The stronger
the interdependence in terms of both the number
and degree of interdependencies, the more difficult it becomes to solve the technical problems that would lead to a realization of the
ideal decentralized decision-making system. One
serious problem is the difficulty of defining
operationally meaningful organizational goals
(see Tuggle, 1978, chapter 2). As Pfeffer
(1978) points out, the real problem of achieving coordination is political, involving issues
of power and governance. Given that there may
not be a single overriding goal, various coalitions within the organization having coalition
goals will push and pull to achieve their
goals. The existence of conflicting goals means
that various units will attempt to exercise
their power in order to achieve their goals.
There will be clashes and disagreements. The
headquarters group and supervisors at all levels will be forced to retain control in order
to exercise power to achieve their goals. These
conflicting interests and the resulting problems of the distribution of activities and power are constrained, however, by the organization's need to take advantage of the interdependencies among the divisions. As explained
by Simmons (1978, chapter 3), power and its
exercise involve trade-offs between persons. If
Headquarters, for example, seeks to get Division A to do something it would not ordinarily
do, Headquarters' actions to have Division A
do it involves exchanges. On the one hand, Headquarters wants it done, and on the other, Division A has things it wants from Headquarters.
Each may want something positively valued or to
avoid sanctions that are negatively valued. So,
in order for Headquarters to get Division A to
do what it wants, there will be some bargaining. Interdependence insures some mutual accommodations between headquarters and its divisions. This accommodation can often be described as a political process.

For example, a university whose funding is dependent upon the number of students and which is faced with declining enrollments might seek to have its school of business launch a part-time or off-campus program leading to an M.B.A. degree. The dean of the school of business, faced with personnel shortages, may not wish to start up such a program. The university president and the dean may have to bargain about what extra resources will be made available to the school of business in order to launch the new program. The interests of the president are to gain increased revenues at minimal added costs. The interests of the dean are to gain increased resources for his school for minimal increases in workload. The ensuing negotiations can take several years, involve many committees, and entail numerous commitments by both sides. If the dean does not really desire the new programs and if the president really wants them, the dean can drive a hard bargain, especially if he is not too worried about remaining dean or playing organizational "workup" to a higher administrative level. But if the dean and his faculty are in favor of the new programs, or if the dean desires to maintain good relationships with the president, the president can settle the issues on terms more favorable to him.

ECONOMIC CONCEPTS OF CENTRALIZATION-DECENTRALIZATION

There seem to be two meanings for decentralization in the economics literature. The first, stemming from microeconomic theory of markets, is the concept of a perfectly competitive market. The second is the economic literature of transfer pricing that stems from Hirshleifer (1957) and is summarized by Morris (1968). Related to both of these is the macroeconomic analysis of comparative economic systems (see Marschak, 1965). The two views mirror, in part, the structural and managerial views.

To some, a perfectly competitive market is the ultimate in decentralization. In a perfectly competitive market, there are four main assumptions. Henderson and Quandt (1958, p. 86) state these:

1. Firms produce a homogeneous commodity, and consumers are identical from the seller's point of view, in that there are no advantages or disadvantages associated with selling to a particular consumer.
2. Both firms and consumers are numerous, and the sales or purchases of each individual unit are small in relation to the aggregate volume of transactions.
3. Both firms and consumers possess perfect information about the prevailing price and current bids, and they take advantage of every opportunity to increase profits and utility respectively.
4. Entry and exit from the market is free for both firms and consumers.

The first condition assumes the anonymity of firms and consumers in that one would gain no knowledge of identity of the seller if one knew the identity of the buyer, and no knowledge of the identity of the buyer if one knew the identity of the seller. The second condition ensures that many sellers face many buyers. The production of an individual seller or the consumption of an individual consumer does not affect the price of the homogeneous product. Individual buyers and sellers act as if they have no influence on the market price and each adjusts production and consumption to market conditions. The third condition states that both sides of the market have perfect information with respect to the quality and nature of the product and the prevailing price. This condition ensures a single price prevailing in the perfectly competitive market. The fourth condition makes provision for the flow of resources between alternative users in the long run. Both firms and consumers move in and out markets in

order to maximize profit or net utility. There
is little "friction" to impede the flow of human and money resources in a perfectly competitive market.

Structurally, a perfectly competitive market
is an all-channel where the contacts between
sellers and buyers are indirect because of the
market. Even though there is no direct contact
between a seller and all other sellers or all
possible buyers, the market participants are
indirectly in contact because of the market.
By condition one, simple buying and selling of
a homogeneous product defines the single type
of structure in a perfectly competitive market.
By condition three, there is full exchange (in
terms of quality and price), ensuring perfect
knowledge, and by condition four the list of
participants changes easily, with inefficient
firms being eliminated in favor of efficient
firms.

The concepts of decentralization in the perfectly competitive sense are so close to the
structural concepts that measures of group
structure in the communications network experiments can be extended to measures of market
structure (see Bernhardt and Mackenzie, 1968).
Perfectly competitive markets become less decentralized as the four conditions are weak-
ened. For example, monopoly and monopsony are
considered centralized markets with respect to
selling and buying respectively. Intermediate
cases of oligopoly and oligopsony and imperfect
competition are of great interest to economic
theorists because the behavior of sellers and
buyers changes with the type of relaxation of
the four main conditions.

The papers by J. Hirshleifer (1956, 1957,
1970), on transfer pricing and the economics of
the divisionalized firm, expanded some techniques of microeconomic theory and welfare
economics to analyze the imperfect correspondence between the profits of the divisions of a
firm and the profits of the entire firm. The
main question in this literature is, for a

given problem such as transfer pricing, to in-
vestigate under what conditions, and for what
goals, does goal-maximization on the divisional
level lead to an optimum for the firm. The
technical question of how to devise a scheme
for one of a number of control problems in a
divisionalized firm is the heart of the literature on decentralization in such a firm. The
book by Morris contains numerous examples of
such problems: the design of capital budgeting
systems, search for investment opportunities,
evaluation of investment projects, degree of
control of funds by headquarters to its operating units, determining the project cost cutoff
point where in all projects above this thresh-
old are reviewed by headquarters and projects
below this cutoff are left to the operating
subunits, and transfer pricing problems.

To illustrate the technical problem, consider
a bicycle manufacturer that manufactures its
own bicycle frames and can either purchase
components from other companies or make its
own. For the sake of simplicity, let us assume
that there is a bicycle assembly plant that
must use wheels made by a division of the company. The assembly division will "purchase"
wheels from the wheel division. What should the
price be for transferring wheels from the wheel
division to the assembly division? The transfer
price will affect the profits of both divisions. The higher the transfer price, the
greater the profits of the wheel division and
the lower the profits of the assembly division.
If headquarters decides to reward each division
manager on his profit performance, the possibilities for conflict can be easily seen. The
transfer price may not affect the profits of
the bicycle company (unless each division adjusts its production in order to maximize its
profits), but it can certainly affect the performance appraisal of its managers.

Numerous intracompany pricing schemes have
been advanced. These include selling the wheels
at the market price for wheels, the marginal

cost of producing the wheels, the variable
costs of producing the wheels, actual or standard costs of producing the wheels, and a
negotiated price. Bierman (1959, p. 358) argues
that "the choice of method to be used can only
be made after the purpose for which the information to be used is determined." B. E.
Goetz (1967) argues that incremental costs,
rather than market prices or average historical costs, be used for transfer prices. Gould
(1964) analyzes the transfer pricing problem
when there are costs of using an outside market. Samuels (1965) and Bernhard (1968) argue
for using opportunity costs for transfer
pricing, which can be calculated using techniques such as linear programming.

Although this discussion only scratches the
surface of this rich literature, the confusions
and inconsistencies among purposes, models,
methods of analysis, and techniques of transfer
pricing make it difficult for both headquarters
and its operating divisions to agree on a
scheme, even if they only accept the issue as
a technical one. Transfer prices do get set,
but the process by which they are set may or
may not correspond to what appears, at the
time, to be a reasonable solution from the
point of view of microeconomics. The issues
raised are interesting, and the various propos-
als for analysis yield valuable insight into
the underlying technical problems. However,
despite the promise of this approach, the real
issues for managers are best analyzed as political processes wherein a balance is struck between information-overloading, reasonableness
and consistency with past practices, and needs
for control by the various parties within the
organization. Furthermore, technical analyses
are best viewed as weapons to be used to advance one's interests in a continuing power
struggle.

A third economic view for a comparison of
decentralized versus centralized economics will

be discussed later in this chapter. We now turn to an analysis of decentralization-centralization from the viewpoint of making a decision to delegate, in the face of conflicting needs to control and to prevent information overload.

THE DECISION FOR THE DEGREE OF DECENTRALIZATION AND CENTRALIZATION

VIEWPOINT OF MULTIPLE STRUCTURES

One of the first ideas introduced in chapter 1 is that an organization has multiple structures. A second idea is that each structure can describe the direction, frequency, and content of the interaction pattern. A third idea is that task processes and group structures are closely related. A fourth idea is that structures represent need-satisfying patterns of interaction, and structures can and will change. These ideas are discussed and shown to be relevant for a number of structural problems. They can also be applied to the problems of centralization and decentralization.

An immediate consequence of these ideas is a new conception of the main issues involved in decentralization-centralization problems. The line between x_1 and x_2 in Figure 6.5(a) appears on a typical organization chart. It is one-dimensional and indicates neither the content nor the frequency of the interactions. It would be more accurate to represent the relationships between x_1 and x_2 as a whole set of lines, one corresponding to each dimension of the relationship, as in Figure 6.5(b). Comparison of the single line in (a) with the set of lines in (b) highlights the difference between a one-dimensional concept of group structure and the multi-dimensional concept of group structures. Using the more comprehensive view of group structures, the main issues in the

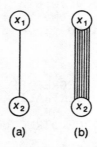

(a)   (b)

FIGURE 6.5

decentralization-centralization decision can be
described in terms of which dimensions and
what direction and frequency of interactions
are necessary between any pair of organizational members.

Delegation means that the interactions between the higher position, x_1, and the lower
position, x_2, have been altered either to cut
out some of the dimensions or to reduce the
volume of interactions from x_1 to x_2 relative
to those from x_2 to x_1. By cutting out some of
the dimensions or by changing the flows, x_2 has
gained relatively more autonomy. The more dimensions between x_1 and x_2 that are cut away
and the lower the volume of interactions from
x_1 to x_2 relative to those from x_2 to x_1, the
more the relationships between x_1 and x_2 become decentralized. Thus, the issues in the decision to decentralize or centralize involve
issues of kind (which dimensions), degree (how
much interaction is required), and direction
(who initiates the interaction).

For example, suppose x_1 represents headquarters and x_2 the head of an operating division. One arrow in Figure 6.5(b) represents
capital budgeting interactions. If x_1 and x_2
are centralized for this dimension, x_2 sends
each investment proposal to x_1 for approval. If

x_1 and x_2 are fully decentralized on this dimension, x_2 makes all of his own decisions without obtaining approval or even notifying x_1 of his decisions. The dangers in either extreme are clear. If the decisions are fully centralized, the volume of work for x_1 may become too large, the costs of transmitting all agreements and documents to support each request may be high, the inevitable delays could result in lost opportunities, and so on. However, if this decision is fully decentralized, control by x_1 could be lost, investments could be made by x_2 that have much lower payoffs than those of other divisions, there could be waste because of duplication of equipment and facilities, and so forth. One possibility lying between these extremes is to set a policy that all projects involving more than a given value, say $10,000, are to be forwarded to x_1 for approval and to allow x_2 to make all decisions for projects whose cost is less than $10,000, up to some total amount, say $150,000. That is, a *size-gate system* (see Morris, 1968, chapter 7) can be created that allows the operating divisions to make investments without further consultations with x_1, provided each of the sums required is less than the gate value (e.g., $10,000) and the total of the sums is less than total size (e.g., $150,000). Such a policy allows the organization to pick a middle ground between extreme centralization and extreme decentralization for interactions involving investments. In terms of Figure 6.5(b), the arrow between x_1 and x_2 for investments still exists, but the volume of the flows of interactions has been reduced.

CAPACITY AND SPAN OF CONTROL CONSIDERATIONS

Chapter 4 was devoted to an analysis of the span of control for a person in an organization. Each person has a limitation on how much information he can possess within a specified time. This maximum capacity reflects his

capacities as well as the norms of the persons
with whom he interacts. We discussed a number
of ways to increase the maximum span of control. However, as was shown even in a little
laboratory group, when the span of control required by the situation was larger than the
capacity of the hub, the group would take steps
to alter its structures in order to find one
that works better. It is also pointed out that
the manager could lose control when he lacked
sufficient capacity to handle his volume of
interactions. That is, inadequate capacity
could lead to a loss of control. Thus, a manager who is overloaded may have to take steps to
reduce his overload. He is thereby placed in a
situation where he must give up some control in
order to maintain control. One way of doing
this is to decentralize partially. He can give
up some of the dimensions that take up his time
or he can reduce the volume of interactions on
a dimension.

Conversely, if a manager has excess capacity,
he could handle a larger volume of interactions. The existence of this excess capacity
could come about because of a more competent
staff, a less time-consuming management information system, a routinization of previously
new problems, a reduction in the range of products and services for which he is responsible,
and so on. The existence of this excess capacity could lead to steps taken by the manager to
increase his degree of centralization with respect to his subordinates. And if he is a
middle manager with an overloaded superior, he
could take on more responsibility and thus become more decentralized with respect to his
superior and more centralized with respect to
his subordinates.

MAINTENANCE OF POWER AND CONTROL

Casual observation, interviews with managers,
and common sense suggest that it is reasonable
to expect each manager to attempt to maximize

his own power and discretion. If he is being
judged by the results of his division's operations, he wants to be able to control the behavior and processes of his subordinates in
order to exert some control over the results
and, hence, his evaluation. Some persons just
enjoy being in charge and exerting power.
Miner (1965, 1968, 1971) and Rizzo, Miner,
Harlow, and Hill (1974) present results generally confirming the proposition that the motivation for power correlates well with success
in hierarchical situations but not in nonhier-
archical situations. But since most larger organizations tend toward hierarchy (see chapter
4) and many managers are motivated by success,
it is not at all unreasonable to expect managers to seek *at least* to maintain power and control whenever it is possible.

Consequently, an important factor in the decision to centralize or decentralize is how to
maintain or increase power and control in the
face of possible overloading. The manager is
constrained by those above and below him and
by his own capacity. It is unlikely, at least
in a pluralistic society, that he can increase
his power without limit before he gets reined
in by these counter-forces. It is also unlikely
that he will relinquish his accumulated power
and control without resistance.

One of the author's pastimes is to talk with
managers about decentralization. The main impression is that if there are a number of levels with Manager A on top, Manager B in the
middle, and Manager C below Manager B, there is
a consistent pattern of preferences for decentralization. Manager A does not want to decentralize. Manager B wants Manager A to decentralize so that Manager B has more autonomy,
but he does not seek to decentralize with respect to Manager C. Manager C is in favor of
both Managers A and B decentralizing so that
he has more control, but Manager C is not as
enthusiastic about decentralizing with respect
to his subordinate Manager D. There are

exceptions to this pattern of preferences, especially in organizations where the rewards for advancement up a hierarchy are small in relationship to the increased loss of personal freedom. However, even in places such as universities, there seems to be a large supply of willing recruits into the hierarchical control positions and these persons, while affecting more complex rationalizations, do not seem to provide many counter-examples to this preference structure for where to begin decentralization.

Thus, although we acknowledge exceptions, it seems useful to assume that each person in a hierarchy attempts to increase his personal power and control in those aspects of his job over which he believes he should be in control. Because there are conflicting views over who should control what activities and persons, power struggles are not at all uncommon. In many cases, this power struggle takes place within the context of decisions about the nature and degree of decentralization and centralization.

The main proposition is that *typically, each manager seeks to be more decentralized with respect to his superior and to keep or increase the degree of centralization with respect to his subordinates.* A corollary to this proposition is that a manager will decentralize when he has to but will avoid decentralizing if he can. There are numerous constraints inhibiting the processes of these power struggles. There are rules and regulations that constrain the range of possible issues. The domain of such rules and regulations is one area for carrying out the struggle, because persons will seek to alter them in order to benefit their position. Availability of resources and the interorganizational competition for scarce resources provide constraints.

Existing technology also places limitations. When the time lag for exercising control is large relative to the time lag for changing conditions for which the control is relevant,

the organization will be forced to be more decentralized in order to maintain its control.
But when this relative time lag for communicat-
ing is short, the organization can centralize.
For example, Roman consuls in provinces distant
from Rome could not be highly centralized because it was difficult for Rome to contact
them. If the Roman emperor wanted to tell the
consul in Britain to do something, it might
take several months for messengers to deliver
this message. The lag of months and the dangers
for a messenger to get through meant decentralization was forced on the emperor. The Romans
built roads and maintained extensive systems to
speed up communications within their empire.
But in present conditions, the leader of a
country can contact his ambassadors and
commanders quickly by telecommunications. Current systems can be much more centralized because of communications technology. Instead of
building roads, like the Romans did, many
modern orgaizations build extensive communications systems. Computers and better information-processing can lead to a shortening of the
time to evaluate a problem and to reach a decision. These tend to foster more centralization.

However, no matter what the communication and
information-processing system, there is always
the underlying problem of information overload.
The situations change, and even if a previous
set of problems could be effectively controlled
by a modern control center, the tendency to
recentralize and for problems to change, plus
the inevitable errors that occur and the power
struggles, leads eventually to overload. One
indirect result of excessive centralization is
the creation of subordinate managers who are
not trained to think beyond narrow limits.
This, in turn, increases the information and
decision-making burden on the central control
center. So, although improved technology can
ameliorate a situation of maintaining control,
it does not remove the necessity to make

trade-offs between information overload and the degree of centralization.

The essence of this trade-off between the degree and type of control and information overloading can be described in terms of Figure 6.5(b). This figure shows a number of different dimensions to describe the range of activities over which the two positions interact. Each of these dimensions takes up time and each involves control. Some require more time than others. Some involve more important variables in terms of power. But power is relative and depends upon the needs of the actors. If x_1 wants to get x_2 to do something, he may not have much difficulty if x_2 also wants to do it. But if x_2 does not want to do it, x_1 will want to have the means to encourage x_2 to reconsider. He may be able to reward x_2 or to punish x_2. The willingness of x_2 for the rewards offered by x_1 or his willingness to avoid sanctions are offset by the needs by x_1 for x_2 to do what x_1 wants and what x_2 can do for or to x_1. Person x_1 is relatively more powerful than x_2 if x_2 wants what x_1 can give or wants to avoid the sanctions by x_1, more than x_1 wants to get what x_2 can give or to avoid sanctions by x_2.

The range of possible issues between x_1 and x_2 is not fixed and involves many uncertainties. If x_1 is being held responsible for what x_2 does, x_1 will want to maintain his bases of power over x_2 in case he needs them. One of the more effective sources of power for x_1 is his control over the promotion of x_2, provided that x_2 seeks promotion. However, if x_2 is in the position of making an evaluation of x_1 through a personal contact with x_1's superior, x_1 will have to be very careful. The range of activities or dimensions for the relationship between x_1 and x_2 shown in Figure 6.5(b) can include budget, approval or disapproval of projects, facilities, promotion, recruitment, retention, transfer of personnel, deciding the nature and amount of products and services to be offered by x_2's organization, use of the computer, rewards for performance, long-range planning, and so on. New issues will arise as circumstances change. One common source of such changes is governmental action and inaction. For example, affirmative action and various pollution laws and interpretation of pollution laws by the courts have caused numerous structural changes in both public and private organizations. This variability and how to cope with changes provides one good reason for the need felt by managers to keep as strong a basis of control as they can. One simply cannot accurately forecast when one will need to exercise power.

Each activity or dimension for interaction has two characteristics important to our analysis of the decentralization-centralization problem: each requires time, and each involves some basis for exercising power. When a manager is faced with an overload, he is going eventually to have to cut down on the time spent in interactions. A good rule of thumb is to try to decentralize on those issues involving large amounts of time and small erosions in one's power base. This way one does the most to reduce the problem of information overload with the least loss of power. If the manager remembers that his power base depends both upon what he can do and what the other person wants, the decision for what issues to decentralize on and to what degree to make this decentralization will involve judgments.

Keeping control over budgets is probably the last dimension one should give up. Budgets do not take up too much time and they give tremendous leverage on a continuing basis for exercising control and power. Budgets have several side effects that are beneficial to maintaining power. First they provide a basis for evaluation; second, arbitrary little changes can usually be justified without having to exercise one's power overtly; and third, the budgeting process involves arcane rituals that give an

experienced incumbent important advantages over
beginners. One can, for example, legitimately
claim that while final approval lies elsewhere,
one will try to "fight" for x_2. Poor x_2 can be
made to feel grateful that someone offered to
fight for him. Then x_1 can adjust how he
"fights" to match how "reasonable" x_2 is on
other issues. The experienced x_1 may know that
budgets will be eventually increased 10%. He
can generously offer x_2 6% and then have x_2
bargain away other issues to get a total of
9%. To a more cooperative subordinate, he can
give 12% after offering 8%. The main technique
here is to withhold full information and maintain control over the uncertainty about how the
budgeting process will end up.

OTHER FACTORS AFFECTING THE DECISION FOR HOW MUCH TO DELEGATE

The emphasis in the previous section is on the
trade-off between maintaining control and power
while accommodating the capacity of the individual to handle his volume of interactions.
The main advice is to rank in terms of time the
issues that would be saved and the power bases
that would be lost. Then give up first on issues that would save a lot of time with low
erosion of the power base. Those issues involving relatively small amounts of time and
large losses of potential power should be the
last to go for two reasons: (1) it will be hard
to exercise control as newer issues arise, and
(2) the lack of power base may result in having
to spend extra time to gain cooperation. This
analysis is more political than technical. This
is not to minimize the importance of more technical analyses--they are important and they can
encourage cooperation because they seem fair.
The analyses themselves can illuminate the
underlying problems, and this knowledge can be
helpful. However, underlying these analyses is
the implicit recognition of the need to balance

the needs to exercise control and power, and
the limitations to this control and power. Although the advice may seem somewhat "wicked"
to the inexperienced, reflection and experience
will help one keep the technical aspects of
these problems in perspective.[2]

There are a number of subsidiary issues affecting the decision for the nature and degree
of centralization. Information-handling time
and costs are important. Unless one is vigilant
one may spend more money and time processing
information than the information is worth to
the operations of the organization. It is not
always possible to communicate judgments and
the bases for the judgments to another who is
unfamiliar with your problems. There may be so
much information to process that one cannot do
it with existing technology. For example, a
firm with 10,000 products, operating in 19
countries, and having 74 subsidiaries would
find it exceedingly difficult to maintain an
information system that would permit effective
centralization.

It takes time to assemble, process, dissemi-
nate, and circulate information. If this time
is large relative to the time during which
important information can change, some decentralization will be necessary in order to
maintain a tactical ability to respond. Many
organizations decentralize tactical and short-
run adjustments, and use a headquarters group
to do longer-range planning. Another well-known
strategy is to establish a filtering system in
which important changes involving the larger
organization are passed on but minor and local-
ized changes are handled by the operating division.

Many problems facing an organization are initially poorly understood and involve complex
processes engaging many persons and subunits.
But as the problems and how to deal with them
are more accurately comprehended, standard
operating procedures can be devised to make

them more routine. The routinization of heretofore complex tasks reduces the burdens on information-processing and provides a basis for recentralizing (see Tuggle, 1978) for a discussion of standard operating procedures).

Many problems are analogous to accidents in that they appear to occur randomly and involve varying costs and benefits. Just as insurance companies can pool risks over a large population of clients, so can organizations pool resources to cope with problems. For example, a death in a family can be a financial catastrophe for the family when it lacks the resources to cope. However, if an insurance firm has 100,000 clients, each paying a small premium, the problems of one family are offset by no problems in thousands of other families. Consequently, using the same principle involved in pooling risks by an insurance company, an organization can centralize some of its operations. Legal services, keeping a cash reserve, research and development, and personnel services can be centralized. Take the case of legal services. Each operating division may expect not to be sued but, overall, the organization can expect to be engaged in some litigation. Instead of such operating division maintaining its own legal services, the organization's headquarters can do this and lower total costs. Research and development is a risky business. Any given project can fail, but enough new ideas and products can be produced overall so that the failure on one problem is balanced by successes on others. Thus, the need to pool risks and to absorb uncertainties, which are major for a subunit but relatively minor for the overall organization, leads to centralization of some activities.

One major risk is the rate and type of technological change. This type of issue (discussed fully in Pfeffer, 1978), has an effect that encourages more decentralization. The need to hedge against being trapped with a product line that is vulnerable to technology encourages product diversification. But when an organization becomes too diversified, it is difficult for a central headquarters to maintain a centalized operation. Rapid technological change encourages the formation of an organization that learns to accommodate changes by designing its task processes so that it will not have to make a lot of changes when changes do occur. To keep flexible and to be able to adjust rapidly, the organizational structures and processes tend away from centralization and towards decentralization.

Threats and outside pressures on the organization can lead to decentralization. Because it presents more targets, an organization having many operating units can localize external threats. So, even if one is endangered, there are enough other divisions to keep the organization going. For example, if a firm has a number of production facilities, a strike at any one, unless it is a company-wide union, may not cripple the organization. On the other hand, if the threats and outside pressures can be applied to the organization as a whole, it may be forced to centralize in order to protect itself. For example, if an organization is seriously threatened by a lawsuit about its hiring practices, it may be forced to centralize its personnel functions in order to insure consistent compliance with the law. Such pressures create the need for consistency, and the easiest mechanism for insuring consistency is to centralize.

COMPARISON OF COMPETITIVE MARKETS AND SOVIET-TYPE ECONOMIES

Up to this point, the discussion of centralization and decentralization has been described in terms of: (1) the structures, (2) delegation, (3) technical issues such as transfer pricing, and (4) markets. There is another literature of centralization and decentralization in the

field of economics in which a purely competitive (fully decentralized) economy is compared
to a purely socialistic (fully centralized)
economy. No one pretends that either extreme
actually exists, but it is instructive to compare these extremes. The comparison demonstrates how the issues of centralization and
decentralization can be extended from pairs of
persons to whole economies. The description of
a Soviet-type economy (as it existed in the
late 1950s) requires elementary knowledge of
input-output analysis (Leontief, 1953). But
once we have this, we can demonstrate how an
enormous buroid for economic planning is actually functioning as a large computer. This
comparison of a competitive and a Soviet-type
economy is useful in extending our understanding of both the issues of centralization and
decentralization and those of bureaucracy
(chapter 5). We begin by first describing elementary input-output analysis. We then examine
how a Soviet-type economy solves this problem.
This is then contrasted with a purely competitive economy.[3]

INPUT-OUTPUT ANALYSIS

W. Leontief (1936, 1941, 1951, 1953) presented
and elaborated a system of analysis to take
account of general equilibrium phenomena in
the empirical analysis of production for an
economy. The basic method is called input-output analysis. In the open model, demand theory
plays no role. The problem and analysis are
technological. Input-output analysis "seeks to
determine what can be produced, and the quantity of each intermediate product which must
be used up in the production process, given the
quantities of available resources and the
state of technology" (Baumol, 1972, p. 503).
    The following assumptions are made in input-
output analysis: (1) an economy consists of a
number, n, of interacting industries; (2) each
industry produces a single good and uses only

one process of production to make this good;
(3) in order to produce its good, a given industry needs as inputs goods made by other industries, labor, and perhaps external goods
(such as imports); (4) each industry must produce enough to supply needs of other industries
and to meet external demand (consumers, exports, etc.); and (5) the required input of any
factor is directly proportional to the level of
production.

If there are n industries, let y_{ij} be the
amount of good i needed by industry j, let b_i
be the exogenous demand for good i (i.e., consumers and exports), and let x_i be the amount
industry i must produce exactly to meet its
demands. Then, assumptions 1, 2, 3, and 4 result in:

$$x_i = \sum_{j=1}^{n} y_{ij} + b_i \quad \text{for every industry,} \quad (6.1)$$

and assumption 5 means that:

$$y_{ij} = a_{ij}x_j \quad \text{for all } i \text{ and } j, \quad (6.2)$$

where a_{ij} are a technical coefficient for the
amount of inputs from industry j to produce one
dollar's worth of the output for industry i.
The a_{ij} are assumed to be constant. Substitut-
ing equation (6.2) into (6.1), one obtains:

$$x_i = \sum_{j=1}^{n} a_{ij}x_j + b_i \quad \text{for each industry.} \quad (6.3)$$

Because there are n industries and n unknowns,
and the a_{ij} and the b_i are known, the problem
of determining the n values of the x_i is to
solve n linear equations in n unknowns. Procedures from linear algebra are used to solve
this system of equations.

Mathematically, if A is an n by n table of
technical coefficients, b is a vector of the n
values of b_i, and X is a vector of the n values
for the x_i, then:

$$X = (I - A)^{-1} \tag{6.4}$$

where I is the identity matrix and $(I-A)^{-1}$ is the inverse matrix of $I - A$. Waugh (1950) showed that, under reasonable conditions, the values of X can be solved by a simple series of expansion or:

$$X = b + Ab + A^2 b + \ldots \tag{6.5}$$

where $A^2 = A \cdot A$, and so on.

The result by Waugh greatly simplifies the computational problem of solving equation (6.4) for the n values of X. Equation (6.5) also provides an interesting interpretation of an input-output system. Consider an economy with just a coal and a steel industry. Let b_1 and b_2 be the consumer demand for coal and steel respectively. The matrix of technical coefficients, A, is:

		Purchasing industry	
		Coal	Steel
Producing industry	Coal	a_{11}	a_{12}
	Steel	a_{21}	a_{22}

The first term of equation (6.5) is $\binom{b_1}{b_2}$ which is the amount of coal, b_1, and the amount of steel, b_2, needed by consumers. The second term of equation (6.5) is:

$$= \begin{pmatrix} a_{11} & a_{12} \\ a_{21} & a_{22} \end{pmatrix} \begin{pmatrix} b_1 \\ b_2 \end{pmatrix} = \begin{pmatrix} a_{11}\, b_1 + a_{12} b_2 \\ a_{21}\, b_1 + a_{22} b_2 \end{pmatrix}$$

The term $a_{11} b_1$ is the amount of coal needed to produce b_1 units of coal. The term $a_{12} b_2$ is the amount of coal needed to produce b_2 units of steel. Hence the first row of Ab is the amount of coal needed to produce b_1 units of coal and b_2 units of steel. This term reflects the fact that it takes coal to produce coal and coal to produce steel. The second-row terms have similar interpretations: the term $a_{21}b_1$ is the amount of steel required to produce b_1 units of coal and $a_{22}b_2$ is the amount of steel required to produce b_2 units of steel. So up to this point, we have needed:

$$d_1 = a_{11}b_1 + a_{12}b_2$$

units of coal to produce b_1 units of coal and b_2 units of steel. Similarly we need:

$$d_2 = a_{21}b_1 + a_{22}b_2$$

units of steel to produce b_1 units of coal and b_2 units of steel. But it takes coal and steel to produce d_1 and d_2 units of coal and d_2 units of steel. The third term of equation (6.4) is:

$$A^2b = A \cdot d = \begin{pmatrix} a_{11} & a_{12} \\ a_{21} & a_{22} \end{pmatrix} \begin{pmatrix} d_1 \\ d_2 \end{pmatrix} = \begin{pmatrix} e_1 \\ e_2 \end{pmatrix}$$

This type of reasoning extends to needing coal and e_1 units of coal to produce d_1 and d_2 units of coal and steel and e_2 units of steel to produce d_1 and d_2 units of coal and steel. But, under normal conditions,[4] each successive term becomes smaller and smaller. At this stage we have needed $b_1 + d_1 + e_1$ units of coal to produce b_1 units of coal and b_2 units of steel and $b_2 + d_2 + e_2$ units of steel to produce b_1 units of coal and b_2 units of steel. But actually we need more coal and steel to produce e_1 and e_2 units of coal and steel, and so on.

There are numerous nasty problems in defining the quantities in b and A, and picking the set of n industries. A modern economy is highly interrelated and there are difficulties in defining a product and an industry, handling imports and exports, changing inventory levels, and defining the boundary of an economy. These topics are far beyond the scope of this chapter, but one can find an elementary discussion in Miernyk (1966) and more technical discussions in Fisher (1958), Evans and Hoffenberg (1952), Tiebout (1962), and Florence (1948).

SOVIET-TYPE ECONOMIES

The famous article by J. M. Montias (1959) described the economic planning problem faced by the U.S.S.R. in the mid-1950s. The problem was how to solve Equation (6.4) for the levels of production of each industry in the U.S.S.R. in the absence of markets and a flexible price system as we understand them in a capitalistic society. Although there is no evidence that the Soviets saw their problem in terms of input-output analysis, their procedure is consistent with the series expansion described in Equation (6.5).

The Soviets' general plan is called GOSPLAN and uses a Council of Ministers responsible for economic planning. Under the Council of Ministers is the Planning Commission, whose job is to prepare preliminary balances of essential materials. They examine latest production figures, forecasts of productive capacity, and the labor force. The total production is broken down into categories and sent to the subordinate Industrial Ministries (Glavki). The Industrial Ministries then send specific production targets to their subordinate enterprises who do the actual production. This first set of specific production targets corresponds to our term b in Equation (6.5). Given their target, b, the subordinate enterprises then send estimates of material inputs required to hit the cited production targets. This round corresponds to the term $A.b$ in Equation (6.5). These are sent to the Industrial Ministries, who then consolidate the requirements, which are then sent to the Planning Commission. There, care is

taken to see that total inputs equal total outputs (after allowing for changes in productive
capacity and inventories). The planning commission then sends this to the Industrial
Ministries, who then send more detail production plans to the subordinate enterprises. This
iteration corresponds to A^2b in Equation (6.5).
The iteration process continues.

While there are more efficient methods for
inverting $(I - A)$ (for example, they could
start with total volume of finished product
and then work backwards to raw materials), it
is interesting that the elaborate planning
apparatus and its planning iterations could be
viewed in terms of solving Equation (6.5). The
system has numerous problems, such as checking
the production assumptions, estimating all
of the technical coefficients, and determining
the y_{ij}. But the system is flexible because
it allows humans to intervene to change coefficients, examine possible bottlenecks, set
and change economic priorities, and decide
how much of the production should go to consumers. An example of a bottleneck is the lack
of pipes for oil pipelines should they decide
to increase the production of crude oil. At
first glance, this system for planning appears
cumbersome and inefficient. The U.S. went into
a similar system in order to mobilize and arm
itself for World War II. As there was not much
of a domestic market for tanks, 8-inch guns,
machine guns (except maybe in Chicago), sub-
marines, aircraft carriers, and so on, the U.S.
Government felt that it had to intervene to
shift the consumer-oriented economy to a war-
time basis.

There are a number of obstacles to this type
of economic planning because of problems of
transmitting all data, and errors in fulfill-
ing the plan. The system is so complex that
it is vulnerable to unrealsitic technical
norms, obsolescence by technological innovation, difficulties in aggregating allowances
for repairs and maintenance, and frequently
changing specifications of products.

The system is also vulnerable to changes in demand, time lags during which all of the calculations are made, failure of producers to notify consumers of production breakdowns which cause postponed deliveries, and thence production delays. The system lacks the simple incentives of profit maximization and can be upset by changing priorities. New factories, scheduled for completion during the planning period, may not get completed in time to meet their scheduled quotas. The problems with such a system are clear but the system is saved, in part, by large inventories that buffer production problems.

A simple example is a shoe factory that uses leather for its shoes. A technical norm could be written in terms of the amount of shoe leather the plant must use in manufacturing its quota of shoes, as measured by the total amount of leather used. There are running shoes, dancing shoes, street shoes, work shoes, ladies' shoes, children's shoes, bicycling shoes, hiking boots, ski boots, and so on. To control production, a plan might specify how the shoe leather is to be divided among these various types of shoes. Suppose that a plant is to produce street shoes. A smart manager might produce only size 14 shoes. This way it could meet the production quota easily for the total amount of shoe leather required. To guard against such decisions, there would have to be further details on the production norms for the shoe factory. It is doubtful that any specification of detail production norms could ever prevent some smart plant manager from finding some way to meet his quotas by a socially silly plan of production. If the plant manager is rewarded for meeting his quotas and not for efficiency, such absurd production as all size 14 shoes is not at all unlikely. In fact, the Soviet newspaper *Pravda* often contains stories like the factory with only size 14 shoes. The author remembers seeing a cartoon of a nail factory that made a nail as long as the factory. The manager met his total tonnage of nail

production efficiently by making one giant
nail. The plant managers do not have to sell
their shoes or nails because the production has
already been allocated according to the plan.

COMPETITIVE ECONOMIES

The owner of the shoe factory in a competitive
economy relies on a price system to make his
production decisions. If he made too many size
14 shoes and no size 8 shoes, the price of
size 14 shoes would tend to decrease and the
price of the size 8 shoes would tend to increase. In his attempt to maximize his profits,
the entrepreneur running the shoe factory would
have an incentive to reduce the production of
size 14 shoes and increase the production of
size 8 shoes. But if he made no size 9 or 10
shoes, he might be forced to alter production
to take advantage of the rise in the prices of
these sizes.

Ideally, in a competitive society there is a
central agency, but it is called a *market* rather
than a planning commission. The market trans-
mits information about prices to the entrepreneur. Given the factor input and product
prices, the entrepreneur adjusts his production
to increase his profits. The production enters
the market in the form of increased supply.
The market reacts and a new price is established. The entrepreneur then adjusts his production, the market adjusts its prices, and so
on.

Marschak (1965) and Hurwicz (1960) have shown
that in terms of what we in the West would consider reasonable social welfare functions (such
as Pareto optimality)[5], the competitive economy
is more efficient than a Soviet-type economy.
But a competitive economy may take longer to
reach equilibrium prices and production. The
relative advantages are also dependent upon the
computational efficiency of the planning system. It is not inconceivable to consider a number of possible scenarios whereby the Soviet-
type economy could be more efficient than a

economy. But right now, in terms of output per worker, competitive societies are more productive.

The main advantage of a competitive society is that it has much lower requirements for technical information than the Soviet-type society. Each housewife, plant manager, and so forth, performs these calculations rather than some central planning agency. Housewives and managers all compute simultaneously in terms of their net utility and profits. Information autonomy is permitted managers. There is no need to compute all of the technical coefficients and then transmit them to some higher level. The market, acting as the central agency, need only be concerned with total excess demands for each commodity; it does not need to know the demands and supplies of the individual plant manager. And whenever the central agency (the market) communicates with managers, it need only announce a vector of prices.

However, such a system can produce "bads" as well as "goods." Does society really need 6,000-pound automobiles? Do we really need all varieties of pornography? Handguns? How you feel about these questions defines your social welfare function. Within broad limits, many would rather make these decisions for themselves. Others, with perhaps more wisdom (and certainly more hubris), feel that they should make such decisions for us. This debate is at least 45 years old and involves all of the issues raised in this chapter about the relative advantages and disadvantages of centralization and decentralization, plus explicit assumptions about what one feels is a suitable welfare function.

ACTUAL ECONOMIES

One of the themes of this chapter is that most well-run firms are neither fully centralized nor fully decentralized. Most fall in between in an attempt to balance advantages and disadvantages. It should come as no surprise, then, to observe that modern competitive societies exist within a framework of laws and regulations and that modern socialist societies have sizeable competitive sectors. Both systems adjust. Both Adam Smith and Karl Marx would scarcely recognize the United Kingdom or the U.S.S.R. if they could see them today. The United Kingdom has nationalized several industries. Canada, for example, has numerous "Crown Corporations" that are competitive firms running under direct control of the government. In the U.S.A., most public utilities are regulated as local monopolies. The number of private enterprises in communist Yugoslavia and in sections of the U.S.S.R. is substantial.

STRATEGIES TO AVOID DECENTRALIZING

One of the main reasons for decentralizing is to avoid information overload. Meier (1965) and Churchill (1965) discuss a number of ways of cutting down on the amount of information to be processed:

1. Storing incoming requests in order of their arrival. This creates a waiting line or queue. But persons do not like being placed in a queue and some persons and some requests are more important than others. The judgment of the relative importance of difference types of incoming requests may be political as well as strictly functional. These problems lead to:
2. The setting of priorities for requests in the queue. For example, in a hospital, emergency cases or illnesses of very important persons, such as a donor who serves on the hospital's board of directors, will take precedence over nonemergency cases or those low in influence. Minor injuries and those with postponable treatment needs can be given low priority. The high priority requests

get treated first. In a sense, if one
thinks of a queue in terms of lining up at
a ticket office, high priority requests
move to the front of the line. But as the
queue continues to grow, some of the requests will have to be ignored. This leads
to:

3. Eliminating the lowest priority requests.
   This is done by never giving attention to
   such requests or promulgating rules and
   regulations to discourage lowest priority
   requests from ever occurring. This can help
   for a while, but the pressure from requests
   can continue to increase. There are different types of requests and there are variations in the request rate for the different
   types. Taking advantages of these variations results in:

4. Setting up special files to take advantage
   of redundancy of the type of request. A
   frequently recurring request can be given
   special treatment in the queue and a system
   can be created to handle it efficiently. For
   example, some hospitals maintain special
   sections for different types of cases such
   as pediatrics and intensive care units.
   Libraries can handle surges in demand by
   students for popular textbooks by creating
   special reserve rooms. But, if this works
   for a while, as demand continues to climb
   the central location can become overloaded.
   This leads to the next strategies:

5. Creating special branch facilities. Branch
   facilities are generally located to take
   advantage of geographical clustering of
   those with special requests. For example,
   the branch libraries for the engineering,
   business, and psychology faculties place
   these collections closer to the users.
   Branch facilities reduce the opportunity
   costs (in terms of time) for the users as
   well as siphoning off the demands placed on
   the central office. This strategy helps reduce overloading but often, despite valiant

efforts, it does not eliminate the problem.
A next step is for some entrepreneur to
step in by offering special services. Thus,
we come to the sixth strategy of:
6. Admitting middlemen into the system. One
   must remember that one's organization is
   likely to be experiencing overloading problems that are shared by other organizations.
   Middlemen can enter to offer services that
   reduce the overload to the organization and
   reduce costs to both the users and the organization. Middlemen abound in computing
   and clerical services. Middlemen help, but
   backlogs occur and are not distributed
   equally throughout the organization. One way
   of coping with the unequal backlogs is:
7. Creating a mobile reserve. Mobile reserves
   are special task forces that can be assembled on a temporary basis for handling backlogs or anticipated surges in requests. For
   example, sales staffs are beefed up for
   special sales. Fire and police departments
   man special emergency units as a mobile reserve. Sometimes corporate staff groups such
   as legal services, management science
   groups, and research and development groups
   act as a functioning mobile reserve. Mobile
   reserves can be plugged into gaps, but if
   pressures continue to increase, they can
   help but they cannot overcome a poorly designed system. The system can learn to
   begin:
8. Tolerating defects and simplified procedures. Much of the time taken in existing
   procedures is economically wasteful because
   the direct money and time costs of having
   the system work perfectly exceed the estimated costs if some reasonable errors could
   be allowed to happen by simplifying the system. By studying current procedures, one
   can often find ways of simplifying them.
   However, these simplifications often mean
   that some defects will occur in the system.
   One example occurs in university promotion

systems in which research and publishing
are mistakenly equated and the measure of
quality of one's research is equated with
the quantity of work published. Every party
to such discussions knows that the system
is illogical, but most feel that while it
is overly simplified, it at least is a good
surrogate. The next stage in the overload
problem is to:

9. Reduce standards of performance. The rules
   for maintaining performance standards get
   relaxed and even ignored. The game of managing is almost lost when this type of
   strategy is followed. The organization begins to unravel. The interdependent members,
   depending upon the proper performance by
   others, can no longer do so. Errors creep
   in and seem to accelerate in number. By
   the time this stage is reached, the organization is ready for a miracle worker. Miracle workers often have some magic formula
   to offer as a remedy. Thus, we enter stage
   10 in which the organization searches for
   some magic formula to solve the problem.
   The failure of the American Stock Exchange
   to meet the excess demands in early 1959
   brought out the magic cure of using computers for the branch office record-keeping
   and clerical jobs at brokerage firms. Sometimes the magic formula consists of scape-
   goating ethnic or managerial groups. Magic
   formulae seldom work and the organization is
   left with mounting overloading. Often the
   only hope is:

10. Escaping. Because, by this point, those
    within the system are convinced that they
    cannot cope with it any longer, they begin
    to resign. Sometimes the escape takes the
    form of bankruptcy, giving up on key litiga-
    tion, not fighting attempts to take over
    the organization. Another form of escape is
    to blur the boundary between employees and
    clients. Customers wanting service have to

serve themselves and may even have to help the organization provide the service. But sometimes escape is made impossible by legal, moral, and financial reasons. The strategy, then, is to:

11. Hang on and follow the rules. Breaking the rules is more risky than following them. For if one obeys the rules, no matter how silly, it is the rule-makers who are to blame rather than those who follow the rules. When one breaks the rules, one is always liable to severe sanctions. It takes optimism and some faith in the future to knowingly break rules. It is easier, when one has lost hope, to hang in there by following the rules in a hope that the problems will cure themselves. It is hard for a large buroid to break down completely. Parts of it manage to function. One reason to hang on is that when the organization is collapsing, one can still benefit from attempts at:

12. Salvaging the component parts of the organization. The larger organizations may become subdivided into new smaller organizations. Parts may be disbanded and other parts may become absorbed into other organizations. Those hanging on can often find tenure after the reorganization, if they have "kept their noses clean" by following the rules.

One possibility that can prevent final collapse is that as the overload increases, the quality of service begins to deteriorate. If alternatives for getting these services exist for the clients and customers, they can shift their requests to other organizations. They can even form new organizations to obtain the services. These alternatives cut down the demand and can soften the overloading by diverting requests to other organizations.

Another possibility is to cut demand by

raising the price of having a service provided. As the price increases, the amount of service requested at that price will tend to decline. This decline in demand reduces the overloading and can help the organization survive. As we pointed out in chapter 8, the inability to cope with problems is often a powerful weapon to extract more resources out of a ruling body. In fact, one of the strongest forces for obtaining more resources is demonstrated failure to complete the job with existing resources.

Many organizations create temporary organizations such as task forces and committees to handle novel problems (see chapter 2). These temporary organizations are formed to answer a specific need and they sometimes disband when the needs have been met. Swinth (1971), in his paper on complex novel problem-solving discusses procedures for forming temporary organizations to solve such problems. These temporary organizations allow discussion of problem and policy to take place while the rest of the organization is functioning. This not only reduces the organization disruptions caused by a new problem, but it also is a way of maintaining the present system.

Another procedure, used in the United Kingdom, is called "hiving-off." When a ministry becomes too complex and its operations too cumbersome, some of its functions can be "hived off" to private sectors or to other ministries. The same procedures are seen in the U.S.A. when companies shed subsidiaries or reduce the range of products to a more easily managed number.

NOTES

[1]Tuggle (1978, chapter 2) discusses goals and how goals are formed. Pfeffer (1978) points out that different coalitions within an organization have different goals. The problem of achieving goals is probably less important than deciding which goals are to be served.

[2]This point is made repeatedly by Pfeffer (1978) in his analysis of organizational design.

[3]The reader can skip the next section and still get the main ideas of how a capitalistic and a Soviet-type economy illustrate extremes of decentralization and centralization in their pure forms.

[4]Technically, $\lim_{k \to \infty} A^k = 0$.

[5]The distribution of consumer goods is Pareto efficient if every possible reallocation of goods among consumers results in the reduction of the satisfaction of at least one consumer.

REFERENCES

Baumol, W. J. *Economic Theory and Operations Analysis.* 3d ed. Englewood Cliffs, N.J.: Prentice-Hall, 1972.

Beauchamp, M. A. "An Improved Index of Centrality." *Behavioral Science* 10 (1965): 161-63.

Bernhard, R. H. "Some Problems in Applying Mathematical Programming to Opportunity Costing." *Journal of Accounting Research*, Spring 1968, pp. 143-48.

Bernhardt, I., and Mackenzie, K. D. "Measuring Seller Unconcentration, Segmentation, and Product Differentiation." *Western Economic Journal* 6 (1968): 395-403.

Berge, C. *The Theory of Graphs and Its Applications.* London: Methuen, 1962.

Bierman, H., Jr. "Pricing Intercompany Transfers." *The Accounting Review*, July 1959, pp. 429-32.

Churchill, L. "Some Sociological Aspects of Message Load: 'Information Input Overload and Features of Growth in Communications-Oriented Institutions.'" In *Mathematical Explorations in Behavioral Science*, edited by Masserik and Ratoosh, pp. 274-84. Homewood, Ill.: Irwin, 1965.

Evans, W. D., and Hoffenberg, M. "The Interindustry

Relations Study for 1947." *The Review of Economics and Statistics* 36 (1952): 97–142.

Fisher, W. D. "Criteria for Aggregation in Input–Output Analysis." *The Review of Economics and Statistics* 40 (1958): 250–60.

Florence, P. S. *Investment Location and Size of Plant.* Cambridge, U.K.: University Press, 1948.

Goetz, B. "Transfer Prices: An Exercise in Relevancy and Goal Congruence." *The Accounting Review*, July 1967, pp. 435–40.

Gould, J. R. "Internal Pricing in Firms When There Are Costs of Using an Outside Market." *The Journal of Business* 37 (1964): 61–67.

Harary, F.; Norman, R. Z.; and Cartwright, D. *Structural Models: An Introduction to the Theory of Directed Graphs.* New York: Wiley, 1965.

Henderson, J. M., and Quandt, R. D. *Microeconomic Theory: A Mathematical Approach.* New York: McGraw-Hill, 1958.

Hirshleifer, J. "On the Economics of Transfer Pricing." *The Journal of Business* 29 (1956): 172–84.

_____. "Economics of the Divisionalized Firm." *The Journal of Business* 30 (1957): 96–108.

_____. "Internal Pricing and Decentralized Decisions." In *Contemporary Cost Accounting and Control*, edited by G. J. Benston. Belmont, Calif.: Dickenson Pub., 1970.

Hurwicz, L. "Optimality and Informational Efficiency in Resource Allocation Processes." In *Mathematical Methods in the Social Sciences*, edited by Arrow, Karlin, and Suppes, pp. 27–46. Stanford, Calif.: Stanford University Press, 1960.

Leavitt, H. "Some Effects of Certain Communication Patterns on Group Performance." *Journal of Abnormal and Social Psychology* 46 (1951): 38–50.

Leontief, W. W. "Quantitative Input–Output Relations in the Economic System of the United States." *The Review of Economics and Statistics* 18 (1936): 105–25.

_____. *The Structure of American Economy, 1919-1929.* New York: Oxford University Press, 1941.

_____. *The Structure of American Economy, 1919-1939.* 2nd ed. New York: Oxford University Press, 1951.

Leontief, W. W. et al. *Studies in the Structure of the American Economy.* New York: Oxford University Press, 1953.

Lewin, A. Y., and Tapiero, C. S. "The Concept and Measurement of Centrality—An Information Approach." *Decision Sciences* 4 (1973): 314-28.

Mackenzie, K. D. "Structural Centrality in Communications Networks." *Psychometrika* 31 (1966): 17-25.

_____. "Decomposition of Communication Networks." *Journal of Mathematical Psychology* 4 (1967): 162-72.

_____. *A Theory of Group Structures, Volume I: Basic Theory.* New York: Gordon and Breach Science Pub., 1976a.

_____. *A Theory of Group Structures, Volume II: Empirical Tests.* New York: Gordon and Breach Science Pubs., 1976b.

Marschak, T. A. "Economic Theories of Organization." In *Handbook of Organizations*, edited by J. G. March, pp. 423-50. Chicago: Rand McNally, 1965.

Meier, R. L. "Information Input Overload: Features of Growth in Communications-Oriented Institutions." In *Mathematical Explorations in Behavioral Science*, edited by Masserik and Ratoosh, pp. 233-73. Homewood, Ill.: Irwin, 1965.

Miernyk, W. H. *The Elements of Input-Output Analysis.* New York: Random House, 1966.

Miner, J. B. *Studies in Managerial Education.* New York: Springer, 1965.

_____. "The Managerial Motivation of School Administrators." University Council for *Education Administration Quarterly*, Winter 1968, pp. 57-72.

_____. "Personality Tests as Predictors of Consulting

Success." *Personnel Psychology* 24 (1971): 191–204.

_____. "Motivation to Manage Among Women: Studies of Business Managers and Educational Administrators." *Journal of Vocational Behavior* 5 (1974): 197–208.

Montias, J. M. "Planning with Material Balances in Soviet-Type Economies." *American Economic Review* 49 (1959): 963–85.

Morris, W. T. *Decentralization in Management Systems: An Introduction to Design*. Columbus: Ohio State University Press, 1968.

Pfeffer, J. *Organizational Design*. Arlington Heights, Ill.: AHM Publishing Corporation, 1978.

Rizzo, J. R.; Miner, J. B.; Harlow, D. N., and Hill, J. W. "Role Motivation Theory of Managerial Effectiveness in a Simulated Organization of Varying Degrees of Structure." *Journal of Applied Psychology* 60 (1974): 31–37.

Sabidussi, G. "The Centrality Index of a Graph." *Psychometrika* 31 (1966): 581–603.

Samuels, J. M. "Opportunity Costing: An Application of Mathematical Programming." *Journal of Accounting Research*, Autumn 1965, pp. 182–91.

Simmons, R. E. *Managing Behavioral Processes: Applications of Theory and Research*. Arlington Heights, Ill.: AHM Publishing Corporation, 1978.

Swinth, R. L. "Organizational Joint Problem Solving." *Management Science* 18 (1971): B-68—B-79.

Tiebout, C. M. *The Community Economic Base Study*. Committee for Economic Development, 1962.

Tuggle, F. D. *Organizational Processes*. Arlington Heights, Ill.: AHM Publishing Corporation, 1978.

Waugh, F. V. "Inversion of the Leontief Matrix by Power Series." *Econometrica* 18 (1950): 142–54.

Evolution of Organizational Structures

7

The first six chapters have stressed numerous
theoretical concepts and theories about organizational structures and their application
to a number of managerial problems. The new
ideas in these chapters permit one to look at
the development of organizational structures
in terms of the problems, structures, and task
processes of the organization. This chapter is
both a summary of the first six and an attempt
to extend these ideas to the evolution of organizational structures from the simple line
organization to more modern organizational
forms.

SUMMING UP THE BASIC THEORY

STRUCTURES, TASK PROCESSES, ROLE MATRICES, AND HIERARCHY

An organization is made up of individuals with
varying needs. Some of these needs are met

while they behave in an organization. They are
difficult to define, hard to measure, and contingent upon what happens on and off the job.
Jabes (1978) presents an excellent discussion
of motivation, and Simmons (1978, chapter 3)
analyzes many problems in applying these ideas
to organizations. Consequently, this book has
made no attempt to present a theory of motivation. Instead, it starts with the assumptions
that needs exist, that they are important, and
that persons will interact in order to further
the satisfaction of these needs. Group and organizational structures are need-satisfying
patterns of interaction. Results from laboratory experiments consistent with this basic
proposition are reported in chapters 2, 3, and
4. These experiments established that preference for channels over which to interact and
for different types of structures involve
monetary, time, and social needs.

Formally, a group structure is defined by
the expression $S = (X_n; R)$ where X_n is the list
of participants in the organization and R is
the table of interactions between all possible
pairs of participants. The choice of X_n and the
entries in R depend upon the purposes for
studying an organizational structure, the
methodology for making the study, and the theory one is using. Most groups have more than
one structure. This fact has far-ranging consequences in the study of organizational structures. Organizations can have different structures for different organizational task processes and different organizational structures
for different phases of a given task process.

Each task process describes the sequence of
steps taken by the members of a group in order
to solve some specific problem. In the theory,
there is a logic to solving group problems. A
group problem defines a set of problem stages
which are called group milestones. These milestones can be ordered in terms of logical precedence. Whenever a group interacts to solve a
problem, its progress defines a movement

through these milestones. This movement or trajectory describes the task process of the group as they solve the group problem.

Groups learn how to reach the milestones, to relate them logically, to organize their problem-solving by discovering the sequence of milestones, and to correct deviations from that sequence. In short, with experience the group develops its task processes. An important part of this learning is setting up structures to facilitate the fulfillment of member needs while completing the solutions to the group problem. The development of group structures occurs at the same time the group increases its understanding of how to solve a problem. Thus, the group's structures and task processes develop together. Accordingly, although one can separate, for analytical purposes, the development of structures and task processes, the two actually interact and overlap.

Groups and organizations work on more than one kind of problem. For each organizational problem there are milestones, structures, and task processes. Different subgroups can work on different organizational problems, with some members working on more than one. For example, most organizations have persons working on production processes, personnel processes, governance processes, administrative processes, accounting and data processes, maintenance processes, marketing processes, and so on. These processes vary in importance for different organizations and suborganizations. The more vital the process is considered, the higher the rank of the person who is engaged in overseeing that process. Organizations are at least partially hierarchical in their authority structure. However, many of the task processes cut across the hierarchical lines of authority because different parts of the organization are involved. One example concerns the accounting and bookkeeping functions; another deals with those production processes involving scheduling. If a firm has organized its production processes according to type of product or technical production process, the processes of production will affect and be affected by marketing, accounting, and financial processes, among others. Thus, when one expands the ideas of this book from little laboratory groups to larger organizations, the key facts of life involve the existence of numerous processes and the crisscrossing of the task-process structures.

It is possible to examine a person in terms of his position or level in a task process, his position on a variety of task processes, and how these task processes are ordered for the whole organization. What Simmons (1978, chapter 2) calls an operative, and what we call a worker, is an individual who is at the lowest level of a hierarchy for a single task process. The supervisor's supervisor may be involved at different levels in a number of task processes. Theoretically, the chief executive is at the top level in each of the task-process hierarchies. If the highest-level person who actually does the work in a task-process hierarchy has relatively low organizational rank, that task process is also ranked relatively low by the organization. Conversely, if the person at the highest level of a specific task-process hierarchy has high rank, then that task process is relatively very important to the organization. Thus, one's organizational rank in an authority hierarchy is a surrogate for the relative ranking of the organization's task processes.

This extension from a group performing one or two task processes to an organization performing a number of task processes has a number of useful applications. It can account for the fact that even those on a low level in the authority hierarchy can feel important. Such persons can be on the top level for a relatively low-ranked process. Examining what persons at different levels do provides immediate clues about which duties the organization considers important. For example, not very long ago the chief officer for academic affairs, often called a vice chancellor, was just below the university's chancellor and was involved in numerous task processes (teaching, research, academic policy, goal-setting, recruitment of faculty and students, etc.). Today, with larger budgets and increasing vulnerability to changes in budgets, the academic vice chancellor has a number of colleagues on the same hierarchical level and is often below an executive vice chancellor. There may be more than one executive vice chancellor who works for the chancellor. The office of academic vice chancellor has been downgraded in many universities. Thus, the changes in the administrative structures yield direct evidence of the changing rank order of functions to the vitality of an organization. The upgrading and downgrading of the authority level of each task-process head receives careful scrutiny in the organization. For one thing, members in a task-process hierarchy rise and fall organizationally with the upgrading and downgrading of the authority or rank position of the top person in their task authority. This idea of multiple hierarchies and how they crisscross the organization can also be used to describe why executives on different levels have different types of responsibility. The higher levels involve a greater variety of task processes and often, because there are more task processes, the executive at a higher authority level is less involved in terms of how he allocates his time to each task process than an executive at a lower level. A lower-level executive spreads his time over a smaller number of task processes. Presumably, the "big picture" that so many refer to when describing the higher authority positions is a way of saying that more task processes, and hence more connections across task processes, are involved in the higher levels of an organization.

Now let us return to the theoretical description of the theories on group structure. This

description involves a much more limited range
of task processes than one would expect to
find operating in a larger organization. However, the theories can be applied to the more
extensive case. Attempts to study the entire
organization without a reasonable theory for
how the parts operate have not been very successful. There are too many persons, processes, and issues to comprehend. The result is
usage of summary data such as number of workers, data from questionnaires from a sample of
persons, and amount of sales. Lost are the
task processes, the way in which the task processes are performed, the relationships between persons and task processes, and any real
understanding of how the organization functions. Weick (1974) has argued that the best
way to develop a theory of organizations is
not to study organizations. However, once one
has a useful and reasonably comprehensive theory to apply, the process of studying organizations is greatly simplified. If one knows what
one is looking for, how to look at it, and how
to relate what one finds, one is more likely
to find out what one is looking for and more
likely to understand what is found.

In his youth the author was an amateur but
enthusiastic collector of reptiles and insects.
I found that when I knew the habits of the
various creatures and how they fit into their
environment, I was more successful in finding
them. I could go out to a farm or a stream
where no one had ever found a snake and come
back with twenty of them in just one morning.
I could locate and capture rare species more
easily because of knowing where to look and
what to look for. I also used the proper equipment. Similarly, when one has a coherent view
of organizational structures and task processes and when one has the right tools, it is much
easier to locate, capture, and use information
about organizations. It is also easier to detect and to analyze trends. Thus, while it is
obvious that what is learned from little groups

is not always the same as what one expects to
find in larger organizations, it is also reasonable to expect to find out more about organizations if one fully understands the laws
governing their component parts. So, let us
return to the theory.

A problem defines the types of milestones.
Persons interact in order to reach milestones.
For each group milestone, there is a corresponding group-milestone structure. The task
process, which describes how and in what succession these group milestones are met, defines behavior as being timely, redundant, and
untimely with respect to the reaching of the
group milestones. Task processes are used to
calculate problem-solving efficiency and numerous performance measures. The task processes,
combined with the milestone structures, define
the group's role matrices. Just as there are
timely, redundant, and untimely behaviors,
there are also timely, redundant, and untimely
role matrices. For this book, the redundant
and untimely role matrices are combined and
called the untimely role matrix. Thus, the
timely group role matrix and the combined untimely group role matrix are used to describe
the group's structures and task processes.

The reader will recall from chapter 1 that a
role matrix is a table whose rows represent
the participants and whose columns represent
the activities performed by the participants.
Originally, the role matrix is just a useful
way of rewriting and displaying the information
contained in the group-milestone structures.
But it is then rearranged, compacted, and re-
examined to yield more information about the
group. One can determine the organizational
levels of each member of the group by examining
the timely role matrix. This information is
used to rearrange the role matrix in order to
place the members in descending order to the
person or persons on level one at the top of
this role matrix and persons on the lowest level at the bottom. Many of the half-channels are

not used and some of the possible group milestones are bypassed in the actual task process.
So one can squeeze or compact the original role
matrix into fewer columns. One can also examine the task processes to determine whether
or not a member takes responsibility for an
activity. A member, for example, can take responsibility for a set of activities, even
though he does not perform them himself.

When calculating the level of each person in
the task-process hierarchy, defined by the
timely role matrix, the main question is whether one person is the immediate superior,
immediate subordinate, on the same level, or un-
related to, every other person. A person is
the immediate superior to another if his set of
activities includes all those of an immediate
subordinate plus some in which the immediate
subordinate does not engage. The immediate
superior and immediate subordinate must also
interact about their common activities. The result of applying these ideas is a reordered
timely role matrix in which the role of each
person, represented by a row in the timely role
matrix, is ordered to reflect his level.

The immediate superior-subordinate relationship is only one of those possible. For members
on the same level, there are cousin relationships for interactions and overlapping of activities for members on the same level. Between
adjacent levels and for those not in an immediate superior-subordinate relationship,
there are uncle-nephew relationships. Uncle-
nephew relationships are caused by cousin relationships between the uncle and the immediate superior of the nephew.

Once one has the role matrix, the levels for
each person, the cousin and uncle-nephew relationships located in the timely role matrix,
one can easily construct diagrams such as
Figure 7.1 (in a later section) that show the
relationships and give the details about the
activities involved in each of these relationships. One can then calculate the number of

timely cousin and uncle-nephew relationships.
From the untimely role matrix one can obtain
the number of untimely and redundant behaviors.
These quantities (timely, T, cousin, C, uncle-nephew, U, and untimely and redundant, U_T) can
be used to calculate the degree of hierarchy.
   The degree of hierarchy, H, is defined in
chapter 1 as:

$$H = 1 - \frac{C + U + U_T}{T + U_T} \qquad (7.1)$$

This measure is strongly and positively correlated with the degree of task-process efficiency, E_T. The degree of hierarchy is also
significantly correlated with a number of performance measures. In fact, empirically, the
value of H is always less than or equal to the
value of E_T.
   H is unity when each milestone structure is
purely hierarchical, each milestone has the
same structure, and the task-process graph is a
pure chain. Any departures from a structural
hierarchy create uncle and cousin relationships. As the values of U and C become larger,
the value of H decreases. Similarly, any departures from a pure chain the task-process
graph mean that there are redundant and untimely behaviors. These are represented by U_T. The
greater the number of redundant and untimely
behaviors, the lower the value of H. Thus, a
group that is structurally hierarchical, as in
a pyramid of authority, can have low degrees of
hierarchy, H, if its task processes generate
large amounts of redundant and untimely behavior.
   Experimental groups act as if they seek to
increase their degree of hierarchy, H, when
they are asked to be efficient. They learn how
to solve the problems and thereby reduce the
number of redundant and untimely behaviors.
They also learn how to organize themselves to
reach the milestones and they do this by

cutting down on the number of cousin and uncle
relationships. Thus, with experience the term
$C + U + U_T$ tends toward zero, and as it does,
H tends toward unity. And, as H tends towards
unity, the groups are more efficient, spend
less time, make fewer errors, and send fewer
messages while they solve their problem. A
goal, then, of increasing the degree of hierarchy, H, operationally defines what the group
can do to increase its efficiency and perhaps
its effectiveness.

Each task process has its own milestones and
role matrices. One can calculate the levels of
each person and the degrees of hierarchy and
task-process efficiency for each milestone.
Large-scale complex organizations, called
buroids in chapter 5, may have many different
task processes occurring simulatensouly
throughout the organization. Operatives tend to
be restricted to one of these task processes
and executives are involved in more. Persons
can be described in terms of their levels within the subgroup engaged in each task process
and in terms of their level in the authority
hierarchy. An executive on the third level from
the top in the authority hierarchy could be
above the top level on some task processes, at
the top level on other task processes, and at
a lower level on still other task processes. If
resources are scarce and there is competition
for them, hierarchies will tend to form for
each task process and across task processes.

As pointed out in chapter 3, in the section
on committee formation, there are usually gaps
between the task-process system (as defined by
the various timely role matrices) and the authority-role system. A continuing problem, operationally and politically, for any organization is how to resolve problems falling into
this authority-task gap. This class of problems, called authority-task problems, has been
overlooked in most books on organizational decision-making. The explicit identification and
recognition of such problems is one of the

fruits of a more comprehensive model of organizational structures. Once recognized, the
existence of authority-task problems seem obvious. It may be stretching an analogy, but
the obvious existence of electricity, magne-
tism, nuclear radiation, and other well-known
phenomena was not recognized until very recently. Once recognized, scientists could study
them. It is still too early to tell, but it is
not unreasonable to posit that once authority-
task problems are explicitly recognized, organizational theorists will begin to study
work on methods to resolve them.

It is well within the realm of possibility
that there exist other gaps such as an *account-
ing-authority gap* that, when studied, could lead
to new ways of designing management information systems. There may be very different
structures for how the accountant records and
aggregates data and how the task-process or
authority-role system is set up. The existence
of such gaps can confuse a manager about how
to solve a problem arising from the accounting
system. What exactly should he do, for example,
when he learns that the cost of goods sold has
risen 15% in six months, but he neither has
the authority to address the problem nor is
even in the appropriate task-process hierarchy?
And, even if he is in a position to take action, his action to solve the problem could
upset other task processes. The problem could
be a direct effect of a change in accounting
procedures and not a problem of production.

STRUCTURAL CHANGE

A structure represents a need-satisfying interaction pattern. The structures of a group
change as the members adjust their behaviors
towards greater need satisfaction. Experiments
reported in chapters 2 and 3 demonstrate just
how these structural changes can occur. The
idea that organizational structures, like steel
bridges, are rigid and stable is simply

254 Organizational Structures

incorrect, except in rare and limiting cases.
It is possible to study the processes for how
a group goes about changing its structures.
Pfeffer (1978) organizes his analysis of organizational design about the the theme that
organizational changes result from the political processes engaged in by the members to increase or maintain personal influence. His
work, focusing on organizations as arenas for
influence attempts, analyzes structural changes
as the result of political processes.

This book, on the other hand, is more micro
in its orientation, especially for chapters 1
through 4. Consequently, the emphasis is on
discovering and defining structural change
processes in terms of the logic of influence
attempts. Each behavior is seen as an implicit
or explicit source of influence. Attempts to
influence are called *votes*. The votes are related to issues and to usage of half-channels
and entries in the timely role matrix. An
algebra for how such influence attempts are
processed by the group members has been developed and employed to analyze structural
change processes. This algebra, called a *behavioral constitution*, has proved useful in studying
structural change processes. The basic constitutional process begins with an *elected state*
(which could be the state of the role matrix
at the time the analyst takes his first look).
A vote to change one of these states places the
elected state into a *recall*. The votes are
processed according to voting rules which describe the outcome of a vote and a state. The
influence process when resolved, results in an
election process. These influence attempts are
seen as continuing processes and the number and
type of recalls, and the success at creating
or blocking changes, can be used to explain
and predict both the rate and timing of structural changes.

In the experiments reported in chapters 2
and 3, it is easy to compare the structure of
each group on its first problem with those at

the end of the voting processes. The final
adopted structure usually differs from the one
at the beginning. Thus, the changes and the no
changes in half-channels are highlighted. One
merely has to compare the pairs of structures.
There were recalls for the changes and there
may have been recalls for the no changes. The
initial recall for a change may have been defeated and then brought up again. There may
have been a succession of recall, voting, and
elections that ended up with no net change. It
is possible to reexamine each vote in light of
the final outcome and to classify each according to whether it was for or against the final
outcome. Votes that are consistent with the
final outcome are called favorable votes and
those that are inconsistent are unfavorable
votes. We know which person made each vote and
so we can calculate for each person the fraction of favorable and unfavorable votes per
unit time. These numbers are a surrogate index
of influence. The greater the fraction of a
person's favorable votes, the more successful
his influence attempts, all other factors being held constant. A person who votes and
loses on most issues is less influential in
his influence attempts.

Unfavorable votes always mean that a recall
was proposed and then defeated. While it may
have taken several elections, the fact that it
was unfavorable in the end means that it was
defeated. Favorable votes could result in a
final election in just one round. However, a
favorable outcome could result from a long
sequence of elections in which the final outcome is in serious doubt at least once. One
can examine the number of favorable and unfavorable votes per unit of time, which we
call favorable and unfavorable vote intensities. If the number of favorable votes is
large relative to the number of unfavorable
votes, there were fewer recalls and elections.
If the number of favorable votes is small
relative to the number of unfavorable votes,

there were more recalls and elections. It takes time to vote and have elections. Thus, one should expect to find that the larger the number of favorable votes relative to the number of unfavorable votes, the more rapidly a group adopted its structures. Data and results of a test of this data are consistent with the reasoning. Thus, at least under the conditions of the experiments, the rate of adoption of a group's structures can be explained in terms of the number and type of influence attempts made by the group's members.

The votes, type of problems, structural conditions, electoral states, and the capacity of a key person to handle the job could be combined in a decision model that allows one to predict the occurrence of structural changes on a later problem based upon knowledge of the group's processes on the previous problem. This function, called a *mapping function*, tells how to combine the crucial aspects of the group's processes in order to predict the outcomes of these processes.

Thus, it is possible to predict both the rates and occurrences of certain structural changes based upon knowledge of the task process, the type of problem, and the behavioral constitution. These ideas can be extended to more complex organizations. It is also possible that ideas such as these underlie, and could be used to define, how group members process those influence attempts which Pfeffer (1978) calls "political." The mapping function, although rather primitive as yet, is a prototype organizational model for combining the relevant aspects of a structural change situation.

Although little laboratory organizations can differ in many ways from large buroids, the fact that behavioral constitutions have been so useful in analyzing influence attempts to change structures in these experiments suggests that it might be possible to extend the idea of behavioral constitutions to buroidal structural change processes. Political influence processes may be just a species of a more general class of influence processes. The hope that one can discover simple algebras for describing how these influence attempts are processed by the members, and then use these algebras to study behavior, leads to a number of exciting areas of research: (1) discovering the core or basic set of behavioral constitutions; (2) discovering rules for switching behavioral constitutions as conditions change; (3) applying these to study group problem-solving to obtain a more useful class of models than currently available; (4) analyzing social judgments made about others in terms of the skill with which they use the appropriate behavioral constitution; (5) examining cross-cultural contact problems in terms of conflicting behavioral constitutions; (6) discovering possible underlying theories for how behavioral constitutions evolve and why they are maintained; (7) deriving empirically testable hypotheses about group behavior from knowledge of behavioral constitutions; and (8) attempting to assess the degree to which interpersonal behavior is governed by such constitutions.

It is, for example, surprising to discover the extent to which problem-solving behavior involves influence attempts. Thus, even though Pfeffer cannot yet give solid empirical data to support his ideas about the importance of political processes in studying organizations, this author believes that, based on his own research, it is likely that Pfeffer is correct. It is even possible that Pfeffer is understating the importance and pervasiveness of influence processes in organizations. In any case, we now have a new class of hypotheses and a new methodology for studying them. Only after a great amount of research will management science, as a field, be able to assess the degree to which and the conditions under which one could use behavioral constitutions and other

influence models to analyze organizational
behavior.

SPAN OF CONTROL

The fundamental principle of the discussion of
span of control in chapter 4 is that each person in an organization has only a limited
amount of time to devote to his duties. This
time is consumed by: (1) his interactions with
subordinates, (2) interactions with nonsubordi-
nates such as peers and clients, (3) problem-
solving and other "internal calculations," and
(4) a provision for slack or buffer time to
smooth out demands on his time. The time taken
for interactions is assumed to be directly
proportional to the volume of the interactions.
The coefficient of proportionality is called
interaction ineffectiveness. The volume of interaction is the product of the number of interactions and the average content of an interaction. The time taken for internal calculations
is assumed to be directly proportional to the
volume of these internal calculations. This coefficient of proportionality is called *problem-
solving effectiveness*. These factors, when summed,
yield an expected amount of time required for a
person to perform his organizational activities.
    Unfortunately, the total time taken may not
equal the total time available. Total time
available represents a group norm for the maximum time the person is allowed for performance
of his activities. When the maximum allowable
time is greater than the actual time taken,
the person is said to have *excess capacity*. When
the maximum allowable time equals his total
time taken, the person is said to be operating
at his *maximum span of control*. Finally, when the
maximum allowable time is less than his total
time taken, the person is said to have *insufficient capacity*. A person with insufficient capacity is said to be *overloaded*.

It is argued that different organizational consequences occur when a person has excess capacity than when he is overloaded. Persons with excess capacity tend to increase their activities to the point of maximum span of control. Persons who are overloaded take steps to decrease this overload and when they cannot do so, their failure triggers attempts to change the task processes and hence the organizational structures. It is also argued that many common (and some bizarre) managerial practices and principles can be seen as devices for increasing an individual's capacity.

This capacity limitation is used to describe a short theory for why and under which conditions a hierarchy will form. It is also part of the mapping function for structural change. Experimentally manipulated violations of the maximum span of control have consistently resulted in structural change. Knowledge of the maximum span of control is also a key factor in predicting the occurrence of structural centralization and decentralization.

BUREAUCRACIES AND BUROIDS

Chapter 5 contains a description of a pure bureaucracy based on the works of Max Weber. A bureaucracy is described as an idealization or benchmark to which one can compare an organization. To define a pure bureaucracy, one starts with some administrative or organizational problem requiring coordinated efforts by a number of persons. Given problems, one should analyze and rationalize them in order to determine what must be done, how it should be done, and what it would take to insure that the problems are solved satisfactorily. This task rationalization should be done with respect to achieving some criterion of efficiency. Thus, the two *antecedent conditions* for a pure bureaucracy are: (1) task rationalization, with respect to (2) a criterion of efficiency. Once

these two conditions are met then there are a
number of *implementation conditions* to insure that
the task processes defined by the antecedent
conditions are carried out. The implementation
conditions ordinarily include: (1) a hierarchy
of authority, (2) a division of labor, (3) a
system of consistent rules and regulations,
(4) formalistic impersonality wherein each
member subordinates his personal needs to those
of the organization, and (5) employment as a
career. The first three implementation conditions are shown to be consistent with the concept and measure of the degree of hierarchy
presented in chapter 1.

An organization meeting the antecedent and
implementation conditions is called a bureaucracy. Bureaucracies are quite rare but organizations having some of their properties are
common. These not-quite-bureaucracies are
called *buroids*. A key theme in the discussion
is that buroids strive to become bureaucracies
but never quite make it, because the conditions
under which the buroid operates are continually
changing. A second theme is that many of the
commonly expressed criticisms of buroids can be
traced to the fact that they are buroids and
not bureaucracies. Thus, buroids are seen as
organizations undergoing continual structural
and task-process changes.

COMMITTEES

One of the consequences of buroids' not being
bureaucracies is that the task-process system
describing who performs what activities with
whom is usually inconsistent with the authority
system describing who is responsible for the
performance of each activity and with whom one
should be working. Both systems are usually out
of synchronization with the formal organizational chart allocating persons to authority
positions. The result of these inconsistencies
is an *authority-task gap*. The existence of authority-task gaps is tolerated because the members

act as if there is a behavioral treaty among
them. Behavioral treaties are sort of "live
and let live rules." As long as there are no
serious departures from the terms of the
treaty, the organization runs smoothly. But,
once the issue is raised that lies in the authority-task gap, the organization is confronted with an *authority-task problem*.

Authority-task problems bubble up out of the
organization and need to be resolved. The resolution involves a technically feasible reallocation of the activities in the task-role
system. Hence, resolution will bring up issues
of structural change. Each party to an authority-task problem acts as if he evaluates each
of the disputed activity assignments. Generally, a member is in favor of a solution that
enhances his role set and is against one that
detracts from his role set. The issues involved
in one authority-task problem may involve directly or indirectly issues in other areas of
the authority-task gap. Thus, the person having
to resolve an authority-task problem must consider the reactions of those involved. These
reactions include accepting, resisting, and
spreading the issues to other areas in the
authority-task gap. Thus, a feasible solution
must consider both the technical problem and
the problems of obtaining implementation. A
set of factors including whether or not the
problem needs to be solved, whether or not the
administrator knows a solution or has the authority to solve it, whether or not there are
standing committees for this type of issue,
whether or not there is sufficient time, whether or not a solution can be negotiated, and
whether or not it is feasible to have a consultant is considered. From our theory of
group structures, it is possible to define a
mapping function that can predict which of
seven choices an administrator will take for
different combinations of the factors to be
considered. In its present form there are 11
such factors. The seven choices are: (1) do

nothing, (2) solve the problem, (3) appoint a committee, (4) appoint a task force, (5) give the problem to a standing committee, (6) pass the buck, and (7) hire a consultant.

The apparent increase in the number of committees in buroids such as universities, large businesses, and governmental units can be examined with such a theory and model. Because authority-task problems are so common and because they are often unavoidable, the procedures for solving them has become a major issue in organizational change. The theory presented in chapter 2 has been tested at a major Midwestern university, using nineteen senior administrative officers, and it predicts the choices quite accurately. Although this does not necessarily mean that the theory is correct, it does indicate that the theory and model are at least a useful approximation. It should be noted that the theory does not explicitly assume either that the administrators are economically rational or that they are decent. The theory, model, and results of its application give more evidence in support of Pfeffer's (1978) basic thesis as well as supporting the basic theory of structural change contained in this book.

DECENTRALIZATION AND CENTRALIZATION

Chapter 6 begins the discussion of the issues of decentralization and centralization by differentiating among the ways in which these words are used. There is one meaning in small group studies in which centrality refers to the degree to which a group is structurally centralized. Basically, a wheel structure is centralized and an all-channel structure is decentralized. There are several meanings in economic theory. One interesting aspect is how a market is decentralized in the degree to which it is perfectly competitive, and centralized to the degree to which economic planning and control is exercised by a buroid. There is a comparison between capitalistic and Soviet-type economies in chapter 6. A third meaning is the degree to which the decisions of a multibranch firm are centralized in a central office. This literature examines the various economic trade-offs existing as long as one headquarters group does the decision-making. This literature is technical; it is clear that although there has been progress in understanding the essentials of the technical problems, there is not unanimity. The managerial literature stresses the problem of delegation and is most closely allied in terms of its problems to the technical economic literature on decentralization. However, the difficulties in formulating and solving these technical problems have made the application of technical solution methods uncertain. This means that the problems involve politics and power plays in a sense used by Pfeffer (1978).

The discussion of decentralization and centralization is cast in terms of span of control considerations and loss or gain in power. The lines on an organization chart are multi-dimensional, involving a number of different activities. Each of these takes up time. It is argued that most executives desire to have as many of these activities under their control as possible. But the single executive may not have the capacity to handle all of these dimensions. Some take up more time than others and some are stronger bases of power than others. Hence, the main problem in deciding the degree of decentralization is deciding which can be given up with the lowest loss of potential power. It is argued that the first candidate for delegation is an activity whose savings in time, if given up, are large compared to the loss of potential power. The last ones to be surrendered are those whose savings in time are small relative to the loss of potential power. Budget allocation, for example,

is one activity that is almost never given
up.

Because delegation involves a reassignment
of activities to persons lower in a structural
hierarchy, the issues of delegation are those
of structural change. The influence attempts,
to work on the activities to be delegated, are
essentially political but involve the kinds of
considerations included in the theory of structural change. But because this analysis depends
upon the information-processing capability of
the person doing the delegation, the resolution
of delegation disputes also depends upon available information-processing technology. This
includes the existence of useful models, availability of relevant information, the degree to
which changes in problems and situations are
capable of being handled by the technology, and
the usefulness of computers and other information-processing devices. Thus, if the information technology is inadequate, organizations
tend to delegate. But when the information
technology improves, there is a tendency to
recentralize.

EVOLVING ORGANIZATIONAL STRUCTURES

The most startling difference between an industrial firm today and one of a century ago is
the greater size of the modern firm. General
Motors alone is larger, in terms of gross revenues, than the Gross National Product of most
countries. The size of government has also
grown, and its agencies are also larger. Whether one measures size in terms of the number and
distribution of types of employees or in terms
of its gross receipts, buroids in present-day
North America and other industrialized economies have tended to grow. Growth, however, is
just one of the changes taking place. Modern
firms are also involved in a greater number of
auxiliary tasks. There are demands from employees and government for a greater variety of

personnel services. There are more rules and
regulations that constrain the organization.
The tendency to diversification and integration has led to more products. Many firms compete in a variety of different industries.
There is a deeper and broader pool of trained
talent for organizations to use. There are
radically different methods of gathering,
filtering, routing, and processing information.
The management sciences have provided new ideas
as well as new techniques for managing a
buroid. And in some cases there has been more
than "lip service" paid to the idea that perhaps the organization should seek to benefit
its employees rather than to view labor as one
more economic input.

The greater variety of auxiliary tasks, the
greater the variety of activities in which the
organization can engage, the increasing complexity of its functions, the complexity and
constraints introduced by government and labor
unions, and the less simple motivations and
values of its employees are related to the
growth of the organization and those with which
it interacts. These changes set off modifica-
tions in the organizational structures and task
processes. It is conceptually improbable that
there will ever be a simple one-to-one relationship between a structural change and an
environmental or technological change. There
is no such relationship even in little laboratory organizations operating under very simple
conditions. One can state and test theories
about the processes by which structural changes
occur. But that is very different from claiming
that a change in variable x will always result
in a change in y. The mapping functions and
other structural change processes do offer the
hope that it is possible to study the change
processes and even to intervene to affect them.
However, a process model that considers the
multiple chains of contingency is different
from the sort of simple causation that event
x will produce change in y. Instead, event x,

concurrently with other events, sets off a
sequence of behaviors whose end result will depend both upon the events that start the processes off and how those in the system behave
in response. One is faced with complex, time-
dependent, contingent sequences of events and
responses and not just simple, one-step, stimulus-response behaviors. While it is very possible that the basic process theories are
relatively simple, a chain of basic processes
can produce very complex behaviors. Thus, this
author believes that the formulations that assert or seek to identify how an event x should
result in change in y are obsolete. Process-
based explanations will have to replace simple
causation explanations if we are ever to understand organizational behavior.

A CASE STUDY OF AN ATTEMPTED STRUCTURAL CHANGE

Taking a process perspective leads one to examine the evolution of aggregate organizational
structures as many separate experiments in
structural change. Just as there is a wide
variety of events demanding some sequence of
responses by an organization, there is also a
wide variety of structural responses. Lables
for patterns of responses such as line-staff,
organic, matrix, and participatory organizations abound in the literature. Most of these
are at minimum lables and at maximum social
movements. Within each of these broad labels,
there are so many subvarieties of organizations that the labels are at best indications
of organizational structure. For example, the
author was involved in an attempt to make an
academic faculty into a matrix organization.
The simple idea seemed reasonable, but as the
design work unfolded it turned out that there
were major differences over what a matrix organization should be. The label, matrix organization, was operationally confused. It did have
emotional meaning and involved deep values

among the participants. It was easier to list
the changes and to point at how each faction
was to benefit than it was to agree on the
meaning of the label, matrix organization. The
political realities and perceived political
realities were important. Apparently, one of
the virtues of a matrix organization over a
line-staff is that it can bestow more positions
with authority and titles such as director,
chairman, and head.

The organization in question was an academic
school with a dean and four department chairmen. The school, henceforth called the School
of Management Sciences,[1] ran undergraduate and
master's degree programs. The School of Management Sciences was new and wanted to improve itself academically. It had the usual mix of
established faculty and "Young Turks." The
credentials of the Young Turks tended to be
better than those of the older established
faculty. There was a substantial number of
senior faculty who desired to improve the
school's reputation. Each of the four departments was reasonably autonomous and the department chairmen exercised wide discretion in
how they ran their departments. The departments
were interdependent because of common core
courses such as accounting, organizational behavior, and quantitative methods. There was a
problem in upgrading these core courses. There
was also the problem of bringing in professors
with established reputations to give leadership in the development of each of the core
areas.

Since it was a new school, it was difficult
to attract and keep this sort of professor.
Therefore, the idea of having someone called Senior
Professor in each area seemed good. This would
provide the potential for leadership in each
area and would make the School more attractive.
Hence, on paper there would be the usual dean,
department-chairmen, faculty-member authority
hierarchy vertically and senior professor for
each area horizontally. In principle this is a

matrix organizational structure. An original
short memorandum suggesting this was well received. A structures committee was appointed
to study the problem and to come up with a
solution. A much larger report was drafted by
the structures committee. It was reasonably
well received but several problems of governance arose. The sensible questions of who
would be responsible for what activities, who
would have what type of authority, and how the
inevitable conflicts would be resolved caused
some confusion. This led to more questions and
then to another committee which produced a
lengthy report of sixty-three pages of text
and many pages of appendices.

The lengthy report was circulated for discussion and objections and suggestions. Although there were some interpersonal problems
among some of the members of the school, it
appeared that with compromises, the school
might get reorganized. However, another process
taking place outside the school caused an
intervention. It turned out that the president
of the university had another structures committee examining the entire university. One of
its recommendations was to form a School of
Social Sciences which would include the departments of the School of Management Sciences.
If this recommendation were accepted, there
would be no School of Management Sciences, and
hence, no reason for coming to a matrix organization. Thus, this report preempted the Structures Committee report. The report of the
Structures Committee immediately became a "dead
letter" until the recommendation for the School
of Social Sciences was resolved. The School became more united because it sought to take
steps to block implementation of the report
suggesting the formation of a School of Social
Sciences. If the school were successful, it
would improve the chances for the implementation of the report of the Structures Committee.

This brief description of the problems and
complex processes of formulating an acceptable

response to an organizational problem is only
a shadow of the real processes that took place.
For example, one of the possible senior professors was fired, the dean had a mild heart attack, a new temporary dean was appointed who had
a nervous breakdown, one of the department
chairmen took another job, another resigned,
and so on. Each of these events is related to
the structural change process and each had an
effect on it. All in all, most of those involved had the best interests of the school in
mind and each was trying to look after his own
interests. The sequence of events was very complex and the original problem and the beginning
processes were modified continually as the
structural change process unfolded. It is interesting to note that two of the professors
had extensive experience in matrix organizations elsewhere and one argued that the other
"did not really know" what a matrix organization was. Thus, the label "matrix organization"
or "project management" was unclear when it
came to translating the ideas behind the label
to actual school structures.

This example illustrates why theories of
structural change should not be stated in
terms of whether or not problem x should result in change in y. There are many problems,
and the structural change processes are affected by the processes themselves. In addition,
other new problems from outside the organization can affect the structural change processes. The technical aspects usually take a back
seat to the political aspects in organizational
structure changes that formally rearrange the
task-role matrix and the authority structure.

EVOLUTION OF ORGANIZATIONAL STRUCTURE TYPES

The most ancient type of organizational structure is called the *line organization*. A line organization is a structural hierarchy to carry
out a task process. A boss, subbosses, and
operatives are arranged structurally in a

hierarchy. This organizational form can be very efficient. The lines of authority are clear and each person's position is well defined. However, as the organization's functions and activities become more complex, the burdens on those in the hierarchy to manage the many separate and related task processes becomes increased. A role matrix for a line organization would look like Figure 7.1a in a pure case. The organization chart for this organization is given in Figure 7.1b. Note that, in principle, a line organization has no uncle or cousin relationships.

A variation of the simple line organization is the *functional organization* by F. Taylor. In this organization, there are more complex technical skills required and a specialist in each acts as a functional foreman. Thus, each operative has a number of supervisors, one for each of the technical skills. A pure functional organization has the following type of role matrix, as shown in Figure 7.2a. The organization chart corresponding to the role matrix is given in Figure 7.b. In Figures 7.2a and 7.2b each functional foreman x_1 does activity a_1

Activities

	a_1	a_2	a_3	a_4	a_5	a_6	a_7	a_8	a_9	a_{10}	a_{11}	a_{12}
x_1	1	1	1	1	1	1	1	1	1	1	1	1
x_2	1	1	1	1	0	0	0	0	0	0	0	0
x_3	0	0	0	0	1	1	1	1	0	0	0	0
x_4	0	0	0	0	0	0	0	0	1	1	1	1
x_5	1	1	0	0	0	0	0	0	0	0	0	0
x_6	0	0	1	1	0	0	0	0	0	0	0	0
x_7	0	0	0	0	1	1	0	0	0	0	0	0
x_8	0	0	0	0	0	0	1	1	0	0	0	0
x_9	0	0	0	0	0	0	0	0	1	1	0	0
x_{10}	0	0	0	0	0	0	0	0	0	0	1	1

FIGURE 7.1a The typical role matrix of a pure line organization.

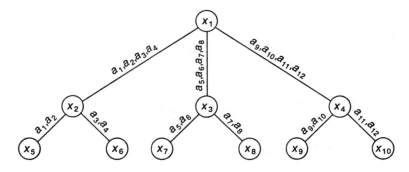

FIGURE 7.1b The organization chart of the pure line
organization in Figure 7.1a.

with x_4, activity a_2 with x_5, activity a_3 with
x_6, activity a_4 with x_7. Activity a_5 is his
planning activity. Figure 7.2b can be rewritten
in terms of three separate hierarchies, one for
each functional foreman. This is shown in Figure 7.2c.

The functional organization allows for a
division of labor according to functional
skill. As can be seen in Figure 7.2c, a functional organization essentially creates a set
of parallel and simultaneously functioning
structural hierarchies. It has the problem,

Activities

		a_1	a_2	a_3	a_4	a_5	a_6	a_7	a_8	a_9	a_{10}	a_{11}	a_{12}	a_{13}	a_{14}	a_{15}
Functional foremen	x_1	1	1	1	1	1	0	0	0	0	0	0	0	0	0	0
	x_2	0	0	0	0	0	1	1	1	1	1	0	0	0	0	0
	x_3	0	0	0	0	0	0	0	0	0	0	1	1	1	1	1
Workers	x_4	1	0	0	0	0	1	0	0	0	0	1	0	0	0	0
	x_5	0	1	0	0	0	0	1	0	0	0	0	1	0	0	0
	x_6	0	0	1	0	0	0	0	1	0	0	0	0	1	0	0
	x_7	0	0	0	1	0	0	0	0	1	0	0	0	0	1	0

FIGURE 7.2a A typical role matrix of a pure functional
organization.

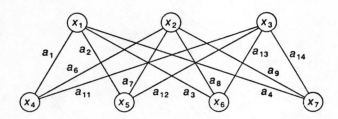

FIGURE 7.2b The organizational chart for the pure functional organization in Figure 7.2a.

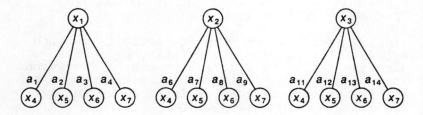

FIGURE 7.2c A decomposition of Figure 7.2b into the functional hierarchy for each functional foreman.

however, of having many uncles and cousins and a low degree of overall hierarchy. Technically, if these separate hierarchies can be maintained and problems do not arise cutting across the various workers or functional foremen, a functional organization can achieve a high degree of efficiency. However, conflicts do arise, the task processes change, persons seek promotion, and the functional foremen could interfere with each other and with the task processes. This form of organization is now very rare and it represents a stage beyond the simple line organization.

A variation of the line organization that tries to maintain the authority system while retaining some of the advantages of the functional organization is the *line-staff organization*. In this organizational form, the ideal is to

keep the staff members out of direct contact
with other subordinates while benefitting from
their expertise. Problems of line-staff organizations were discussed in chapter 4 and in
Tuggle (1978, chapter 8). It is sufficient
here just to mention that the distinction between line and staff is blurred in practice
and that there are many different meanings attached to the relationships between line personnel and staff personnel. For example,
Browne and Golembiewski (1974) recently reex-
amined the concept of line and staff according
to the image held by organization members about
line and staff.

Ideally, a line-staff organization will have
a role matrix such as the one in Figure 7.3a
and an organization chart such as the one in
Figure 7.3b. The line organization is that of
x_1, x_2, x_3, x_6, x_7, x_8, and x_9. The staff positions, x_4 and x_5, would normally perform
duties that do not interfere with the functions
of the line directly. But in some organizations, the staff have direct contact with the
line in an advisory, consultative capacity,
and even in capacities involving more direct
influence. But the activities involving both
the line and the staff are usually only a subset of the line activities and the relationship is intermittent. This variation is illustrated in the role set of Figure 7.4a and
the organizational chart of Figure 7.4b. Here
the line-staff relationships can be considered
as cousin and uncle-nephew relations. For example, in Figure 7.4a, there are cousin relationships between x_2 and x_4, between x_3 and
x_4 and between x_3 and x_5. The cousin relationship between the staff member x_5 and the line
member x_3, causes an uncle-nephew relationship
between x_5 and x_9, who is x_3's immediate subordinate.

A modern variant of both the functional organization and the line-staff organization is
the *matrix organization*. A matrix organization is
a double hierarchy and is a functional organization where each operative has two functional

foremen. There is usually a staff attached to some of these functional foremen. Thus, two functional foremen can give direct supervision to a task process and a staff can be maintained for less vital processes. This organization has proven useful in project management or in the creating of temporary task forces. Galbraith

Activities

	a_1	a_2	a_3	a_4	a_5	a_6	a_7	a_8	a_9	a_{10}	a_{11}	a_{12}	a_{13}
x_1	1	1	1	1	1	1	1	1	1	1	1	1	1
x_2	1	1	1	1	0	0	0	0	0	0	0	0	0
x_3	0	0	0	0	1	1	1	1	0	0	0	0	0
x_4	0	0	0	0	0	0	0	0	1	1	0	0	0
x_5	0	0	0	0	0	0	0	0	0	0	1	1	0
x_6	1	1	0	0	0	0	0	0	0	0	0	0	0
x_7	0	0	1	1	0	0	0	0	0	0	0	0	0
x_8	0	0	0	0	1	1	0	0	0	0	0	0	0
x_9	0	0	0	0	0	0	1	1	0	0	0	0	0

FIGURE 7.3a A role matrix for a typical line-staff organization under normal conditions.

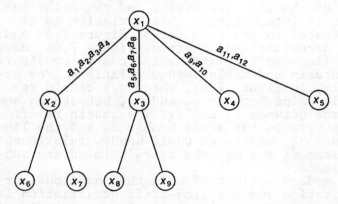

FIGURE 7.3b An organization chart for the line-staff organization in Figure 7.3a.

Activities

	a_1	a_2	a_3	a_4	a_5	a_6	a_7	a_8	a_9	a_{10}	a_{11}	a_{12}	a_{13}
x_1	1	1	1	1	1	1	1	1	1	1	1	1	1
x_2	1	1	1	1	(1)	0	0	0	0	0	0	0	0
x_3	0	0	0	0	0	(1)	1	1	1	1	(1)	0	0
x_4	0	0	0	0	(1)	(1)	0	0	0	0	0	0	0
x_5	0	0	0	0	0	0	0	0	0	0	(1)	1	0
x_6	1	1	0	0	0	0	0	0	0	0	0	0	0
x_7	0	0	1	1	0	0	0	0	0	0	0	0	0
x_8	0	0	0	0	0	0	1	1	0	0	0	0	0
x_9	0	0	0	0	0	0	0	0	1	1	(1)	0	0

FIGURE 7.4a A role matrix for a typical line-staff organization with three cousin and one uncle-nephew relationships between staff and line. These are found in the circled entries.

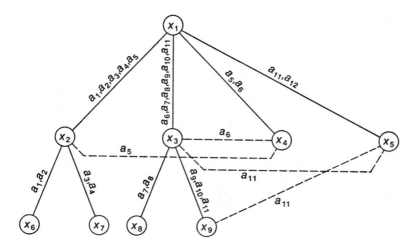

FIGURE 7.4b An organization chart for Figure 7.4a. The cousin and uncle-nephew relationships between line and staff are indicated by dashed lines.

(1973) reports its use in the aircraft industry. If the issues of governance and division
of labor can be sorted out, this organization
is capable of high efficiency. Because members
can be temporarily assigned, it provides flex-
ibility to the organization. However, it may
not always be possible to work out the governance and division of labor problems. When
these are not resolved, the ensuing conflicts
can create large drops in efficiency.

Burns and Stalker (1961) give an example of
still another organizational form, called the
organic organization. The organic organization has
no particular organizational structure. Rather
the structure changes as the needs of the organization change. This organizational concept
is very close to one that is consistent with
the analysis of group structures and task processes present in this book. However, because
there is no set form, it is difficult to analyze its features in idealized terms as we did
for the other structures.

Some authors have advocated *participatory organizations* where there is no formal authority
and the members are free to interact as equals.
This can be operationally unsound if interpersonal influence processes are prevalent and
if supervision based on technical skills is
essential. It was tried in a firm called *Non-
Linear Systems* (Malone, 1975), for 1960-65. Pri-
or to the experiment, the firm operated with a
board of directors, president, vice presidents,
production manager, sales manager, and managers
for accounting, inspection, quality, purchasing, engineering, and shipping. There were
engineers, superintendents, technicians,
draftsmen, foremen, and so on. It was a line-
staff organization making electrical measuring
instruments. When it began the experiment,
three "zones" of management were set up: (1)
trustee management including the four members
of the board of directors and the president,
(2) general management including seven members
chosen by the president, and (3) departmental

management including thirty department units. The responsibilities of Zone One were to determine basic policies and the basic course of the business. The purpose of Zone Two was to establish operating policies; to plan, coordinate, and control the business; and to appraise the results. There were seven vice presidents in the executive council, which operated as a unit. Members of the executive council did not control subordinate operations individually. Decisions were advisory and by mutual consent of those present. The departmental managers in Zone Three ran their own shop. Thus, the organization had some hierarchy and some division of labor. In 1965, Non-Linear Systems reorganized. It established properties similar to those of a bureaucracy. The analysis of the failure, by Malone (1975), is enlightening. One of the chief problems with the experiment was the separation of the managers from their responsibility. Apparently worker satisfaction increased but supervisor satisfaction fell. Malone speculates that perhaps it was because of the unique qualities of the president that the experiment lasted so long.

There are many other labels that can be attached to the enormous variety of organizations that evolve. These labels can simplify the identification of principle features of an organization. These labels can also mislead one who is attempting to manage or analyze an organization. Rather than describe each possible label and discuss its relative advantages or disadvantages, it is more helpful to think of an organization in terms of its authority, task, and organizational-chart role systems. Problems change and the conditions faced by the organization change. Hence, the labels become increasingly irrelevant over time. So, rather than analyze the labels, it makes more sense to analyze the organizational processes affecting organizational structures.

Processes of adapting and diffusing change in organizational structures are vital to

understanding organizations. These processes
are discussed more fully in the next chapter.

NOTES

1
  This is not the actual title.

REFERENCES

Browne, P. J., and Golembiewski, R. T. "The Line-Staff
Concept Revisited: An Empirical Study of Organizational Images." *Academy of Management Journal* 17
(1974): 406-19.

Burns, T., and Stalker, G. M. *The Management of Innovation*. London: Tavistock, 1961.

Galbraith, J. *Designing Complex Organizations*. Reading,
Mass.: Addison-Wesley, 1973.

Jabes, J. *Individual Processes in Organizational Behavior*. Arlington Heights, Ill.: AHM Publishing Corporation, 1978.

Malone, E. L. "The Non-Linear Systems Experiment in
in Participative Management." *The Journal of Business*
48 (1975): 52-64.

Pfeffer, J. *Organizational Design*. Arlington Heights,
Ill.: AHM Publishing Corporation, 1978.

Simmons, R. E. *Managing Behavioral Processes: Applications of Theory and Research*. Arlington Heights, Ill.:
AHM Publishing Corporation, 1978.

Tuggle, F. D. *Organizational Processes*. Arlington
Heights, Ill.: AHM Publishing Corporation, 1978.

Weber, M. *From Max Weber: Essays in Sociology. Translated by H. H. Gerth and C. W. Mills*. New York:
Oxford University Press, 1946.

Weick, K. E. "Amendments to Organizational Theorizing."
Academy of Management Journal 17 (1974): 487-502.

Adoption and Diffusion of Change

A book on organizational structures must be concerned with change because structural changes are inherent in organizations. Indeed, in every chapter of this book, concepts of change, processes of change, and problems of change have played a pivotal role. The stress on individual and group processes is rooted in the necessity and occurrence of change. For if there were no changes, there would not need to be an emphasis on process rather than simple causation (e.g., stimulus-response) explanations.

Despite the importance of change to the theories, results, and speculations in this book, there has been no systematic development of a theory of the concept and measurement of change. Furthermore, there have only been indirect references to the processes of adoption and diffusion of change. Only those aspects of the concept of change and the rate and timing of change (chapter 2) that were directly related to structural change are mentioned. The purpose of this chapter is to correct these omissions. The first section discusses the concept of change; the second presents a model for the adoption of a group structure. The third section presents a theory for the adoption and diffusion of change. Finally, we examine some aspects of organizational change.

THE CONCEPT OF CHANGE

Each person in an organization is viewed in terms of his activities. The activities of each person are represented in his role set or equivalently his row in the group role matrix. Every consumer, club member, producer, and organization can be seen as engaged in activities. A new practice, a new idea, a new product, a new technique, an altered set of participants, and even a new ideology are events that can be called *innovations* from the point of view of the person or organization facing them. A product such as a new computer may be new only in the sense that it is new to the person or organization that is facing the decision of whether or not to accept it. For another person or another organization the computer might be "old hat." If a group of managers have never heard of linear programming, then, although linear programming is approximately 30 years old, it is an innovation to them. A 10-speed bicycle might be an innovation to a habitual car driver and not one for a "bike freak." An idea such as the simple wheel can be an innovation to an isolated culture such as the one recently discovered in the Philippines.

An innovation should be described in terms of the changes in activities that might be expected to occur if it were to be adopted by a user. The emphasis is on behavior rather than on the technological description because behavioral responses to an innovation vary with the person or organization during the adoption.

There is no simple relationship between the technological description of an innovation and the behavioral responses. Very trivial technological events can create havoc to the adopters and major technological changes can have little or no effect. In fact, the same technological event can have different effects according to which potential adopter one is referring to.

Consider the case of a new, solid-state color television. As a technological event, the development of such a T.V. receiver is a significant advance on the black and white vacuum-tube television. But for the person buying it, the only real effect may be a loss of money when it is purchased, some inconvenience when it is installed, and perhaps a loss of sleep because the new set is watched more. Essentially, the T.V. owner pulls a knob and the desired program appears on the screen. The changes in his activities are probably very minor. But, for the T.V. repairman, the new technology means that he will have to stock new parts, learn a few new skills, and adjust his advertising and prices. The change in activities for the T.V. repair shop are probably greater than those of the consumer. But the changes for the T.V. repairman are trivial compared to the activity changes required of the manufacturer. He needs new engineers, new production input factors, new assembly lines, and so forth. He may even need new forms of financing. He has to retrain some of his personnel, deal with new suppliers, etc. However, the changes in activities of a competitor, who has only the capability of producing the older type of T.V., may be even more drastic. He could, for example, be driven out of business.

Just as a stone cast into a pond creates ripples outward from the impact point, an innovation can set off a long chain of sequentially dependent events. For example, if more persons own the new T.V., there will be an increased demand for color programs. This will,

in turn, create demand for new television cam-
eras and processing equipment. But new kinds
of video equipment also affect the movie industry. The shift in demand for the new television could create shortages in other product
lines because the rare earth elements needed
for the new T.V. are scarce. This shortage
could lead to higher prices, and to avoid
higher prices other technologies would be developed. The various regulatory bodies of
government could become involved. But the new,
solid-state technology is not the only source
of innovation that could affect all of these
persons and organizations. Someone could in-
vent a wall screen and set off a whole new
round of changes.

Changes in activities due to the adoption of
an innovation are only part of the problem.
These changes in activities have *consequences*
that are crucial to understanding the relative
resistance to or acceptance of the innovation.
The changes in the activities are called the
nature of the change. The evaluation placed on the
nature of the change define the *consequences of
the change*. It is possible that an innovation
which is minor in terms of its nature could
have significant consequences. It is also possible that an innovation involving large
changes in activities will have minor consequences. In order to understand the problems of
the adoption and diffusion of change, one has
to consider both the nature and the consequences of the change as viewed by the potential adopter.

EXAMPLE 8.1 Suppose that we have described the role
set of a participant in two successive problem-solving
periods. Let his role sets be given by the two sets of
entries:

Activity

	a_1	a_2	a_3	a_4	a_5	a_6	a_7	a_8
Period T	1	1	1	1	0	0	0	0
Period $T+1$	1	1	1	0	1	1	1	1

He added activities a_5, a_6, a_7, a_8, and he dropped activity a_4. He did not change activities a_1, a_2, and a_3. The nature of the change is defined by those activities he added (a_5, a_6, a_7, a_8) and by those he dropped (a_4).

It is important to consider both those activities added and those dropped, because the consequences of each may be evaluated differently. As we shall see when we discuss the consequences of the change, the differential evaluation is an important feature to understanding the adoption process. A Venn diagram of the nature of a change is presented in Figure 8.1. Set A depicts the set of activities before the innovation is introduced and set B depicts the set of activities that are expected to occur after the innovation is adopted. The shaded part of set B corresponds to those activities added. The shaded part of set A corresponds to those activities which have been dropped. The intersection of sets A and B represent those activities for which there are no expected changes.

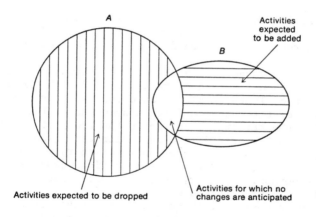

FIGURE 8.1 A Venn Diagram of the nature of the change expected when changing from A to B.

EXAMPLE 8.2 Suppose a group structure, given by Figure 8.2a on problem I, becomes the structure given by Figure 8.2b on the next trial. The circled entries in Figure 8.2a are those half-channels dropped when the group shifts its structure to the one in Figure 8.2b. The circled entries in Figure 8.2b are those half-channels added during the change in structure. Note

$$
\begin{array}{c}
\begin{array}{ccccc} x_1 & x_2 & x_3 & x_4 & x_5 \end{array} \\
\begin{array}{c} x_1 \\ x_2 \\ x_3 \\ x_4 \\ x_5 \end{array}
\begin{bmatrix}
0 & 1 & \textcircled{1} & \textcircled{1} & 0 \\
1 & 0 & 0 & 0 & 1 \\
\textcircled{1} & 1 & 0 & 0 & 0 \\
\textcircled{1} & 1 & 0 & 0 & \textcircled{1} \\
\textcircled{1} & 1 & 0 & \textcircled{1} & 0
\end{bmatrix}
\end{array}
\qquad
\begin{array}{c}
\begin{array}{ccccc} x_1 & x_2 & x_3 & x_4 & x_5 \end{array} \\
\begin{array}{c} x_1 \\ x_2 \\ x_3 \\ x_4 \\ x_5 \end{array}
\begin{bmatrix}
0 & 1 & 0 & 0 & 0 \\
1 & 0 & \textcircled{1} & \textcircled{1} & 1 \\
0 & 1 & 0 & 0 & 0 \\
0 & 1 & 0 & 0 & 0 \\
0 & 1 & 0 & 0 & 0
\end{bmatrix}
\end{array}
$$

FIGURE 8.2a A structure of a group.

FIGURE 8.2b The structure of the same group as Figure 8.2a at a later time.

that there were 7 half-channels dropped and 2 half-channels added. Thus, the nature of the change consisted of these 9 half-channel changes. This example can also be shown in a Venn Diagram. The set A in Figure 8.1 corresponding to the structure in Figure 8.2a, and the set B in Figure 8.1 corresponding to the structure in Figure 8.2b can be depicted in Figure 8.3.

The consequences of a change are estimates of the expected benefits and costs associated with the nature of change. There is always uncertainty about both the nature of the change and its consequences. For example, the structural change in the group of Figures 8.2 and 8.3 resulted in a centralization (see chapter 6) of the group structure about person x_2. Previously, two persons (x_1 and x_2) were receiving messages from every person. Person x_1 sent it to all except x_5, while x_2 sent messages only to x_5. Also, x_4 and x_5 exchanged messages. These extra messages decreased hierarchy because they created cousin relationships and they also reduced efficiency. However, the real consequences of the change to the group members may have been the elimination of a struggle for control by persons x_1 and x_2. When x_1 "lost out" to x_2, the structure could centralize and become more efficient. If both x_1 and x_2 sought to be the hub, then the consequence to x_1 was a net loss, to x_2 a net gain, and

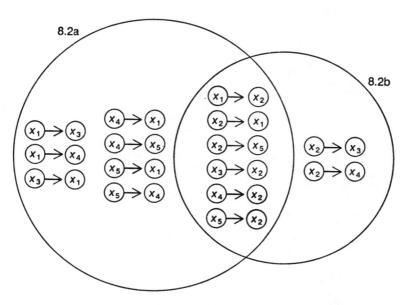

FIGURE 8.3 A Venn Diagram of the half-channel changes in Figures 8.2a and 8.2b.

to x_3, x_4, and x_5, a net gain. But these gains and losses are uncertain because it may turn out that x_2 cannot do the job well. And if he cannot do well, there may be another series of structural changes. Person x_1 could end up back on top and x_2 would be discredited as a rival. It is also possible that x_1 and x_2 were struggling to *avoid* becoming the hub, and x_1 wins.

The inability to know how each person sees the innovation (in the example, centralizing about a person) and to estimate the benefits, costs, and probability distribution of these benefits and costs in a real situation, makes it difficult ever to calculate with precision the consequences of a change. Persons can think strategically, and thinking ahead several moves further complicates the problem of determining the consequences of a change. Accordingly, one seeks to find a theory and model that does not rely on detailed estimates of the nature and the consequences of a change.

In the case of structural change, the best way is to posit processes by which these half-channel changes occur in terms of influence attempts by the group members. This is accomplished by inventing a behavioral constitution for how the members process and determine the outcomes of the many influence attempts. The next step is to formulate a measure for the change and to use votes or influence attempts as a probable cause for these changes. This formulation leads to a model for the rate of change. This model can then be empirically verified or rejected using actual data.

In the case of economic issues such as the adoption of producers' durables (e.g., new machines for producing a product line), the consequences can be estimated by expected changes in costs and revenues. The innovation could, for example, reduce costs of production. It could also allow the firm to produce new products or better products that could increase revenues. Finance theory provides numerous techniques for estimating the consequences of investing in producer's durables. These probable consequences can then be used to estimate the rate of adoption of a specific producer's durable in a specific industry. Generally, the greater the expected advantages of adopting, the more quickly adoption will occur.

However, as Pfeffer (1978, chapter 7) points out, it is only an assumption that an economic determination of consequences of a change is the one that best describes the acceptability of an organizational change. The real issue may be whether or not the adoption leads to a change that benefits politically or increases the content of a coalition within the organization. Those coalitions which would have an increase in control if the innovation were adopted will tend to favor it. Those which would suffer a loss or would see a competing coalition gain because of the innovation will tend to resist it. Pfeffer (1978) argues persuasively that considerations of altering the distribution of control and authority may outweigh economic or technical factors. Thus, a good idea that makes sense to one group, say the stockholders, may not be accepted because it would reduce the control of a dominant coalition. Professional managers could be more interested in protecting their interests than in producing high dividends for their investors. A labor-saving machine will be resisted by a coalition of employees who fear loss of jobs even though the firm would be able to reduce its manufacturing costs.

A MODEL FOR THE RATE OF ADOPTION OF A GROUP STRUCTURE

Since this is a book on organizational structures, and structural change is a key theoretical problem area, let us derive the diffusion function used in the literature on diffusion of innovation by examining structural changes. This result is used in the studies reported in chapter 2.

Suppose that a group has n members. There are, at most $n(n-1)$ half-channels whose state could be either opened or closed. Let j_1, $j_2, \ldots, j_{n(n-1)}$ represent the states of every half-channel for a structure in some given time period. The value of each of the states is 1 if the half-channel is open and 0 if closed. So, $j_1 = 1$ if the first half-channel (i.e., from x_1 to x_2) is open and $j_1 = 0$ if the first half-channel is closed. Next, let $\ell_1, \ell_2, \ldots, \ell_{n(n-1)}$ represent the states of every half-channel for the same group at a later time period. The values of these states are defined the same way as the values of the previous states. For example, $\ell_1 = 1$ if the first half-channel is open and $\ell_1 = 0$ if it is closed.

There are four possible cases for any half-channel if we compare 2 time periods: (1) the half-channel was open and remained open, or $j_1 = \ell_1 = 1$; (2) the half-channel was closed and remained closed, or $j_1 = \ell_1 = 0$; (3) the half-channel was open during the earlier time period and then closed during the later period, or $j_1 = 1$ and $\ell_1 = 0$; and (4) the half-channel was closed during the earlier time period and then opened during the later time period, or $j_1 = 0$ and $\ell_1 = 1$.

We recall that the nature of the change includes those activities dropped and those activities which we added. The 4 possible results for any half-channel involve 2 types of changes (an open half-channel that gets closed and a closed half-channel that becomes open) and 2 types of no changes (the state of a channel does not change). If we examine the changes we note that either $j_1 = 1$ becomes $\ell_1 = 0$ or $j_1 = 0$ becomes $\ell_1 = 1$. We also note that $j_1 - \ell_1 = 1$ for the first case and $j_1 - \ell_1 = -1$ for the second case. Now, if we take the absolute value of $j_1 - \ell_1$, or $|j_1 - \ell_1|$, the value of $|j_1 - \ell_1| = 1$ for both types of changes. It is also true that $|j_1 - \ell_1| = 0$ for both the no change cases.

Thus, the total number of changes is the sum of $|j_1 - \ell_1|$ for every possible half-channel. The size of the nature of the change is given by:

$$\sum_{i=1}^{n(n-1)} |j_i - \ell_i|$$

Next, consider the largest value of the pair of values for each half-channel. If the first half-channel is open ($j_1 = 1$) and remains open ($\ell_1 = 1$), then the largest value is 1. Similarly, if the first half-channel is closed ($j_1 = 0$) and remains closed ($\ell_1 = 0$), the largest value is 0. If the first half-channel closed ($\ell_1 = 0$) and then becomes opened ($\ell_1 = 0$)

and vice versa, the largest value is 1. In
other words, the maximum value of j_i and ℓ_i,
denoted $\max(j_i, \ell_i)$, is 0 or 1 for every possible half-channel. The value of $\max(j_i, \ell_i)$ is
1 if the ith half-channel was open during
either time period, and 0 if closed during
both. Thus, the sum of all of the $\max(j_i, \ell_i)$ is
the number of half-channels that were open
in either time period.

A simple measure for the *relative change* in
structure during the two time periods is given
by μ where μ is:

$$\mu = \frac{\sum_{i=1}^{n(n-1)} |j_i - \ell_i|}{\sum_{i=1}^{n(n-1)} \max(j_i, \ell_i)} \tag{8.1}$$

Obviously, $\mu = 0$ if there are no changes and
$\mu = 1$ if there is a complete change in half-
channel usage. There is a complete change in
half-channel usage if every open half-channel
in the earlier period becomes closed and if
every closed half-channel in the earlier period becomes opened.

EXAMPLE 8.3 For the two structures in Example 8.2,
the size of the nature of the change is 9. The number
of half-channels opened in either time period is 15.
Thus, the value of $\mu = 9/15$.

There will be a value of μ for each successive time
period. And, if one observes a group working on a
sequence of problems, one observes a sequence of
structures. Between every pair of successive time
periods, there will be a value of μ for the relative
size of the change in structure given by Equation
(8.1). Suppose that after a number of such problems,
the group structure becomes stable in the sense that
the values of μ become zero. One can then take the
state of each half-channel in the stable structure
as an adopted state. There will be $n(n-1)$ adopted
states because there are $n(n-1)$ possible half-channels.

One can then examine the votes in the interaction
process to determine the time when each of the half-
channels becomes adopted. This gives one a sequence
of times for the adoption of the state of every half-
channel.

Those half-channels whose state never changes are
adopted at the beginning of the influence process
causing the structural change. Because they are
adopted before the structural change process began,
they can be ignored in modeling the rate of structural adoption. Let us count as adoptions those half-
channels whose state changes to the adopted state
when the structure becomes stable. The state of a
half-channel can be adopted as open or closed.

Suppose that after allowing for the half-
channels that never change, there are N half-
channels that will be adopted at the beginning
of the adoption process. At any later time t,
suppose there have been exactly n_t half-channels whose stable state has been adopted. There
are n_t adoptions and $N - n_t$ potential adoptions
at time t. At a later time, say $t + \Delta t$ adoptions and $N - n_{t+\Delta t}$ potential adoptions. The
change in the number of adoptions between time
t and time $t + \Delta t$ is given by $n_{t+\Delta t} - n_t$. This
can be calculated from the size of the nature
of the change by defining the state of each
half-channel as 1 if it is adopted and 0 if it
is not adopted. The number of channels yet to
be adopted, $N - n_t$, at time t, includes those
adopted at time $t + \Delta t$. Thus, the denominator
of Equation (8.1) becomes $N - n_t$. Hence, the
relative change between time t and time $t + \Delta t$
is given by $w_{\Delta t}$, where:

$$w_{\Delta t} = \frac{n_{t+\Delta t} - n_t}{N - n_t} \tag{8.2}$$

There is a sequence of values of $w_{\Delta t}$ corresponding to each successive pair of time periods. The next step is to posit some reasonable
explanation for why the values of $w_{\Delta t}$ take on

different values. One simple explanation is that the value of $w_{\Delta t}$ is proportional to the product of the number of prior adoptions at time t and the elapsed time Δt. Hence:

$$w_{\Delta t} = k_1 n_t \Delta t \tag{8.3}$$

where k_1 is the coefficient of proportionality between $w_{\Delta t}$ and the product $n_t \Delta t$. Equating Equations (8.2) and (8.3), one obtains:

$$\frac{n_{t+\Delta t} - n_t}{N - n_t} = k_1 n_t \Delta t$$

This can be arranged to yield:

$$\frac{n_{t+\Delta t} - n_t}{\Delta t} = k_1 n_t (N - n_t)$$

Taking limits as $\Delta t \to 0$, we have:

$$\lim_{\Delta t \to 0} \frac{n_{t+\Delta t} - n_t}{\Delta t} = \frac{dn_t}{dt} = \lim_{\Delta t \to 0} k_1 n_t (N - n_t)$$

$$= k_1 n_t (N - n_t)$$

Or,

$$\frac{dn_t}{dt} = k_1 n_t (N - n_t) \tag{8.4}$$

Equation (8.4) states that the rate of change in the number of adopted half-channels is proportional to the product of the adopted half-channels at time t and the number of half-channels yet to be adopted at time t.

Equation (8.4) is the famous equation for the rate of adoption of an innovation. The solution to Equation (8.4) yields the well-known diffusion equation or logistic function. The solution is found by assuming that at time $t = 0$ (the beginning of the adoption process) there

were no n_0 channels whose state did not change.
The solution is given by:

$$\frac{n_t}{N} = \frac{n_0}{n_0 + e^{a - k_1 t}} \qquad (8.5)$$

where $a = \log_e (N - n_0)$. The graph of Equation
(8.5) is shown in Figure 8.4.

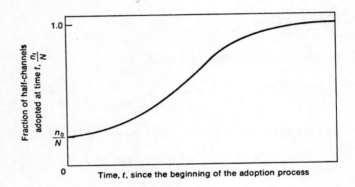

FIGURE 8.4 The logistic function of Equation 8.5.

Some adoption processes are swifter than
others. The more rapid the adoption process,
the steeper the slope of the logistic functions. Two logistic curves are shown in Figure
8.5. The logistic curve on the left of Figure
8.5 represents an adoption process that was
faster than the logistic curve to its right.

The shape of the logistic curves is interesting. The adoption process starts off slowly at
the left, accelerates, and then slows down until reaching full adoption. The curve is "S"
shaped. The slope of the curve is always nonnegative, becoming zero at the point of full
adoption. The constant of proportionality, k_1,
also has an interesting interpretation. One
can take Equation (8.5) and perform some

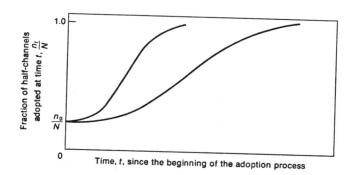

FIGURE 8.5 Two logistic functions for the adoption processes.

algebra to derive equation (8.6) where:

$$\log_e \frac{n_t}{N - n_t} = a + k_1 t \tag{8.6}$$

Equation (8.6) states that the logarithm of the ratio of adoptions to potential adoptions is strictly proportioned to the elapsed time. If one graphs the two curves in Figure 8.5 using Equation (8.6), the result is Figure 8.6. Equation (8.6) says that the logarithm of the ratio of adoptions to potential adoptions is linear and the slope of the curves (in Figure 8.6) is the value of k_1 for each adoption process. The value of k_1 is often referred to as the rate of adoption.

In a study of structural change, there will be a number of groups used. For each group, one can plot the values of $\log_e$ and $n_t(N - n_t)$ and calculate the value of k_1. Because different groups adopt structures at different rates, there will be a number of different values of k_1. The next step is to attempt to explain why different groups have different values of k_1.

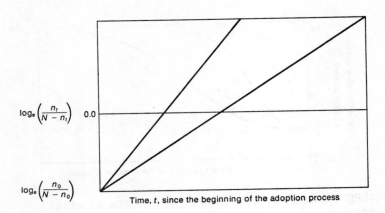

$\log_e\left(\dfrac{n_t}{N - n_t}\right)$ 0.0

$\log_e\left(\dfrac{n_0}{N - n_0}\right)$

Time, t, since the beginning of the adoption process

FIGURE 8.6 The graph of equation (8.6) for the two logistic curves of Figure 8.5.

Although the explanation for why different groups have different values of k_1 may depend upon the experimental conditions, it is not difficult to guess at a simple explanation based on the voting processes governed by a behavioral constitution. In two separate studies of structural change, the value of k_1 was a linear combination of the intensity of favorable and unfavorable votes. The greater the intensity of favorable votes, the greater the value of k_1. The greater the intensity of unfavorable votes, the smaller the value of k_1. Because most groups in a structural change process have both favorable and unfavorable votes, a linear equation such as Equation (8.7) gives satisfactory fits using a simple linear regression statistical procedure:

$$k_1 = \alpha + \beta V_F - \gamma V_U \qquad (8.7)$$

where α, β, and γ are constants estimated by the statistic regression methods, β and γ are nonnegative, and V_F and V_U are the intensities of favorable and unfavorable votes during the structural adoption process.

Equation (8.7) makes sense because, if there are no unfavorable votes, $V_U = 0$, and if only favorable votes occur, there is only one election for each half-channel. But, if there are unfavorable votes, there are a number of recalls, elections, more recalls, and elections. Because each vote and election takes time, the fewer the number of elections, the faster the rate of adoption. Conversely, the greater the number of elections, the slower the rate of adoption. Equation (8.7) and simple variations of it have been shown to explain most of the variance in the adoption rates in experimental groups (Mackenzie, 1976b, chapters 12 and 15).

Another way of interpreting Equation (8.7) is to recall that each group member controls those half-channels that emanate from him. A stable structure represents a unanimity among the group members. If any member does not like a structure, he can always change it by opening or closing any of the half-channels under his control. Suppose the group centralizes about one of its members when it achieves a stable structure. The idea of centralizing and choosing a hub position takes time to be adopted. If one member suggests centralization, he votes for this and ceases to vote against it. If a second member agrees, he votes for the new structure and ceases to vote for others. Now there are two voting for the structure and two less voting for other structures. Their votes can influence another, who then stops voting for a different structure and starts voting for the new structure. Thus, there is a "snowballing" of influence that yields the diffusion of logistic curve of Figure 8.4. But once most of the members have adopted the new structure, there are fewer channels for the group to adopt. Hence the proportion, (n_t/N), of adoptions begins to slow down. This is shown by the upper portion of the curves in Figures 8.4 and 8.5. But the rate of adoption in Figure 8.5 remains the same.

Equation (8.4) can also be interpreted. Each person controls his half-channels, and every person controls the same number. Thus, the number of adopted half-channels, n_t, is proportioned to the number of adoptions who are influencing the adoption process towards the adopted structure. The number of half-channels yet to be adopted, $N - n_t$, is proportional to the number of group members who have not yet adopted the stable structure. Thus, one can interpret the product $n_t(N - n_t)$ as being proportional to the number of contacts between those who have already adopted the structure and those who have not adopted the structure. The more those who have adopted attempt to influence those who have not yet adopted, the greater the relative intensity of favorable to unfavorable votes and, hence, by Equation (8.7), the faster the rate of adoption, k_1.

The value of k_1 is analogous to the rate of contagion of a communicable disease within a population where there are n_t persons interacting with the $N - n_t$ who are susceptible but, as yet, still in good health. Equations that resemble (8.4) and (8.5) have been used to study the spread of communicable diseases such as typhus, venereal disease, chicken pox, etc. Equations resembling (8.4), (8.5), and (8.6) have also been extensively used in the spread of producer's durables, type of seed corn and other agricultural innovations, and for new product introduction by marketing scholars. (For representative discussions of some of the issues involved in the adoption and diffusion of innovation, see Bernhardt and Mackenzie, 1969, 1972, and Rogers and Shoemaker, 1971.

A THEORY FOR THE ADOPTION AND DIFFUSION OF CHANGE

The concept of change is introduced earlier in this chapter. Change is described in terms of: (1) its nature and (2) its consequences. The nature of the change is described in terms of the activities performed by the adopter at the

time the innovation is introduced and those
activities that are expected, should the innovation become adopted. Specifically, the nature
of the change consists of those activities that
are expected to be dropped as a result of adoption *and* those new activities that are expected
to be added. The consequences of the change are
the evaluations placed on the nature of the
change by the adopter.

There is uncertainty about both the nature
and the consequences of the change. There is
less uncertainty about the nature and consequences of the changes that are dropped than
there is about those to be added. Generally,
the potential adopter knows more about his
present circumstances than about possible future states. This uncertainty creates risk for
the potential adopter. An important part of his
adoption process is to search out his environment to gather information that would allow
him to estimate more carefully the nature and
the consequences of a change. This information
search is an important part of the adoption
process and tends to reduce the perceived risks
for adopting an innovation.

He may search in order to learn more about
the nature and the consequences of changes by
consulting peers who have already adopted the
innovation, as well as technical and economic
experts. He may become initially aware of the
innovation through contact with a change agent
or some media message. His relationships with
the change agent and his confidence in the
change agent's competence and honesty have a
bearing on the perceived riskiness associated
with the changes. A trusted and competent
change agent will create less riskiness than
another who is seen as self-serving and less
competent.

For example, if a swimming pool salesman
tells you that your whole life will be improved
by buying his swimming pool, you begin to ask
a lot of questions. You might carefully check
the actual costs of installation, the costs of

running the pool (chemicals, water, heating, etc.), the need for a fence, the number of days per year the pool could be used, how long the lining will last, increased insurance costs, how long the concrete will last before it cracks, the problems of relandscaping the property, the possible effect on tax assessments, the possible resale benefits, and so forth. But if you know and trust the salesman, and neighbors praise his work, and appear happy with this pool, you have information to help you evaluate the consequences of a swimming pool. But if the salesman looks "shifty," represents an unknown company, and your neighbors have many complaints, the possible risk is much higher. Numerous studies (see Rogers and Shoemaker, 1971) have demonstrated the importance of the change agent, the media, the social setting, and the type of product on the rate of diffusion.

Another way of looking at how a potential adopter reacts to the perceived risks of adopting change is to posit how he might evaluate the consequences of the change. Assume that uncertainty implies the existence of a range of possible values for each consequence associated with each nature of the change. For example, if you are told the swimming pool will cost only $8,000, you are pretty certain it will cost at *least* $8,000. The salesman also tells you that pool chemicals will cost only $50.00 per year. This you really doubt. You are told the vinyl liner will last 10 years. Well, it could fail before 10 years and it could last beyond 10 years. You are told that one could swim for nine months. A little voice says "Nonsense! I am not a damn polar bear!" But it could be nine months in a rare year. It could be only six months in another year. You are told how, in the privacy of your own yard, you can enjoy swimming. Balderdash! You *know* that the neighborhood kids will be over. At a minimum, your soft drink costs will increase. You could also be sued.

The range of possible consequences and the uncertainty of each is handled by setting up *safety margins* for each consequence. If you know that costs are at least $8,000, how high are you willing to go before you decline to adopt? You may be willing to pay up to $9,500, provided it is extremely unlikely that the costs will exceed $9,500. On the chemicals, plan on $150 but don't be afraid of $200 if it is a low probability that costs will exceed this. The 10-year vinyl liner should last at least seven years, because you plan to sell your home before then. You are not much interested in the possibility that the vinyl liner could last 20 years. You just want to be very sure that it will last at least seven. You hope that you can get a guarantee on the vinyl liner. The length of the swimming season varies with the person who is swimming and the climate. A nine-month season for a hearty kid may translate into only four months for her parent. This is a tough variable to evaluate—each member of the family has a different length of season and Nature calls the shots unless you have a heater, in which case the gas and oil companies call the shots. You are also receiving a lot of misinformation from your kids, who really *want* the pool and are trying to convince you to get one by exaggerating all of the benefits and minimizing the possible problems. The kids talk as though they are all polar bears, but you know better. So you check an almanac to find the average daily high and low temperature and the average number of days of precipitation. Your estimate is not very precise but you calculate that you should be able to swim some of the time for about seven months. Because there is a public pool that is open three months, you want to be very sure that the swimming period is at least five months.

For each of the consequences, you hedge against the estimate of each value by creating a safety margin, beyond which the probability of going even further is minimal. You tend to

make your decision in terms of whether or not
the consequences fall within the safety margin
for each consequence. You can reduce the uncertainty about the estimates of the consequences by obtaining more information, re-
calculating your financial position, seeking
guarantees, speaking with your friends and
neighbors, and so on. An example of a conceptual representation of a safety margin is
given in Figure 8.7 for the length of the swimming season. You have to have at least five
months a year with probability of greater than
0.9. However, you really expect to have a
seven-month season with a probability of 0.8.
The nine-month claim by the salesman is too
fantastic to believe. So you hedge against the
nine-month claim by ignoring it and setting up
a safety margin of two months between what you
expect and the minimum you will accept.

But the story is not over yet. You go over
and talk to the Smiths, and they are really
enthusiastic about their pool. You kids maintain a constant drumbeat of nagging. The pool
salesman shows you new figures about costs. You
learn that for just a little bit more you could
have the pool company erect a plastic bubble
over the pool. All of these pressures and information tend to reduce your safety margin.
The minimally acceptable time edges towards a
similar number of months and what you really
expect can also increase. Each of these estimates improves the acceptability of the change.

Conceptually, this example is simplified,
because one actually sets safety margins
both the nature and the consequences of the
change. Furthermore, one can make comparisons
across the various types of changes. However,
it does illustrate how the adoption process
involves risks, how one can hedge against risk,
and the importance of both factual and social
information in the decision process.

One's contact with adopters of an innovation
is a very important source of information.
Consequently, the nature and the frequency of

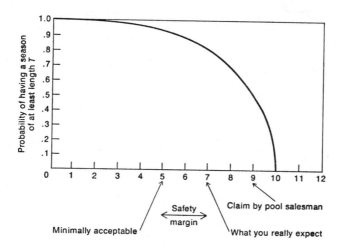

Length of swimming season, *T*, with heater installed (in months)

FIGURE 8.7 A hypothetical inputation of a safety margin.

contact between adopters and potential adopters is a crucial variable in explaining rates
of adoption in a population. These contacts
can provide *experiencing information*. Experiencing
information is the type of information that a
person in similar circumstances can provide
about the nature and consequences of a change.
Experiencing information can be more persuasive
than "objective" information from a trusted
source such as a government agency or a consumer group. For example, if the U.S. Department of Agriculture has a new type of seed
that should increase your yield per acre, you
may believe its figures. But, your farm may not
be exactly the same as the plots where the
studies were conducted. The farmer down the
road, however, can tell you more precisely
what you can expect in your situation. Furthermore, you can look at his fields and talk to

your friends in order to double-check his statements. Some innovations may be resisted because they involve social risks by being illegitimate. Direct contacts can provide *legitimizing information*. Legitimizing information reduces the social costs of adopting. For example, the author recalls the introduction of women's pant suits. The secretaries had adopted pant suits for their off-work social life, but still wore dresses and skirts to work at the university. When the dean's secretary wore a pant suit on Monday, almost all of the secretaries were wearing pant suits by Wednesday. Virtually 100% of those observed by the author wore pant suits by the following Monday. Wearing pant suits for social occasions was already adopted. But wearing pant suits at work was a new innovation. The legitimizing information provided by the dean's secretary made the adoption of pant suits as a work costume possible.

The adoption of ethical drugs is another example of how direct contact reduces the safety margins. If a high-prestige doctor prescribes a new drug and the drug seems to work, other doctors are more likely to prescribe it. The action by the high-status doctor provides both experiencing and legitimizing information to other doctors. Experiencing and legitimizing information tends to reduce the safety margins and to foster the rate of adoption if this information reflects favorably on the innovation.

The impact of adopter-potential-adopter contacts is reflected in the value of the coefficient, k_1, for the rate of diffusion. We first encountered k_1 in Equation (8.3), then later in (8.4), and in Figure 8.6. A model for the value of k_1 for structural change is presented in Equation (8.7). Consequently, k_1 is no stranger to the reader. Because Equation (8.4) is so important and because k_1 is the determinant of the rate of adoption, let us examine a simple heuristic argument for why Equation (8.4) is reasonable.

Suppose that at time t there is a population of size N. The population consists of two types of members: (1) the n_t who have already adopted the innovation as of time t, and (2) the remaining $N - n_t$ who are potential adopters but who have not yet adopted the innovation as of time t. The time t is the length of time since the introduction of the innovation. Now let us suppose that every adopter is influencing every potential adopter by some sort of adopter-potential-adopter contact. The first adopter then has $N - n_t$ contacts. The second adopter has $N - n_t$ contacts. The third adopter has $N - n_t$ contacts, and so on. Because there are n_t adopters each having $N - n_t$ contacts with potential adopters, there is a total of $n_t (N - n_t)$ contacts between the n_t adopters and the $N - n_t$ potential adopters. Let us assume further that once one has adopted, one remains an adopter.[1] Then the source of new adoption grows out of these $n_t (N - n_t)$ contacts. Next, assume that the rate of increase of new adopters is proportional to the number of contacts. Setting $\frac{dn_t}{d_t}$ as the rate of change of new adoptions, these assumptions imply that:

$$\frac{dn_t}{d_t} = k_1 n_t (N - n_t)$$

This is equation (8.4), and note the presence of k_1.

This equation is extremely simple. It assumes that N is constant and that there are no "birth" and "death" processes. It assumes complete mixing of adopters and potential adopters. It assumes that there is no other persistent source of influence outside of the group impinging on the members. It assumes that k_1 is a constant during any adoption-diffusion

process. It is deterministic. Finally, it assumes that eventually every member is a potential adopter. These restrictions can be removed. The mathematical difficulties, however,
are severe and the benefits of a more elaborate
model are more than offset by the increased
problems in solution and in parameter estima-
tion. Bernhardt and Mackenzie (1969, 1972) made
extensive efforts to construct and solve these
problems. After much work, they favored the
very simple model for the reasons that it generates the "S" shape curve and, because of
Equations (8.6) and (8.7), it is very easy to
use and does not require extensive data.

Because the parameter that determines the
steepness of the diffusion curve is k_1, the
best way of understanding the basic process of
diffusion is to explain why k_1 would take on
different values. Essentially k_1 is large when
the nature and consequences of a change are
favorable, when compared to existing alternatives, and k_1 is small when the nature and consequences of a change are less favorable, when
compared to existing alternatives. The parameter, k_1, is a surrogate measure for the effectiveness of the influence on prior adoptions in
creating fresh adoptions. The effectiveness of
this influence is greater when it helps to reduce *safety margins*.

For example, Mansfield (1961) showed that the
value of k_1 for the rate of adoption of twelve
types of producer's durables depends upon a
linear combination of the relative profitability of the innovation and the relative size of
the innovation. He measured relative profitability in terms of the profitability of an
innovation in comparison to other possible investments. Mansfield measured relative size in
terms of the total cost of purchasing and in-
stalling an innovation relative to the amount
of current assets of a firm. Thus a $200,000
machine can be tiny for a large corporation and
huge for a small business. An investment whose

rate of return is 30% may be relatively un-
profitable for a firm with alternatives that
are more attractive, and relatively very profitable for a firm whose investment opportunities involve smaller rates of return. Mansfield
showed that k_1 increased with relative profitability and decreased with relative size. His
equation was similar to that of Equation (8.7).

One interesting side issue with determining
k_1 is the problem of a *technologically tandem innovation*. Some innovations logically·follow another, and if the first is successful, it tends
to reduce the safety margin on the succeeding,
technologically tandem, innovations, thus
speeding up adoption. This suggests a change
strategy called here "bite at a time" strategy.
Making the analogy of a candy bar to a complex
innovation, if the change agent wants to get
the entire innovation adopted, he should proceed by stages, a bite at a time. For if the
whole innovation is considered, the nature and
the consequence of changes are very large. But
if he can introduce the adoption of a first
piece, he reduces the nature and the consequences of the change. This tends to reduce
the safety margin and hence increases the
value of k_1. But, after adopting the first
piece, the adopter's evaluation of the change
of the second piece has been altered. If the
first piece is a success, the safety margin on
the second and technologically tandem piece is
reduced. But if the first piece is unsuccessful, the safety margin on the second piece has
been increased. Each succeeding step or bite,
provided it has been successful, increases the
rate of adoption of the next succeeding bite.
A version of a "bite at a time" strategy is
seen in the computer and office equipment industry. It is also used by politicians to mold
public opinion and to prepare a climate for
escalation of conflicts. In a sense, it is a
strategy with the same problems of an Arab who
lets his camel put his nose inside a tent. The

nose is all right, but if the rest of the
camel gets in, there will be trouble. Change
agents are probably smart to use a "bite at a
time" strategy, but the potential adopters are
wise to be suspicious.

Sometimes there is more than one innovation
being introduced, and these innovations can
conflict with each other. In one experiment
(Mackenzie and Barron, 1970), there was a
business game team with an operations research
graduate student whose job was to get the team
to adopt the optimal operations research technique. While the change agent tried to obtain
adoption of the optimal techniques, conventional wisdom was working against him. The main
prediction of the value k_1 was whether there
were more statements for the optimal techniques than for conventional wisdom. So there
was the innovation of the optimal techniques
working against another set of techniques
loosely called conventional wisdom. The battle
was not one-sided. Conventional wisdom often
beat the optimal operations research technique.
In fact, in at least one case the graduate
student actually adopted the conventional wisdom and disadopted his own techniques. The
model for the value of k_1 was very similar to
that of Equation (8.7) in that statements
favoring the innovation were like favorable
votes and statements for conventional wisdom
were like unfavorable votes from the point of
view of the change-agent operations research
student.

That study also points out the obvious fact
that not all innovations result in progress.
One can diffuse hysteria, nonsense, fear, and
race hatred. One can watch the diffusion of
new fashions, 10-speed bicycles, political
movements, religion, and Monday-night football
viewing. Furthermore, the same theory that can
be used to figure out how to obtain more rapid
diffusion can also be used to slow it down.
Thus, a thorough knowledge of the processes

of adoption and diffusion of innovation is a two-edged sword.

APPLYING KNOWLEDGE OF ADOPTION AND DIFFUSION TO ORGANIZATIONAL CHANGE

The discussion in chapter 2 shows how structural change processes can be modeled using ideas and techniques from the theory of the adoption and diffusion of change. The groups adopted structures, and, by using the concept of a behavioral constitution, one could tabulate the votes for and against the elected structure. These votes could be used to explain why different groups varied in their vote of adoption of structures using an equation such as (8.7). One of the findings is that, within a group, different structures would be adopted at different rates. But in order to predict the occurrence of structural change, it was necessary to augment the adoption and diffusion model with what we called mapping functions in chapter 2.

Pfeffer (1978, chapter 7) has a chapter on organizational change where he provides a much needed corrective to current research. Instead of focusing on the needs for change, the advantage of personal growth and organizational development, and the economic-technical aspects of organizational change, he focuses on the interpersonal struggles for control. He argues that economic-technical considerations are often secondary in importance to the question of redistribution of organizational control. For example, if an organizational change threatens to reduce the power of coalition A and increase it for coalition B, we should not be surprised to find members of coalition A resisting the change and coalition B members supporting it. Although this type of argument could flow directly out of our analysis of the nature and consequences of change (the

consequences were poor for A and favorable for
B), the phenomenon he describes is so important that it deserves a separate chapter. Because Pfeffer (1978) does it, it is only
mentioned here.

A key distinction in organizational change
is whether the changes are informal or whether
they involve a formal reassignment of task responsibility or formal authority. If the
changes are informal, the type of analysis presented in this theory of structural change is
adequate to formulate and analyze most organizational change problems. But if the organizational changes are formal, they involve both
the types of structural change process contained in the book *and* the political objects of
redistributing control discussed by Pfeffer
(1978). If the formal changes merely ratify
and legitimate these informal changes that
have already taken place, the issues of formal
organizational change almost reduce to those
of informal change. But when the formal changes
go beyond the informal change and *really* re-
distribute control, the change involves both
the issues of informal structural change and
problems of implementation. That is, one must
consider both what may be a reasonable solution technically and the problems that we may
expect politically when one attempts to implement the solution.

Another key distinction is whether or not the
person responsible for making the organizational change is working with those below him in
the authority hierarchy to make the system work
better or whether he is working to change the
basic authority hierarchy. If he is working
within the framework of this authority hierarchy, the problems resemble those involved in
the theory of committee formation of chapter 3.
But if he is working to change the basic authority hierarchy, the problems become more
directly political. If he is working within
the system, the solutions and the processes are
more conservative, in that solutions tend to

reinforce or at least to make only marginal adjustments in the authority hierarchy. The other type, where there is an attempt to change the basic system, is more radical and involves the highest organizational stakes. In politics the distinction is between a normal tug and pull of political parties who accept the basic system and fight within commonly accepted rules, and a revolution where the legitimacy of the basic system is in doubt and the tactics and strategies lie outside commonly accepted practices.

Some organizational change issues involve skirmishes and battles. After the battle, one side wins and the organization can lick its wounds and keep functioning. However, there are also *organizational wars*, in which the conflicts are protracted and extend over a wide range of battles.[2] Faculties, for example, have battles over issues such as admission requirements, and course requirements. They engage in organizational wars when the issues are deeper. Business schools, like most professional schools, have internecine organizational wars over the relative emphasis of research and professional practice. These wars, arising out of personal competence, sense of mission, and judgments about how best to serve students, affect almost every organizational battle. It is useful to examine the alignment of the protagonists in each organizational battle. If the line-up of protagonists on either side is relatively stable across organizational battles, one is dealing with an underlying organizational war. Each organizational battle is just one more stage in the protracted organizational war. Organizational changes involve much more if they effect the ability to wage an organizational war. In a war every skirmish and battle advances or detracts from the position of the contending parties. The seemingly innocuous issue of what person to hire is seen as a much more complex issue involving the balance of power of the contending

parties. Thus, in an organizational war the
nature and the consequences of a change are
wider in scope and importance than in an or-
ganizatonal battle. In a stalemated war, it is
harder to achieve an organizational change involving the formal distirubtion of control.
Often, rather than reopen the existing war to
renewed battles, an issue is dropped even
though it would advance the purposes of the
organization. But when one side of the battle
gains control, it is relatively easy to implement formal organizational change. The dominant group simply forces it.

Organizational battles and wars become particularly fascinating to observe (and to participate in) when there is more than one war
going on at the same time. For example, there
is always the Young Turk-establishment war,
the policy A-policy B war, the powerless-power-
ful war. When different persons line up in
different coalitions in different wars, the
mixture of wars and protagonists complicates
each organizational battle. One must continually go around the organization drumming up
support. In a university, those who are active
in research are often at a serious disadvantage because those not engaged in research have
more time for war games. Organizational wars
are serious business but they are also a great
deal of fun. The author is continually amazed
at the ability of organizational wars to arouse
members to incredible levels of energy and effort.

One issue of organizational change that deserves comment is organizational growth. It is
rare to find any organization that does not
seek to grow. Growth can allow the organization to survive by protecting its flanks. For
example, if a manufacturer has a narrow product
line and a small number of customers, he will
want to grow to secure a more stable supply of
inputs, to diversify his product line, to reduce the chance of being caught by technological and market changes, and to increase the

number of customers in order to avoid being
captive to a major customer. As his fixed costs
rise to achieve economies of scale, so does
his vulnerability. Growth is useful for containing organizational wars. By growing, there
are more resources to spread around the warring
camps and so there is less need to battle for
a fixed set of resources. Economic firms grow
to make more profits and they can do this by
offering services. Sometimes growth is pursued
even at the expense of net profits. Studies by
Starbuck (1965, 1971) detail models and processes of organizational growth in firms.

Lately, this author has become aware of a
whole new motive for growth, different from
that of the old "empire builder." In public
service and in universities, there is a new
breed of entrepreneur. He is not an economic
entrepreneur attempting to become rich, but an
organizational entrepreneur seeking to build
his organizational empire. He is rewarded and
admired and even evaluated by his peers in
terms of his ability to increase his budget
and staff. This motivation is shared with the
old-style empire builder. But, the means have
changed. The new breed differs from his prede-
cessors in that his technique is based on
"failure" rather than success.

When we were children, we were rewarded by
hugs, gold stars, grades, medals, money, and
statues when we achieved success. We were un-
rewarded and even punished when we failed. A
student who correctly spells his list of words
gets a gold star. A student who misses lots of
words has to do extra work to make it up. An
athlete who wins a race gets a prize. The loser
gets no prize. So, we tended to equate success
with reward and failure with no reward or
punishment. The economist and rationalist still
believes in this and encourages his students to
be successful. This author prefers this sort of
thinking to the alternative described next, but
we should not allow such a reasonable model to
blind us to the organizational realities of today.

Most persons work in buroids, and many of these are relatively immune from the continual discipline of the marketplace. Such persons, if they are in positions of responsibility, have a budget. Money is always scarce, and so there is a continual struggle to get more. In this milieu, if one is successful in operating one's organization and does not spend all of the money in the budget, the budget is likely to get cut in the next fiscal period; because if you did not spend it, you must not have needed it. So, right away success breeds failure. So operating success can cause organizational failure. The real problem of the organizational entrepreneur is to increase his budget. The budgeting process is very political and involves many organizational entrepreneurs, each attempting to succeed by increasing his budget. The person responsible for the amount each of these entrepreneurs receives only has so much to give. It is rare that he has more to allocate than is demanded. Therefore, in order to obtain more budget, one must come forward with a justification for why more money is needed.

The best form of justification is to fulfill an organizationally desired need. Usually, this means that one should expand one's services. The systems approach, for example, is always good for an elaborate justification for more resources. But, if one is successful in carrying out one's official duties with the current budget, he cannot effectively justify an increase. Accordingly, in order to be successful, the organizational entrepreneur must seek reasons why he cannot be successful with what he already has on hand. To be successful in the funding game, he must document why he could be operationally more successful if he had more resources. Thus, in order to succeed as an organizational entrepreneur he has to demonstrate how and to what extent he is an operational failure. Hence, failure causes success.

This reversal of the reward-success, failure-punishment theory is relatively recent. One sees examples every night on the news program. Four hungry waifs are shown. The camera then cuts to a senator or administrator who points out how he could eliminate the operational failure represented by the four hungry waifs if only he had more resources. When the Vietnam war was going poorly, the armed forces in the U.S. grew rapidly. When the war was ended, there were massive cutbacks. The Canadian forces, for example, have been cut back to 78,000 including all branches, active and militia. They are there to maintain peace. They have been successful and so they are not allowed to increase. The Department of Health, Education and Welfare is a spectacular failure. Naturally, its budget increases each year with all sorts of new programs.

One school of business in California launched an off-campus M.B.A. night program in a neighboring city. To start the program it had to stretch its resources. The program was started and unfortunately, it was a howling success. The dean had over an inch of "letterhead" letters praising the program. In fact, in terms of direct cost to students and to the university, the program is the least expensive in the whole state. The dean then went to the chancellor to report on the program. He emphasized its success, showed the letters, and generally made a good case for why its success should be reinforced. But the chancellor, who was obviously pleased that someone was doing a good job, mentioned the university's budget problems. The computer center needed newer equipment, the library needed more books, etc. So the chancellor thanked and praised the dean but gave him no money. Because he was doing such a good job with the resources at hand, any excess resources should be used to further the needs of the less successful departments. The dean's operational success was an organiza-

tional entrepreneur's failure. It is only
speculation, but had the program in the neighboring city been an operational failure, the
dean would probably have been able to obtain
more resources.

The new breed of entrepreneurs, the organizational entrepreneur, is steadily reversing the
classical success-reward, failure-punishment
conditioning process. Thus, today one of the
most powerful dynamics of organizational growth
is operational failure. Even the police now
have a vested interest in crime. The more
crime, the more police the police department
needs. The more policemen are needed, the
higher the salaries they can extract from the
public.

This author is a direct beneficiary of organizational failure. If there were not so
much of it, there would be no need for so
many books on organizational behavior. On the
whole, however, he has tried to be decent about
it. He has restrained himself from attempting
to extort more resources from others to correct
the failure of his theories; he seems slightly
schizophrenic. The taxpayer and conservative
part of him protests the organizational tom-
foolery all about him. On the other hand, the
researcher part of him is delighted. He has, in
fact, really included these cynical observa-
tions only to emphasize that he sides with the
angels.

NOTES

[1]In the epidemiology literature the situation is more
complex because sick persons can die, they can become
well and catch it again, or they can become well and
immune. Models for such complications have been denied
in this literature.

[2]The author is indebted to Paul Swingle for the
idea of organizational war.

REFERENCES

Bernhardt, I., and Mackenzie, K. D. "Acceptance of Change: A Theory with Models." In *Management Science in Planning and Control*, edited by J. Blook, Jr., pp. 321-50. Special Technical Association Publication No. 5. New York, N.Y.: Technical Association of the Pulp and Paper Industry, 1969.

_____. "Some Problems in Using Diffusion Models for New Products." *Management Science* 19 (1972): 187-200.

Mackenzie, K. D. *A Theory of Group Structures, Volume II: Empirical Tests*. New York: Gordon and Breach Science Pubs., 1976b.

Mackenzie, K. D., and Barron, F. H. "Analysis of a Decision Making Investigation." *Management Science* 17 (1970): B-226—B-241.

Mansfield, E. "Technical Change and the Rate of Imitation." *Econometrica* 29 (1961): 741-66.

Pfeffer, J. *Organizational Design*. Arlington Heights, Ill.: AHM Publishing Corporation, 1978.

Rogers, E. M., and Shoemaker, F. F. *Communication of Innovations: A Cross Cultural Approach*. 2d ed. New York: The Free Press, 1971.

Starbuck, W. H. "Organizational Growth and Development." In *Handbook of Organizations*, edited by J. G. March, pp. 451-523. Chicago: Rand McNally, 1965.

Starbuck, W. H., ed. *Organizational Growth and Development*. Baltimore: Penguin Modern Management Readings, Penguin Books, 1971.

Name Index

Subject Index